The Human Mind through the Lens of Language

Also available from Bloomsbury

Advances in Experimental Philosophy of Language, edited by Jussi Haukioja
Certainty in Action, by Danièle Moyal-Sharrock
Names and Context, by Dolf Rami
The Evolution of Consciousness, by Paula Droege
The Philosophy and Science of Predictive Processing, edited by Dina Mendonça,
Manuel Curado and Steven S. Gouveia

The Human Mind through the Lens of Language

Generative Explorations

Nirmalangshu Mukherji

BLOOMSBURY ACADEMIC

LONDON • NEW YORK • OXFORD • NEW DELHI • SYDNEY

BLOOMSBURY ACADEMIC
Bloomsbury Publishing Plc
50 Bedford Square, London, WC1B 3DP, UK
1385 Broadway, New York, NY 10018, USA
29 Earlsfort Terrace, Dublin 2, Ireland

BLOOMSBURY, BLOOMSBURY ACADEMIC and the Diana logo are trademarks
of Bloomsbury Publishing Plc

First published in Great Britain 2022

ISBN: HB: 978-1-3500-6268-9
ePDF: 978-1-3500-6269-6
eBook: 978-1-3500-6270-2

Typeset by Deanta Global Publishing Services, Chennai, India

To find out more about our authors and books visit www.bloomsbury.com and
sign up for our newsletters.

To
Mohan

Contents

Figures

Preface

My mother used to spend several months every winter knitting woollen garments; all she needed were a ball of wool and two knitting needles, the rest was in her mind. With some crayons and paper, most children can draw some abstract landscapes. Under the Suzuki method, thousands of Japanese children play classical music on the violin. It is well known that if you lift a human being from a Stone Age culture and place him/her in New York, in six months he/she will be playing the stock exchange. The smartest of the animals, chimpanzees, cannot do any of these things.

Call the mind at work *The Generative Mind*. What constitutes the generative mind? For the simplest explanation, suppose the generative mind constitutes a single principle that puts ideas together in different domains, apparently without limit; call it *Principle G*. How do we characterize Principle G?

No doubt, in terms of spread and social significance, human language is the most obvious and dominating example of the generative mind. Some classical philosophers suggested that language is the mirror of the mind. Moreover, after centuries of investigation beginning with Panini and the Greeks, we know something about how the linguistic mind works. So maybe we can find an entry into the intriguing phenomenon of music – not to mention the elusive phenomena of knitting and painting – by studying the generative structure of language. Thus, in this work we propose to examine the generative mind through the lens of language. For example, we will inquire if the generative principle of language, called *Merge*, may be viewed as Principle G.

It is unlikely that, beginning with the study of language, we will be able to cover, within the space of a book, the largely uncharted ground to the distant phenomena of knitting, cooking, yoga and gardening. Yet there is a strong intuition that, at some abstract level of design, these things exhibit the same human competence. The hope is that the method of inquiry might at least suggest a meaningful direction for a wider coverage beyond language. In that sense, this work essentially sketches a programme for mapping out the territory of the generative mind for further exploration. The basic steps of the project are sketched in the Introduction.

A preliminary study of these themes was attempted nearly two decades ago in a largely hesitant and incomplete monograph which remained unceremoniously stacked in the warehouse of an old building (Mukherji 2000). There are glaring problems of organization and presentation in that book, yet I was surprised to find recently how much of it continues to be valid. The present book vastly extends the scope of that early study. Although bits and pieces of this book are borrowed from earlier publications, especially in Chapters 1, 2 and 5, most of the work reported here remained unpublished. In fact, very little was discussed in seminars and meetings because this work was mostly pursued in the shadows.

Some of the research reported here was carried out in several extended visits to the Indian Institute of Advanced Study located in Shimla. There were also shorter visits to the Institut Jean Nicod in Paris and the Institute of Advanced Studies in Durham University, England. I am grateful to the directors of these institutes – Peter DeSouza, Pierre Jacob, Francois Recanati and Ash Amin – for making these visits very pleasant. Thanks also to Roberto Casati and Wolfram Hinzen for much help during our stay in Paris and Durham, respectively.

Over the long period of gestation of nearly two decades, this work has benefitted from comments, suggestions, criticism and encouragement from many people. For this version in particular, I am indebted to Noam Chomsky, Ian Tattersall and Norbert Hornstein for their detailed, often severely critical, comments on Chapters 3, 4 and 5. I am also thankful to the reviewers for some fine suggestions regarding the organization of the volume. The remaining mistakes have obvious agency.

This volume was scheduled for publication in 2018. Unfortunately, a series of unforeseen events, including long spells of serious illness in the family, delayed the publication by several years. I am indebted to my editors at Bloomsbury for their patience and empathy during this turbulent period. As I look back, I find very little resemblance between what was planned four years ago and the final version. I hope the intervening years added more structure to the otherwise elusive search for the human mind.

.

Introduction

Setting the stage

It is well known that theoretical inquiry into aspects of nature can be conducted only on essentially simple systems; complex systems defy principled inquiry. It has been argued that the basic sciences such as physics could reach such depth of explanation because physicists viewed nature to be simple, orderly and, thus, intelligible. In the practice of physics, such a view of nature was reached by abstracting away from the complexities of ordinary experience in the phenomenal world. Such abstractions, in turn, enabled physicists to use elegant mathematical and other formal devices for describing aspects of nature hidden from common experience. Authors have called this form of explanation in physics the *Galilean Style*.

The restrictions on the possibility of reaching genuine theoretical understanding affect pursuits like biology somewhat more directly than physics. Biological systems are not only immensely complex, but they are also commonly viewed as poor solutions to the design problems posed by nature. These are, as Noam Chomsky puts it, 'the best solution that evolution could achieve under existing circumstances, but perhaps a clumsy and messy solution' (Chomsky 2000a, 18). Given the complexity and apparent clumsiness of biological systems, it is difficult to achieve theoretical abstractions beyond systematic description.

According to Chomsky, the study even of the 'lower form lies beyond the reach of theoretical understanding'. As Chomsky (1994) reports in a slightly different context, an entire research group at MIT devoted to the study of nematodes, 'the stupid little worm', just a few years ago, could not figure out why the 'worm does the things it does'. These remarks have an obvious bearing on the biological system at issue, namely, the mind. 'Chomsky has argued', Daniel Dennett complains, 'that science has limits and, in particular, it stubs its toe on mind' (1995, 386–7).

Since this work aims to extract and articulate a simple and species-specific notion of the human mind, the first methodological task, in view of the Galilean restrictions, is to form some idea of how to control the complexity of the phenomena encountered in the world of ordinary experiences. To that end, this project envisages three broad measures for accomplishing the required abstraction. Given the immense complexity of biological phenomena, we distinguish between cognitive and non-cognitive domains in biology to narrow the area of search for the cognitive sciences. Then, within the broad domain of cognition, we distinguish between cognitive and mental phenomena to isolate the specific class of mental systems, such as language, music and arithmetic, that appears to be restricted to humans. Finally, we try to find some simple principle that characterizes the mind in the mental systems so isolated.

As we will see in Chapter 1, such a focused conception of the human mind was mooted in the Cartesian tradition several centuries ago, even if the tradition did not clearly distinguish the steps, as charted earlier, to show the progressive narrowing of inquiry. As argued in Chapter 2, this narrow conception of the human mind is no longer widely favoured in contemporary philosophy and the cognitive sciences. Thus, one of my goals is to revisit the Cartesian tradition to develop their understanding of the human mind in terms of what we now know after hundreds of years of inquiry.

In that sense, if I may say so, this work resembles the philosophical and methodological goals of Gilbert Ryle's influential work on the concept of mind (Ryle 1949), but from an exactly opposite direction. Ryle wished to exonerate the 'ghost in the machine' allegedly promoted by the seventeenth-century French philosopher René Descartes in his 'official doctrine'. In contrast, I wish to show, among other things, that the first real philosophical and scientific advance on the concept of mind proposed in this book, indeed, goes back to the classic work of Descartes, as the informed reader might have already detected.

Noam Chomsky has often characterized Cartesian ideas on language and mind as the 'first cognitive revolution'. Chomsky has also characterized the influential developments due to the work of Alan Turing, Gestalt psychologists and others in the twentieth century as the 'second cognitive revolution'; Chomsky didn't mention his own groundbreaking work probably out of unwarranted modesty. After acknowledging some of the significant contributions of the second cognitive revolution in our times, this work is compelled to revisit the first cognitive revolution, occurring nearly half a millennium ago, in search of its pedigree. Beginning with a historical perspective on the study of the mind, then, the work progressively narrows down to identify a rather simple conception of the human mind based on the shared property between mental systems such as language, music, arithmetic and the like. It is called the *Generative Mind*, for reasons that will soon follow.

0.1 Mind and cognition

The strict restriction of the concept of mind to humans suggests a sharp distinction between mind and cognition since there is no doubt that non-human organic systems are endowed with a variety of cognitive capacities. Thus, the mind is to be distinguished from the rest of the cognitive architecture of organisms consisting of perceptual systems and resulting images, consciousness and subjective awareness, intentionality, representations of distal stimuli, memory, feelings and emotions, depressions, drives, dreams and the like. The list is obviously incomplete and I am unsure if all of these things coherently fall under the single label 'cognition'; but I am sure that none of them belong to the mind unless there is a strong presence of human language or kindred systems in them.

The distinction between mind and cognition places severe restrictions on the conception of the mind. Consider the 'five aggregates' doctrine of the mind proposed in some versions of Buddhism: material form, feelings, perception, volition and sensory consciousness. If we grant a bit of volition to an animal, it'll otherwise satisfy the conditions for a fine Buddhist mind; even lowly animals such as nematodes are likely to qualify. According to the narrow conception of mind I am proposing, the Buddhist doctrine is not a doctrine of mind at all; it is at best a doctrine of cognition. A very similar remark applies to much of what is called philosophy of mind insofar as the primary focus of the discipline is on perception, attention, consciousness, feelings, desires and the like. The study of mind is also disengaged from what may be broadly called the cognitive sciences insofar as these sciences cover cognition as understood above.

The complexity of cognitive phenomena is a natural starting point for developing the distinction between mind and cognition. Even the least developed organisms such as unicellular bacteria are endowed with some forms of sensory systems to grasp relevant parts of the world. As we go up the evolutionary ladder, cognitive effects seem to abound everywhere: a variety of sharp and acute sensory reactions; complexity of locomotion; identification of food, prey and predator; location of space for shelter; making of nests; storing of food; search for mates; grasping of environmental cues for time of day, season, year; a variety of call systems for attracting the attention of conspecifics and for marking territory; rearing of offspring; display of emotions; and the like.

Most organisms show signs of consciousness and some ability for what look like goal-directed behaviour, often appearing to be planned in advance: a classic example are the birds, such as acorn woodpeckers, who store nuts in holes for consumption during the winter. The phenomenon explodes in diversity and richness when we reach the mammals. We will see many impressive examples of smart behaviour across the animal kingdom. For now, let us suppose that humans share many aspects of these cognitive effects with other animals, although it is likely that these effects also have human-specific components: nest-building and grain-storing seem to vary widely between humans and birds.

It is plausible to hold that the resources of the so-called basic sciences, like physics, chemistry, and even biology, are currently largely inadequate to harness the cognitive phenomena just listed. Cognitive phenomena seem to be governed by things like mental images, representations, memory, associations, reflexes, alertness, goal-directedness (intentionality), consciousness and some degree of voluntariness. It is totally unclear what these things mean in the terms of the basic sciences. Imagine that a specific cluster of neurons fires or a particular chemical reaction occurs when an organism becomes aware of some familiar predator. We may be able to secure accurate images of such happenings in the brain, and identify the hormones that flow on such occasions, as recent studies suggest.

Yet, we have no idea what these images mean, what it means for neurons or chemical reactions to grasp predator information themselves in the absence of the curious human interpreter. Hence, a new form of inquiry – call it *Cognitive Science* – is called for; such an inquiry is new in that it incorporates within its explanatory vocabulary terms such as *images, representations, stimulus, reactions* and the like. To emphasize, insofar as *these* cognitive effects are concerned, cognitive science covers both human and non-human organisms.

Nevertheless, it is also pretty obvious that human mental phenomena are markedly distinct from general cognitive phenomena. Except for humans, no other animal builds fires and wheels, navigates with maps and tells stories to other conspecifics, not to mention the human abilities of cave painting and song making. We can witness this unique feature of the human mind in almost everything humans do: cooking, building houses, tailoring, knitting, inventing games including nearly impossible yoga postures, and even innovative sexual practices as depicted in *Kamasutra* and sculptures in the temples of *Khajuraho*. *Prima facie*, it is implausible that the form of explanation for cognitive phenomena such as insect navigation extends to what we are calling *human mental phenomena*, such as cave painting. It appears that, while non-human organisms possess many cognitive capacities some of which also show up in humans, only humans possess the mind.

Given the distinction between cognition and mind, the study of mind appears to fall even beyond the scope of the cognitive sciences as envisaged above. Apart from creating a conceptual space for the (specific) study of the human mind, the distinction between mind and cognition begins to incorporate the Galilean constraint on the availability of scientific studies. Once we disengage the human mind from the vast complexity of cognition of organisms, and try to form a conception of the mind in terms of simple and abstract properties, the study of the mind progressively falls within the boundaries of Galilean science.

Specifically, I intend to show that the human mind consists of systems, such as language, music and others, which are paradigmatic examples of what Descartes called *signs*, which are 'the only marks of thoughts hidden and wrapped up in the body'. It is important to emphasize that although we eventually focus on the Cartesian conception of 'signs' as a perceptual phenomenon encountered in the world, the basic goal is to develop a concept of the human mind 'hidden' in the body. The human mind is distinguished in the organic world in its ability to entertain thoughts entrenched in a variety of sign or symbol systems. This seems to be the central message of Cartesian philosophy.

Human language is certainly the most prominent of these symbol systems in which a specific category of symbols, informally called *words*, are woven in an unbounded fashion to generate a variety of linguistic thoughts. Nevertheless, this work argues that the Cartesian message is far more general; there are symbol systems that generate other varieties of thoughts such as arithmetical thought, musical thought, artistic thought and the like. Each of them is generative in character and none of them are found outside the species. So the claim is that all these thoughts are governed by a single generative principle; call it, Principle G, 'G' for 'generative'. That is the human generative mind.

The task of chipping away from the common thick notion of mentality to reach a thin/narrow notion of the mind proved difficult due to the vast extension of the common concept of mind. Commonly, the concept of mind seems to cover not only many aspects of being human, but it is also often used to characterize almost any cognitive behaviour displayed by (sufficiently) complex organisms. So even if we may hesitate to apply the concept of mind to cockroaches, apes certainly seem to qualify; topics like 'Mentality of the Apes' and 'Does the Chimpanzee have a Theory of Mind' raise no eyebrows. As a result, a large variety of directions are currently pursued under the topic of mind, as we will see in Chapter 2.

0.2 Cartesianism

This is where Cartesianism plays a crucial role. Cartesianism is invoked in this work not merely for some historical support; the basic result about the generative mind could have been stated without recourse to Descartes, as in Mukherji 2010. Descartes is needed in the project because he did propose a concrete concept of mind. If we are able to align the basic result about the generative mind with the imperishable aspects of Descartes' concept of mind, then the apparent vastness of the concept of mind will be partly addressed. The clue is that Descartes did not ascribe mentality to animals at all; it follows that Descartes recommended a narrower notion of mind only for humans. The link between the Cartesian notion of mind and the generative mind arises as follows.

So far, I have mentioned two basic Cartesian themes: (a) a principled distinction between human and non-human organisms, and (b) an intimate relation between the conceptions of language and mind. The distinction between mind and cognition binds these two themes in categorical terms, so to speak. Humans have both mind and cognition, animals have only cognition; the human mind is uniquely constituted of structuring principles of language and related kindred systems. Despite the obviousness and familiarity of the Cartesian postulation of the mind for separating humans from non-humans, my contention is that this specific concept of mind *as distinct from cognition* has not really been studied in the otherwise exploding literature in the cognitive sciences. In fact, as we will see in the opening chapter, Descartes himself was confused between mind and cognition when he proposed too broad a conception of mind that included consciousness, vision, language and a variety of ideas, among other things.

In contemporary times, the Cartesian themes (a) and (b) have generally motivated the Chomskyan linguistic inquiry, as noted; Chomsky initiated the contemporary Cartesian era with his book *Cartesian Linguistics* (1966). However, as I will now argue, Chomsky's appeal to 'Cartesian doctrines' falls short of the distinction between mind and cognition. Thus, while incorporating some of Chomsky's insights, especially his formal work on human language (Chapter 5), the specific conception of mind proposed in this work departs in many ways from Chomsky's 'Cartesian' turn in linguistics and philosophy of mind.

In fact, some of Chomsky's thoughts on the human mind, especially his idea of the modularity of mind, are directly opposed to what I propose here. The standard conception of the mind held by Chomsky and others views the mind as vast and dense and complex; the mind, for Chomsky, includes processes such as language, vision, reasoning and so on. Chomsky holds that each of these mental systems is distinct in terms of its structuring principles; that is basically Chomsky's thesis of the modularity of mind. Insofar as the domain of language is concerned, Chomsky favours the hypothesis that the principles of languages are specific to the domain of language. I will discuss these familiar Chomskyan themes critically as we proceed.

My conception and organization of the mind are very different. On the one hand, I do not think the mind consists of disparate domains such as language and vision whose structuring principles appear to be distinct. On the other hand, I think that the domain of language shares its structuring principles with *kindred* domains such as music and arithmetic. Contrary to Chomsky, then, I will argue that the generative mind consists of a simple operation, Principle G, that is embedded in each of a specific class of mental domains; indeed Principle G defines the class.

To emphasize, although the idea of Principle G emerged during the study of language, the principle itself is *not* specific to human language, although it is specific to a small (as yet unknown) class of what may be viewed as mental systems. It is eminently plausible that Principle G emerged much earlier in the hominid line for the mind to guide the gradual evolution of human language and other mental systems. If so, the postulation of mind gives a new direction to the controversies about the origin of language. I will have more to say on this topic in Part II of the work.

In my view, the suggested notion of the generative mind essentially captures Descartes' conception of mind as the system linking signs with hidden thoughts in a variety of domains. In contrast, the 'Cartesian' turn in the Chomskyan tradition seems to be concerned with the study of language because language is viewed as a largely pre-formed, innate system (Chomsky 1972a, 1986). In my view, the early views of Jerry Fodor on the language of thought also fell in the same genre of innatism (Fodor 1975, 1981). In the Chomskyan tradition, 'Cartesianism' essentially covers the fixed, pre-formed character of cognitive systems of organisms in line with their biological character. In that sense, *all* aspects of cognition fall under 'Cartesianism'; there is nothing specifically 'Cartesian' about language.

I think there are serious conceptual problems in this form of 'Cartesianism'. The problems arise due to the conflict between the species-specific character of language and the general character of innate systems across organisms. In order words, language is 'Cartesian' only in that the language system is viewed as pre-formed along with other cognitive/perceptual systems such as the visual system. Language and vision, in turn, are viewed as components of the mental 'organ', in line with the respiratory and the cardiovascular systems. Hence, the mind is viewed as modular and there is no 'metaphysical divide' between the mind and the rest of organic nature.

Thus, contrary to Descartes, Chomskyan 'Cartesianism' does not distinguish between humans and animals. In an early insightful discussion of the innate basis of various cognitive capacities, Chomsky (1975, 8–10) seamlessly moves from a lucid description of human cognoscitive powers that impressed rationalists like Ralph Cudworth to contemporary results on the 'grammar of vision' of higher animals (Gregory 1970), such as the pioneering work of Hubel and Wiesel (1962) on the cat's visual system. Apparently, all of this falls under 'Cartesianism' for Chomsky.

I am not denying that Chomsky is a leading voice arguing for the species-specificity of human language; one of his recent books is actually titled *Why Only Us?* (Berwick and Chomsky 2016). Yet, somewhat ironically, the unique species-specific properties of human language do not really have a place in the Chomskyan 'Cartesianism'. Perhaps this is because, according to Chomsky, Descartes didn't really have anything specific to say on language. So, Chomsky is attracted to Descartes primarily because of Descartes' internalist perspective on human cognoscitive powers, a prominent theme in rationalist philosophy. To emphasize, according to Chomsky, the study of language is 'Cartesian' *not* primarily because the linguistic system is unique to the species, but because the linguistic system is innate. It appears that Chomsky's 'Cartesianism' amounts just to the claim that language is a biological system. It is no wonder that something like the distinction between mind and cognition never arose prominently in the Chomskyan framework.

In any case, outside Chomskyan linguistics, strong anti-Cartesianism, even in the domain of language, is the ruling doctrine in contemporary philosophy of mind and cognitive science. According to van Gelder (1997, 446–7), the 'anti-Cartesian movements' – supposedly 'spearheaded' by figures as disparate as Gilbert Ryle in Anglo-American philosophy and Martin Heidegger in continental philosophy – are often viewed as one of the 'greatest achievements of twentieth-century philosophy of mind'. This is because Ryle, Heidegger and others have exposed 'subtle, pervasive and pernicious epistemological and ontological misconceptions inherent in the Cartesian picture'. In this palpably hostile intellectual climate, a formulation of an alternative Cartesian conception of the mind is a good reason for writing a book.

Following Descartes and other rationalists, it is natural to trace the uniqueness of the human mind to the endowment of language; rationalist philosophers viewed human language as a 'mirror of mind'.[1] By investigating the structure and function of human language, then, we may form a view not only of human language, but also of the human mind itself as a defining feature of the species. Chomsky (1975, 4) interpreted the rationalist vision as a hope that 'by studying language we may discover abstract principles that govern its structure and use, principles that are universal by biological necessity and not mere historical accident, that derive from mental characteristics of the species'. As we saw, beyond noting the 'biological necessity' of 'mental characteristics', Chomsky never really showed what it means to 'derive' the 'abstract principles' of language from the 'mental characteristics of the species'.

In this work, I will go much beyond Chomsky's interpretation of the rationalist tradition. My goal is to examine whether we may use the Cartesian interest in language and mind to reach an interesting concept of the mind from what we now know about human language. Perhaps the classical intuition was that if the mind is to be a substantive notion, it should be possible to detect its imprint in the most prominent of mental systems: language. I argue that by studying language we not only discover universal and species-specific principles, but we can also use some of the core principles of language to *characterize* the human mind.

The classical emphasis on species-specific mental powers continues to be the most plausible picture of how the mind is organized. Consider language. In the contemporary literature on language acquisition, especially in the connectionist framework, it is often suggested that human children acquire the structural aspects of languages by a 'statistical analysis' of the speech stimuli streaming in from the world. The fact that monkeys, not to mention kittens, do not pick up human languages despite prolonged exposure to (human) speech streams is decisive evidence that they do not have the inner ability (Fitch et al. 2016). This is not to deny that non-human species are endowed with general devices for statistical analysis of recurrent stimuli, among other things, for going about in the world, for acquiring species-specific call systems, selecting mates, locating shelter and so on. But these non-human endowments just do not give rise to language.

In the human case, then, there has to be at least a weak form of inner ability that somehow couples general statistical resources, if any, with the specificity of speech (Lidz and Gagliardi 2015). But even this weak form seems implausible in the face of evidence that deaf and dumb children acquire sign languages (Goldin-Meadow and Feldman 1979; Gleitman and Newport 1995). In this case there is no speech stream available to trigger off statistical resources in the first place.

Even then these children acquire/invent sophisticated generative procedures essentially out of nowhere.

This is not at all surprising since the 'input' to the language system – the *primary linguistic data* – is itself a product of the faculty of language; unlike, say, the visual system, linguistic data is not 'given' by the world. The most reasonable conjecture is that human children are simply endowed with the required mental power to acquire languages; the rudimentary primary linguistic data just fine-tunes the capacity, if at all. As we will see, a similar reasoning applies to kindred mental phenomena such as music and arithmetic. Children do not learn human music by listening to birds; they learn music from instances of human music itself such that some of them are able to give concert performances at age six.

From this perspective, we may view the development of rich systems of thought as a natural effect as the mental systems developed through the advancement of the species. By looking at the structure of human language thus, we form a view of what the human mind looks like. In this specific sense, the concept of mind genuinely applies only to the human case. After over half a century of exciting work on language, primarily due to Noam Chomsky and colleagues, we now know something of the nature of language. However, it remains unclear what notion of the human mind follows from the study of language. Which mind is reflected in the mirror of language?

0.3 Saltation problem

As formulated, the question is nuanced, especially from the evolutionary point of view. The question appears to demand that we postulate *separate* notions of (human) language and mind while showing that they are crucially related to a species-specific mental effect. In other words, although human language and thought systems appear to be distinct mental powers, the evolutionary effect had been such that one led to the other specifically for the species. Even if we agree that the non-human species, especially the primates and other advanced mammals, exhibit impressive aspects of thinking and planning through their inner resources, these non-human resources are likely to be radically different in character from those of humans due to the absence of language. This requires a marked evolutionary *discontinuity* between human and other species, including our nearest ancestors. The concept of mind is designed to highlight the suggested discontinuity.

However, if the inquiry is to have initial evolutionary plausibility at the current stage of knowledge, it is prudent to view the suggested discontinuity as having a minimal but critical basis in an otherwise vast body of continuity in the overall architecture of organic evolution. In effect, we look for just the part(s) of these mental powers, ideally a simple and solitary dynamic principle, that crucially turned the general animal capacities into a specifically human endowment. This is the sense of the focus on the structure of human language to locate the specific form of the human mind.

In this connection, it is interesting that the common conception of the mind is, indeed, typically restricted to something like the generative mind. As noted, the dominant conception of the mind in the philosophy of mind and the cognitive sciences assumes the mind to be an assortment of processes and capacities that range from muscle movement and insect navigation to perception, consciousness, language, thinking and so on. In general, researchers use the notion of the mind to loosely cover what is taken to be the 'mental' aspects of organisms, with no further interest in specifying the boundary of the mental.

The common conception of mind, in contrast, appears to be much narrower and restricted to humans. When we say that someone has a good mind, we do not mean that the person has an acute sense of smell or exemplary attention; we mean that the person displays innovative ways of putting things together, combines ideas in novel ways, throws fresh light on old problems and so on. This usage of *mind* suggests that the mind is commonly viewed as the ability to combine representations or symbols in complex ways to generate ideas and thoughts; the mind is viewed as good when the combination is executed in surprising ways. I have referred to this conception of the mind as the *Generative Mind*.

Interestingly, researchers on animal cognition appear to follow the narrower view of the mind (Andrews 2015; De Wall 2016). When arguing for animal minds, they seldom cite capacities such as agility, muscular strength, visual acuity and stamina; they argue for the ability to count, signs of logical reasoning, evidence for planning, ascription of beliefs and so on. Whether animals do have these abilities is extremely controversial; Penn et al. (2008) claim that, in the animal case, there is not only absence of evidence but also evidence of absence of the mind. As noted, we will be engaged with the issue of animal mind throughout this work, concluding finally in Chapter 6 that they do not have the generative mind.

To sidestep the controversy for now, let us keep the idea of the generative mind to the abilities that are predominantly human-specific. As noted, only humans build fires and wheels, diagnose each other's illnesses and identify remedies and so on. (Penn et al. 2008). In each case it seems that humans are able to put different ideas together to produce thoughts that are used in the world: for example, a diagnosis requires putting together ideas of a symptom and a disease, the idea of a wheel is a combination of the ideas of a circle and ease of locomotion. The examples suggest that, even if human language is the dominant cultural mode for the noted creativity, human generativity extends much beyond the domain of language; in many cases, such as music, cave painting and cooking, it may be meaningless to think of the creativity as a product of human language. It seems that there is a distinction in nature in this respect, and the generative mind marks that divide.

Given the large number of human-specific generative abilities just listed, the massive explanatory problem is that we need to reach some evolutionary account of how these abilities came about. Since they were not available in pre-human systems, it is difficult to view them as quantitative modifications of pre-existing functions. Therefore, each of them seems to require *saltational* explanations at some point of its origin: a saltation is a sudden and large mutational change from one generation to the next, potentially causing single-step speciation. Although saltations do occur in nature for emergence of new biological forms such as polyploid plants, it is an uncomfortable form of explanation for higher-order cognitive abilities, where the required biological explanations are hardly available. The discomfort is enhanced when many saltational steps are needed to account for a large number of cognitive functions of a single species.

In any case, a saltational explanation seems unavoidable for the unbounded generativity of human language, as we will see in Chapter 5. Given the discomfort with saltational explanations, Occam's razor suggests that the entire range of astounding abilities be pinned down to a single saltational principle, if at all. Hence, it is interesting to examine if all human-specific generative principles may have a single explanation based on the generative principle of language. In any case, among the generative systems listed so far, the idea of generativity applies most prominently to the principles of language itself because language is 'one of the few domains of cognitive psychology where there are rather far-reaching results' giving rise to a genuine 'feel of scientific inquiry' (Chomsky 1991). With so much detailed knowledge on human language in hand, it may be possible to examine its generative part with adequate abstraction. So I basically examine the principles of language to see how the mind looks like. Assuming that language is specific to humans, we cannot look for the mind in this form of inquiry where there is no language or related kindred systems.

Following the proposed inquiry, it appears that, in a delightfully narrow sense, the human mind can be identified as the basic structuring principle that constitutes the computational core of language, and related systems such as arithmetic and music. Please note that the conclusion concerns the human mind itself, not just human language or arithmetic or human music. The human mind is just that, a set of structuring principles, probably a unit set, that lies at the core of these human systems. I have called it *Principle G*, 'G' for 'generative'. So the basic conceptual thesis of this work is that Principle G is the human mind; the human mind is a generative mind. In my view, this part of the work is pretty definitive. I reach this thesis by the end of Chapter 4. The rest of the work is an attempt to give a more theoretical shape to the thesis.

The perspective on the human mind just sketched significantly departs from common conceptions of how mind and language are related. As noted, the standard conception of mind and language is that mind is a conglomeration of 'mental' capacities: language, vision, reasoning, consciousness, attention, desires and so on. In this conception, there is no separate notion of mind; the study of mind is exhausted when we have completed the individual studies of these capacities. To look for an independent conception of mind in the standard view is to commit what Ryle (1949) called a *category mistake*. It is a mistake if the mind is thought of, at once, as constituted of and separated from its components, such as thinking of an army as separated from its brigades and divisions that constitute the army.

In the proposed conception of mind, in contrast, we think of the mind as an independent joint of nature that is located in the human cognitive apparatus. So, when we are looking for separate notions of mind and language to study their relation, we escape Ryle's problem by not thinking of language as a component of the mind, while we do think of mind as a delineable part of language and other language-like systems, if any. Each of these complex systems of which the mind is a part is, therefore, to be viewed as a *mental system*. The cluster of mental systems, of course, is deeply embedded in the rest of the human cognitive architecture.

The proposed way of looking at the relation between mind and language thus matches another intuitive requirement. It seems that the standard concept of language, such as Aristotle's idea of language as a system of sound–meaning correlation, is too restricted to carry the entire weight of the concept of mind. The human mind after all cannot be viewed as the same as human language since there is a strong intuition that humans may continue to have the mind even in the absence of crucial aspects of language. In any case, it is implausible to presuppose without detailed argumentation that creatures without language do not have mentality; various mental functions seem to remain intact despite severe language impairment, as we will see.

So, any conception of mind must incorporate the intuition that, as a substantive notion, the concept of mind covers much more than language; as we saw, the standard cluster view of mind, indeed, meets this condition, but with the wrong grain. However, the requirement of species-specificity suggests that we cannot view the mind too widely to include perception, consciousness and the like. So we need some sense of a separation between the mind and language which will also guarantee some sense of intimacy between them. In that sense, the task is to view the mind as reflected in language and other 'language-like' kindred systems: the former condition suggests intimacy, the latter separateness. The proposed perspective on mind and language meets the condition. The discussion thus shifts from language as a whole to just its structuring principle.

In the discipline of biolinguistics, the basic structuring principle of language is known as Merge. Thus, a prominent line of inquiry in this work is to see if Merge carries the weight of Principle G that constitutes the human mind. We will see that Merge does satisfy some of the major conditions that constitute the rationale for Principle G. For example, it turns out on closer inspection that the operation of Merge is not domain-specific. Furthermore, Merge defines the relevant notion of computation such that the computational conception of the mind essentially constitutes Merge. In that way, viewing Merge as the empirical – perhaps, even the evolutionary – manifestation of Principle G is an attractive theoretical inquiry.

Yet, Merge is after all a product of linguistic inquiry; furthermore, even in linguistic inquiry, Merge is a fairly recent invention (Chomsky 1995a) that continues to attract a variety of alternative formulations (Chomsky 2020). It is not prudent to place the conceptual weight of the human mind entirely on the shifting fortunes of a new science. Principle G, then, is best viewed as an adequacy condition for Merge; in other words, the proposal is to so formulate Merge-like operations in a variety of kindred domains as to meet the conceptual requirement of Principle G. In that sense, the conception of the generative mind in terms of Merge-like operations is work in progress. This part of the work is thus more tentative than the earlier conceptual part.

It is worthwhile to emphasize the extremely narrow character of the preceding proposal to distinguish it from apparently similar proposals in the recent literature. For instance, my central claim is not a general one that mind is a recursive system (Corballis 2011). I have several problems with this otherwise undoubtedly narrow conception of the mind. First, as we will see, the first application of Principle G does not generate a recursive structure; it happens only with the second application, if at all. Even for the first application, Principle G is (already) a unique endowment of the species in effecting a particular form of sign–thought correlation. Second, it is not evident that Principle G may be *characterized* as recursive even if it may be so viewed on occasion – *on occasion* because, as we will see in Chapters 5 and 7, it is unclear if the language system is recursive in the sense in which arithmetic is (Arsenijević and Hinzen 2012); in that sense, recursiveness may not be a necessary condition for Principle G.

More fundamentally, notions of recursion and computation seem to be a fallout of Principle G; *we do not have these notions in advance of Principle G*. In other words, Principle G is an empirical discovery concerning human language, and recursion is an abstract idea which makes sense only in the light of Principle G – that is, recursion is a theoretical characterization, if at all, of what Principle G does. In that sense, the project here is exactly the opposite of Corballis' programme of studying language through the 'lens' of thought, as he claims, rather than exploring the human mind through the lens of language as proposed here. This is my basic disagreement with Corballis (2011) who takes the abstract, formally defined notion of recursion to be a primitive in cognitive explanation.

The reversal of the direction of explanation, from the mind to human language, in Corballis' framework creates formidable empirical and theoretical roadblocks. Since his conception of recursion is independent of language in the sense that human language 'borrowed' recursion from somewhere else – namely, from the domain of thought – Corballis is committed to argue for the presence of recursion in thought independently of language. In order to clarify what he means by recursion outside of language but restricted to humans, Corballis needs to also show that non-humans do not have such recursive thoughts.

To that end, Corballis suggests two tests: mental time travel and theory of mind, both of which according to him require recursive thinking without language; assume so. Thus, according to Corballis, animals do not have a sense of past and future, and they cannot read the minds of others. We will see that empirically these claims are not settled at all: some birds can recall dozens of locations where they had stored food in the *past* for *future* consumption, and chimpanzees appear to make intricate inferences about the beliefs of conspecifics (Krupenye et al. 2016). Therefore, Corballis' entire framework collapses if animals turn out to be smarter than he thinks (De Wall 2016). No such problems arise if the operations of mind are viewed with the lens of language. Principle G is what it is, independently of whether it should be called *recursive* or not.

Part I

The background

The Cartesian perspective on the mind

The seventeenth-century French philosopher René Descartes, among others, inaugurated what has come to be known as the Cartesian dualistic tradition in philosophy. I am not concerned either with Cartesian philosophy as such or with the philosophy of Descartes. Although various forms of mind–body dualism were advocated by a range of other Cartesian philosophers, such as Géraud de Cordemoy and Nicolas Malebranche, I will restrict the discussion only to some prominent remarks by Descartes. My aim is to understand the main thrust of the Cartesian tradition for reaching a narrow and species-specific conception of the human mind as desired in the Introduction.

I will suggest that the so-called mind–body dualism initiated in the Cartesian tradition is basically the result of two converging ideas: (a) use of signs by humans to indicate 'hidden thoughts', (b) absence of thought-indicating signs in non-human species. Although by *sign* the Cartesians generally referred to items in human language, the notion of sign is profitably viewed in a more abstract fashion as referring to *symbols*. Once we set aside epistemological and religious noise from the Cartesian discourse, it can be seen that the metaphysical dualism between mind and body was basically meant to capture the distinction between (a) and (b). In that sense, the Cartesians wished to promote the conception of narrow mind as a distinct joint of nature.

As we will see, it is difficult to locate exactly the suggested concept of mind in the complex Cartesian discourse. Descartes held a range of epistemological, psychological and metaphysical views in which the concept of mind was concealed. It is likely that some of his ideas proposed four centuries ago may not survive current scientific scrutiny, especially those ideas which carry clear empirical significance such as whether animals are conscious. So if the concept of narrow mind is to have some durable classical interest, we should be able to set aside the perishable parts of Descartes' ideas. After extracting something like Descartes' core idea, I will keep refining the idea in the light of Descartes' own further reflections and some recent evidence.

Due to my restricted interest in Descartes' work, many popular strands of the literature on Cartesian philosophy have no direct bearing on the inquiry here. These include (i) the notion of clear and distinct ideas; (ii) the conception of God as directing and ensuring the validity of human thought; (iii) the real meaning of, and obscure problems with, his dictum *Cogito ergo sum*, among others; and, oh yes, (iv) innate ideas. I may touch upon these things occasionally as a historical reminder, but they play no significant role in the reconstruction of the Cartesian tradition proposed in this work. In fact, my contention is that over-engagement with these (perishable) aspects of Descartes' work in the philosophical literature might have distracted attention away from his real contribution to philosophy.

In any case, it is not obvious why a creature with a mind must have the ability to entertain clear and distinct ideas because even confused ideas require a mind; as Bertrand Russell pointed out, really wise people are significantly more confused than the stupid ones. Also, the idea that the application of mind requires divine guidance presupposes the existence of mind with God in the driver's seat; this raises the usual question about which mind comes up with such an attractive picture. Furthermore, it is plausible from Descartes' perspective that, since some clear and distinct ideas, such as that of God, cannot be reached through sensible means alone; some of these ideas must be innate. However, in an alternative perspective in which there is no urgent requirement for clear and distinct ideas, including that of God, innate ideas may be dispensed with; it is hard to deny that atheists have a mind.

Finally, though it seems plausible that only a mindful creature can entertain the *Cogito*-thought, it is not clear that the *Cogito*-thought is a necessary condition for having the mind; one need not attain the reflective stature of Descartes in order to be endowed with a mind. Having a mind is not such a risky business that it depends on finding the *Cogito*-thought to be true, or even meaningful. To have a mind, it is enough to entertain a healthy mixture of true and false propositions, and lead a life accordingly; hopefully, omniscience happens naturally (Davidson 1984). So I do not see any harm in separating Descartes' mind–body distinction from other aspects of his philosophy.

I am not denying that, in his own thinking, Descartes might have entertained a strong connection between this distinction and the rest of his philosophical ideas. It could be that, in his time, Descartes had no other means of arguing for the distinction directly; he had to somehow 'derive' the distinction from more abstract philosophical and theological reflections. Alternatively, given the theistic-scholastic tradition that surrounded him, his primary concern might have been to construct a new metaphysical system, rather than developing a theoretical description of the human species. It is likely that Descartes wanted to argue for the mind–body distinction on largely *a priori* grounds and used the human endowment of language to highlight the distinction already reached.

So Chomsky's contention, supported by scholars such as Clarke (2003), that the Cartesians were simply making usual scientific proposals may not be true; the Cartesians could have been indulging in what Chomsky (2000b) derisively calls the 'transcendental' method. Be that as it may, our goal, in contrast, is to begin with the empirically indisputable fact of human language to ground it in a (version of) the mind–body distinction. We will play with this contrast throughout the work.

1.1 From substances to doctrines

The Cartesian themes (i) to (iv) mentioned previously, and set aside, are of interest primarily to professional philosophers (Yablo 1990; Cassam 2008). In the general intellectual culture, René Descartes is primarily known as the original advocate of the so-called mind–body dualism – the idea that mind and the body are separate substances with their own distinct attributes. According to Descartes, literally speaking, the attribute of mind is *thought*, and the attribute of body is (spatial) *extension*. Much obscurity surrounds these notions which Descartes borrowed from the classical scholastic substance-attribute tradition in philosophy. In many instances, though, Descartes objected to the tradition.

For example, he gave a spirited defence of the attribute of extension in his long letter to Henry More (Cottingham et al. 1991, 360). In this letter, Descartes distinguished 'extended substance' from 'perceptible, tangible or impenetrable substance' as suggested in the scholastic tradition. One of his analogical arguments for the distinction is that 'just as man is defined not as an animal capable of laughter, but as a rational animal, so body should be defined not by impenetrability but by extension'. We will see some other instances of Descartes' opposition to the tradition as we proceed (see also, Clarke 2003). Setting complex scholarly disputes aside, the substance of body is often viewed as constituted by *matter*, the realm that occupies (physical) space and time. Consequently, Descartes' conception of the mind is often characterized as *immaterialist* to sharply reinforce the contrast with the body.

The most popular form of argument against the Cartesian mind targets its alleged immaterial character. Since Descartes did propose that mind causes bodily action (=behaviour), his critics, such as Ryle (1949), ask: How can something immaterial cause changes in something material? Descartes' own alleged answer in terms of the mind occupying some specialized zone of the body, such as the pineal gland, is obviously inadequate and perhaps question-begging. I am also setting aside his complicated proposals such as the distinction between two kinds of soul: one that drives the spirit, and the other that drives the corporeal nature. We return to what Descartes could have coherently wanted to do with his concept of mind a bit later.

While Cartesian philosophy flourished for some time in the hands of post-Cartesian philosophers, the growing opposition to it, especially from empiricists and materialists, overshadowed his philosophical legacy. In contemporary philosophy, except for a few authors, a vast majority of philosophers of mind and cognitive scientists adopt some or other form of materialism even if the matter of the mind is now understood in terms of the brain. Materialist thinkers broadly reject the immaterialism of the Cartesian mind. In that sense, these philosophers reject the classical form of mind–body dualism from the mind-side as it were and retain the body.

1.1.1 Collapse of materialism

However, some philosophers reject the mind–body dualism from the body-side along with, or without, retaining the mind-side. As we saw, the materialist's objection to the immaterial mind simply assumes that matter/brain is the only available realm, and all discernible cognitive action must be caused within *this* realm. In other words, Descartes' critics allow only a materialist conception of nature. Is that conception valid or even meaningful?

Thus, concerning the doctrine of eliminative materialism (Churchland 1984), Noam Chomsky (1994c, 84–5) holds that 'nobody can tell you what matter is. Take fields. Is that consistent with materialism? Every physicist says it is, but since we have no concept of matter, there is no way of answering that question.' The point is, once physics introduced the notion of action at a distance and mysterious entities like gravitational fields, the push–pull contact mechanisms, advocated by pre-Newtonian mechanistic philosophers and scientists, collapsed. Since mechanistic philosophy was grounded in materialism, the metaphysics of matter itself lost credibility when mechanistic philosophy failed to explain, say, the phenomenon of gravitation.

Interestingly, the Cartesians themselves questioned the validity of the Newtonian mechanism precisely on these grounds; they held that Newton violated the principles of mechanistic philosophy. So there is some historical truth to the suggestion that Cartesian philosophy identified bodies so closely in terms of mechanical philosophy that they were compelled to postulate a different immaterial realm to explain mental phenomena, such as consciousness. As a result, Cartesian mentalism and Newtonian 'mechanics' were basically on the same non-mechanistic page; yet Descartes is viewed as the principal historical villain. In any case, except for historical interest, the topic of mechanical philosophy grounded in materialism became largely irrelevant once Newton postulated gravitational fields and Descartes postulated the mind.

However, the preceding argument against mechanical philosophy does not show that, therefore, Descartes' mind–body dualism is invalid, as Chomsky seems to hold. The failure of mechanical philosophy only shows that materialism is false; hence, the concept of mind retains its validity. However, the mind–body distinction will be affected by this argument only if it is shown that Descartes' concept of body rested on mechanical philosophy. To see that Descartes' concept of body, and thus the mind–body distinction, escapes this charge, let us carefully examine the steps of Chomsky's argument.

Descartes' notion of a body, Chomsky suggests, was essentially rooted in a philosophy according to which all physical motion is to be explained in terms of mechanical forces acting on bodies in contact. However, it is unclear if Descartes understood mechanical philosophy in terms of push–pull contact mechanics. Descartes held a conception of mechanical philosophy which may be used to explain much of natural phenomena: all of the inorganic world, and much of the organic world, 'including everything about plants and animals and much of the functioning of humans, up to elements of sensation and perception' (Chomsky 1994a, 37).

Now, Chomsky's argument is that, developments in post-Cartesian science, especially Newtonian science, 'not only effectively destroyed the entire materialist, physicalist conception of the universe, but also the standards of intelligibility that were based on it' (Chomsky 2001; also, Hinzen 2006). As we saw, the failure of materialism, viewed as promoting a contact mechanism, possibly explains the non-material character of both gravitational fields and human minds. However, Chomsky's further contention that the force of Cartesian dualism between the mind and body depended on the salience of the materialist, physicalist conception of the universe presupposes that Descartes also held the same mechanical, materialist, physicalist conception of body. This presupposition can be questioned.

Descartes' rather strange conception of a body that includes, as we saw, all of the planets, gyroscopes, plants *and* even sensations suggests that Descartes was possibly not asserting some empirical category to indicate the range of classical mechanistic philosophy; he was perhaps constructing a hypothetical category, in the form of a thought experiment, to sharpen its distinction from the mind. In other words, he was saying that even if we include sensations in the concept of body, we still don't get the mind. From this perspective, it is implausible to view this wide conception of body as an assertion of what Chomsky calls 'mechanical' philosophy; sensations do not seem to 'push and pull' each other. We will see later that Descartes' conception of body need not be viewed as physicalist either. In that sense, Chomsky's criticism of materialism need not affect Descartes' abstract categories.

In recent years, Chomsky has been even more emphatic in rejecting any form of dualism in rational inquiry (Chomsky 2000b, Chapter 4). Science is viewed as a unified enterprise which seeks to develop 'bodies of doctrines' wherever rational inquiry is granted an entry. According to Chomsky, these bodies of doctrines do not affect the assumption of the fundamental unity of nature: 'Certain phenomena, events, processes, and states are called *chemical* (etc.), but no metaphysical divide is suggested by that usage' (Chomsky 2000b, 75). As discussed at length elsewhere (Mukherji 2010, Chapter 1), I find Chomsky's views deeply problematic.

Chomsky seems to encourage a picture of scientific enterprise which proceeds in terms of a cluster of 'body of doctrines' that are looking for unification with each other; hence, there are no metaphysical divides. However, there is no obvious conflict between the notions of a body of doctrines and our conception of fundamental divides in nature; whether to call these divides 'metaphysical' is immaterial. Unification is a very rare occurrence in science anyway. It happened only twice – physics and inorganic chemistry, and organic chemistry and molecular biology – in the entire history of science, and only for small corners of the concerned disciplines. For example, although atomic physics united with aspects of inorganic chemistry, gravitation continues to be an enigma even *within* physics (Mukherji 2017, Chapter 4).

Furthermore, the body of doctrines that concern us here, namely mental and biological, are not even *adjacent* domains unlike physics and chemistry which occupied a Newtonian continuum for centuries (Mukherji 2010, 22–3). So the possibility of unification in these domains is not only not in view, but we also do not even know what it means. All I wish to stress at this point is that Chomsky's conception of a body of doctrines and its relation to scientific unification has no effect on the significance of Descartes' way of making the distinction between the mind and body. Descartes need not be viewed as erecting a 'metaphysical divide' either even if his scholastic discourse suggests so, but he was certainly indicating a fundamental gap in our understanding of nature, as we will now see.

1.1.2 A doctrine for signs

Why exactly did Descartes need a concept of mind as distinct from 'mechanistic' principles? Descartes held that the phenomenon of unbounded and stimulus-free use of 'signs' falls beyond the scope of mechanistic philosophy (Descartes 1637; Chomsky 1966; Leiber 1991). Hence, he postulated the novel substance of mind to account for the use of signs which are 'the only marks of thoughts hidden and wrapped up in the body'. Now that we have given up Descartes' substance dualism, does the rejection mean that we have reached a unified account of 'sensations' as falling under body, and 'free use of signs' in the mind?

As we will see from some recent work in neurolinguistics in the next chapter, there is much support for Chomsky's scepticism that the problem of unification between biological sciences and linguistics virtually remains where it was two centuries ago (Chomsky 2001; Mukherji 2010). Thus, commenting on Edward Wilson's optimism about a 'coming solution to the brain-mind problem', Chomsky (2001) remarks that the 'grounds for the general optimism' regarding 'the question of emergence of mental aspects of the world' are at best 'dubious'. In this light, the puzzle is that, even though mind–body dualism – which was postulated four centuries ago to account for the explanatory gap between physical motion and language – turned out to be untenable in its classical formulation, the subsequent history of science has furnished no optimism that the gap between sign and sensation has been bridged. In that sense, the origins of Cartesian dualism remain unaddressed.

So how do we approach the Cartesian notion of *sign*? The broad research programme of linguistics is often viewed as a revival of the Cartesian tradition in the study of human 'cognoscitive' powers (Chomsky 1966; Leiber 1991). Appealing to the long tradition from Descartes (1637, 1641) to Wilhelm von Humboldt (1836), Chomsky (1966, 72) suggested that 'linguistics and cognitive psychology are now turning attention to approaches to the study of language structure and mental processes' which are often ascribed to the 'century of genius'; the tradition, according to Chomsky, continued 'well into the nineteenth century'. The tradition continued because, although 'Descartes himself devoted little attention to language', the Cartesian tradition on the whole offered 'a coherent and fruitful development of a body of ideas and conclusions regarding the nature of language in association with a certain theory of mind' (Chomsky 1966, 2; Hinzen 2006, Chapter 1). I will argue that this project remains essentially incomplete despite Chomsky's powerful intervention.

As Chomsky's remarks suggest, the Cartesian tradition was invoked essentially for its general programmatic ideas ('approaches'), and *not* for extracting any specific theory of language or of mind. Chomsky did point out some interesting theoretical moves made in the tradition, especially in the tradition of Port Royal grammar: for example, the distinction between deep and surface structures, and the implicit notion of grammatical transformation (Chomsky 1966, 97, notes 67, 68). Still, Chomsky's basic concern was to draw attention to the 'internalist perspective' explicitly proposed in the Cartesian tradition, especially those that underlie the rich expressive capacity of human language (Chomsky 1997).

We will look later in Chapter 5 at how Chomsky and his colleagues have developed the 'internalist perspective' to explain 'the rich expressive capacity of human language'. We do not know whether Descartes would have approved of Chomsky's theory of language because apparently Descartes 'himself devoted little attention to language'. Moreover, it is unclear how Chomsky's theory of language addressed Descartes' general concern about signs. Most importantly, apart from some suggestions regarding an 'internalist perspective', it is unclear how Chomsky's theory of language connects with the envisaged theory of mind.

The core problem for Descartes was that a central aspect of human nature, the use of signs, did not fall under current scientific doctrines (=mechanistic philosophy). This was not just the usual incompleteness of scientific perspectives such as the inability of current physics to explain the mass of a neutrino. The phenomenon of the use of signs appeared to defy the very framework of the science Descartes knew; hence, there was the need to postulate a new aspect of nature, a substance called *mind*. From Descartes' perspective, the notion of mind was needed to develop a theory of signs independently of prevailing scientific programmes.

In this light, even if we set aside the philosophical categories Descartes used to characterize this aspect of nature, his basic reasoning remains unaffected since, as Chomsky has repeatedly pointed out, the problem of unification of 'mental' studies with the rest of science, especially linguistics and current biology, continues to be unresolved. In this sense, Chomsky's own writings on the Cartesian tradition do not quite address the tension I have been trying to point out: on the one hand, Chomsky rejects any form of dualism; on the other, he keeps on emphasizing the explanatory gap between linguistics and biology.

This independence of the putative theory of signs from the rest of human inquiry constitutes our basic interest in the Cartesian framework. Supposing for now that the theory of language proposed by Chomsky at least partly covers the envisaged theory of signs, the unsolved problem of unification between linguistics and biology essentially means that the constructs of linguistics – especially the postulation of C_{HL}, the single computational system of human language – cannot currently be understood in terms of the constructs of biology; that is, the constructs of linguistics are to be understood in their *own* terms (Mukherji 2010, Chapter 1).

If we adopt the intuitive idea that our conception of reality is basically a projection of a true theory (Quine 1969), then assuming the truth of linguistics, it follows that linguistics has unearthed a new aspect of nature (Mukherji 2010, Chapter 7). Thus, I am assuming that Descartes' notion of a (new) substance has just this much force: the notion of a substance captures the fact that the postulates of a body of doctrine on the cognoscitive powers of the human mind cannot be understood in terms of some other body of doctrine. In this restricted sense, Descartes' substance dualism basically amounts to a *doctrinal dualism* (Mukherji 2009a).

I am not suggesting that whatever (current) science doesn't explain constitutes a new joint of nature. It is obvious that science, at any given stage, explains very little in any case. Physicists currently hold that 90 per cent of the universe consists of 'dark matter' and 'dark energy', meaning that current physics explains about 10 per cent of what constitutes the universe, according to Chomsky (2002). If Chomsky is right, dark matter is not a joint of nature at all; it is an expression of ignorance. In contrast, the central discovery of linguistics, C_{HL}, is a postulation based on rigorous scientific reasoning from a variety of directions. So there is a genuine case for deep doctrinal dualism.

Returning to Descartes, we saw that, according to Chomsky, Descartes might not have been fully engaged with the conception of language under investigation in modern linguistics. For example, it is unclear from his writings if he was directly concerned with aspects of grammatical structure, the connection between sound and meaning, and the like, in natural languages such as Latin and French. It is well known that Descartes' philosophical ideas heavily influenced the subsequent development of the universalist, mentalist Port Royal grammars (Arnauld and Lancelot 1975; Chomsky 1966), but it is not definitely known if Descartes himself participated in these developments. In any case, scholarly views on the relation between Descartes and Port Royal are too controversial for a clear historical judgement.

So, what was Descartes primarily concerned about? All we know is that he was basically interested in the (general) notion of *sign* and its relation with 'hidden thoughts' such that humans can indicate the latter with the use of the former; he also held that the 'brutes' do not have this ability. I will presently discuss the relation between signing and thinking in the next section. For now, notice that in making this general comment on mental abilities, it is unlikely that Descartes wanted to direct attention to the chimpanzee's inability to speak Latin.

In fact, Descartes held that animals sometimes vocalize their fear, anger and so on, but this does not amount to (genuine) signing because the 'thoughts', if any, are not 'hidden', it is just 'natural impulse'; again, it is unlikely that he wanted to point out that animals do not scream with French expletives. In that sense, Descartes was basically interested not just in language, but also in developing a species-specific conception of mental abilities, even though the intrinsic connection between sign and language cannot be missed. From another direction, we could say that even if language is arguably the paradigmatic example of sign, theoretically the notion of sign covers more, such as musical symbolism. So I will argue in Chapter 7.

At this point, I confess that I have not been able to locate any scholarly source to show that Descartes was aware that the notion of sign also covered musical symbolism. It is well known though that Descartes did not restrict his notion of sign only to 'words' as units of sound–meaning correlation because 'even deaf-mutes invent special signs to express their thoughts' (Descartes 1970, 60). However, I do not know if Descartes would have extended the notion of sign further to include musical 'signs', probably because it was unclear to him, as it is unclear even now, what 'hidden thoughts' are indicated by musical symbolism.

Nevertheless, it is interesting to note that Descartes did have serious academic interest in the study of music. He wrote an 'excellent' *Compendium on musick* when he was twenty-two; the compendium was published only after his death (Descartes 1961). In this early work, he viewed music as a 'passion of the soul' thus restricting the faculty of music to humans since the brutes did not contain much of a soul. Although he was interested in musical aesthetics, he was more concerned with showing, following the Pythagorean tradition in music, that music obeyed mathematical order in its organization that determined the aesthetics (DeMarco 1999; Jorgensen 2012).

On hindsight, the striking similarities with language cannot be missed. The basic formal property of language is that grammatical structure strongly constrains the range of interpretation available to humans; yet there is no evidence that Descartes saw that. But then, Descartes did not have the formal generative conception of language either. In any case, musicologists of his own time weren't particularly impressed by his attempt to find order in semitones. As far as I know, Descartes' musical explorations did not find much favour in the centuries that followed.

1.2 Thought and consciousness

How does the doctrine of signs relate to the other doctrines in the Cartesian body of doctrines, especially the doctrine of mind–body dualism? The question is complex and an answer will emerge only after a scrutiny of its parts. So let us first ask once again why Descartes needed the mind–body dualism in the first place, and then ask how the doctrine of signs satisfies that need.

1.2.1 Humans and animals

As we saw, Descartes thought that a principled way is needed to distinguish between the cognitive abilities of human and non-human animals; that is the basic thrust of the doctrine of signs. But then he needed a broader conceptual framework to ground this specific doctrine; this is where the mind–body dualism acquired its central role in the tradition. According to Descartes, what distinguishes humans from animals is that humans have both a mind and a body, while animals just have a body. So far, of course, *mind* and *body* are labels marking the required distinction; as yet they do not say what the distinction is. That depends entirely on the conception of mind and body entertained by Descartes.

Even before we go into the details, it is important to be clear about the character of the issue raised by Descartes. I think much confusion prevails here. For example, Mary Midgley (1980, 10) is of the popular opinion that Descartes 'identified the human soul or consciousness so completely with reason as to conclude that animals could not be conscious at all, and were in fact just automata'. Adding a few more angry ideas, Peter Singer (1976, 217) writes: 'In the philosophy of Descartes the Christian doctrine that animals do not have immortal souls has the extraordinary consequence that they do not have consciousness either. They are mere machines, automata. They experience neither pleasure nor pain, nor anything else.'

I cited these as representative samples of a fairly widespread belief that Descartes' philosophical project begins with disdain for animals and a superiority claim of men over them. The very project is, therefore, (morally) inadmissible in the first place. However, Justin Leiber (1991, 152–8), after a painstaking survey of Cartesian texts, failed to find a single shred of evidence that Descartes ever held these views. Quite independently of Descartes, it surely does not make sense to begin an inquiry *from* some superiority claim although Descartes might well have entertained it. There is no absolute scale in which men are superior to animals and vice versa. In some domains, animals are clearly superior. Generally, they have a much acuter vision, hearing and sense of smell. Most run faster, some can run incredibly fast just by wriggling horizontally. Some of them can lay eggs in nests perched on the tops of trees. Some can weave intricate baskets just with a beak while hanging upside down. Some of them can detect slight changes in magnetic fields; others can detect earthquakes developing in the bowel of the earth. Some can swim at great depths without special clothing and equipment. Several species of birds have the impressive ability to store food at dozens of concealed locations from which they can retrieve the food at ease.

So, there is no doubt that animals are far better than humans in many respects, including cognitive feats such as retrieving stored food and locating prey with naked eyes from great distances. The interesting issue is this: do we need to invoke Cartesian signs to explain any of these tested non-human feats? Noam Chomsky (1975) cites the interesting case in which rats outperformed college students in maze running. However, as Chomsky reports further, when the mazes were placed at, say, prime numbered turns, the rats couldn't get started while college students found their way. Interesting questions regarding differences between species, and sometimes between entire groups of them, naturally arise with or without superiority claims.

To take a more recent and fascinating example, consider stone toolmaking by chimpanzees. Most books on animal cognition such as De Wall (2016) mention many examples of sophisticated toolmaking by animals: use of rocks to break nuts, bending twigs to reach termites, joining two sticks for a greater reach and the like. Recent work on chimpanzees, including bonobos, has demonstrated the ability of apes to make hundreds of fine stone tools to be used for various purposes (Roffman et al. 2012); their ability seems to be comparable to that of the early hominids, not surprisingly. However, a long tradition of research in palaeolithic archaeology has established that late hominids since about 1.5–300 KY could produce a far more sophisticated variety of stone tools.

Cutting a long story short, it is now known that hominids of the Late Acheulean period about 300 KY ago produced one set of tools to produce others up to six layers of 'recursive' depth: using shaped bones to detach stone flakes, then using the flakes to cut finer flakes, using finer flakes to chisel stones and so on (Stout 2011; Uomini and Meyer 2013; see Chapter Eight). Roffman et al.'s present-day 'language-competent' bonobo-chimpanzees, Kanzi and Pan-Banisha, do not show even a glimpse of such ability; Penn et al. (2008) viewed such differences between human and non-human species as 'evidence of absence'.

As for the effects of Christian doctrines on Descartes, it is not clear what follows or does not follow from Christian doctrines in these matters, or from Buddhist ones for that matter. Given the time in which Descartes engaged in philosophy, it could be that there was a penchant to link up everything that one says with 'Christian doctrines', just as there is current peer pressure to link up everything that one says with 'postmodernism'. However, Harry Bracken (1993, 66) has shown that Descartes' ideas actually went against the established Christian doctrines; thus, he was under attack from Christian circles once the true implications of his ideas were (belatedly) understood.

In any case, the real issue is to see, independently of Descartes' theological attachments, what ought to follow from a coherent way of interpreting assorted *theoretical* statements made by Descartes. For example, what do we make of the widespread complaint, shared by Midgley and Singer previously, that, according to Descartes, animals do not possess thought and consciousness at all because Descartes was alleged to have held that these things are intrinsically related.

1.2.2 Descartes on consciousness

As far as I can see, Descartes could not have – rather, need not have – *identified* reason with consciousness, as Midgley suggests, to conclude that, since animals do not reason, they are not conscious either. Consider the dictum *Cogito ergo sum*, often translated as *I think, therefore I am*. Launching the well-known method of doubt in his *Meditations*, Descartes argued that most of the truths about the world garnered from experience might be seen to be (contingently) false. Descartes is not arguing that they are, in fact, false; they can be *viewed* as false when we are under the grip of the demon, that is, we can imagine possible worlds in which they do not hold. This point is very clearly brought out in the first of Descartes' six meditations. The trouble is, once such possible worlds are reached in (demonic) imagination, it is hard to see what epistemological moves are additionally available to distinguish them from the real world. This is the crucial point of the *method* of doubt.

However, a certain condition must be assumed in order for the method to apply in the first place: the condition that the subject employing the method *has thoughts,* possibly false ones. This condition is not open to the method of doubt. Unless a thought such as *this table is brown* is first entertained, it cannot subsequently be imagined to be false in a possible world. It is obvious that this *general* condition obtains throughout independently of the specific content of given thoughts. This is where Descartes makes the crucial distinction between humans and animals: humans *have* thoughts, animals do not. To maintain this position, one need not assert further, as Descartes apparently did, that this thought about having thoughts is therefore certain, indubitable and so on. In doing so, Descartes was probably confused between having thoughts and the conditions for having them; calling the latter 'metathoughts' does not improve his case; it was probably a genuine 'category mistake'. In any case, this additional step of Cartesian certainty is not needed, in my view.

Moreover, the focus is on *having thoughts,* rather than on *being conscious.* It is a contingent matter that one possibly needs to be conscious in order to (actively) apply the method of doubt, *possibly* because it is unclear if doubts don't arise during dreaming.[1] But the *force* of the method does not require that one needs to be conscious in order to have thoughts in the first place; it is a separate issue whether the method of doubt may only be consciously applied. In other words, it could be that the method of doubt requires some degree of awareness for the agent to reflect on specific thoughts, but these thoughts themselves might be there without the agent being conscious of them.

Even if we concede that Descartes wasn't particularly clear about the distinction and that he might actually have ignored it at some places, it is difficult to agree that a *conflation* between reasoning and consciousness is central to Descartes' philosophy. Descartes thought about dreams and what are now called *subdoxastic* states (Davies 1989) – such as states of linguistic and visual processing – deeply enough not to see the simple distinction. If one grants, as Descartes surely does, that we think – that is, *entertain* thoughts – while dreaming, and, if those thoughts are taken to be on par with thoughts when we are awake to give rise to the method of doubt, one could hardly conclude that thinking has been identified with consciousness. Yet it could be that the distinction between thought and consciousness is difficult to establish in the human case, so let us look at the issue from a slightly different direction.

Contrary to Midgley and Singer, it is simply false that Descartes denied consciousness per se to animals. His view was more subtle and profound, and it is crucially significant for our project. In his famous letter to Henry More, dated 5 February 1649 (Cottingham et al. 1991, 366), Descartes categorically asserted that animals have 'life': 'I do not deny life to animals, since I regard it as consisting simply in the heat of the heart; and I do not even deny sensation, in so far as it depends on a bodily organ. Thus, my opinion is not so much cruel to animals as indulgent to human beings.' Further, Descartes cheerfully granted that, apart from undergoing sensations, 'all animals easily communicate to us, by voice or bodily movement, their natural impulses of anger, fear, hunger, and so on.'

It is difficult to deny consciousness to creatures which undergo sensations, communicate by voice and express natural impressions such as hunger and fear; paradigmatic inanimate objects like pendulums and gyroscopes cannot do these things. Nevertheless, it is well known that Descartes denied that animals have thoughts, and he was not particularly 'disturbed by the astuteness and cunning of dogs and foxes, or by all the things which animals do for the sake of food, sex and fear; I claim that I can easily explain all of them as originating from the structure of their bodily parts' (360). Given advances in the neurosciences, let us suppose so.

Thus, Descartes kept cognition (=thoughts) and consciousness (=sensations) strictly separate for animals, as demanded by Midgely and Singer.[2] However, Descartes did not keep cognition and consciousness separate *for humans*; earlier in the same letter, Descartes stated that 'thought is included in our mode of sensation' (365). Let us see what it means. Descartes suggests, clearly and categorically that 'the main reason for holding that animals lack thought is the following', and I will cite fully to forestall any ambiguity of interpretation:

> Yet in spite of all these facts, it has never been observed that any brute animal has attained the perfection of using real speech, that is to say, of indicating by *word or sign* something relating to thought alone and not to natural impulse. *Such speech is the only certain sign of thought hidden in a body.* All human beings use it, however stupid and insane they may be, *even though they may have no tongue and organs of voice*; but no animals do. Consequently, this can be taken as a real specific difference between humans and animals (Cottingham et al., 366, emphasis added).

For Descartes, therefore, animals do not have thoughts because they do not use signs. For this reason, although they do undergo sensations, they cannot be conscious in a human way because thought is included in human consciousness; it is not included in animal consciousness. In other words, while animals undergo the same form of orange sensation as humans do, they cannot form the conscious judgement *that there is an orange on the table*. It is for this reason that – otherwise abruptly – Descartes shifted to a quick discussion of lack of speech in animals while discussing whether animals can have thoughts. We return. The present point is that the absence of conscious *judgement* is no reason for denying either phenomenal consciousness or informational consciousness insofar as animals can somehow detect the perceptual differences between apples and oranges.

In any case, independently of Descartes, it is plainly false that animals are devoid of consciousness. In fact, the supposition that animals lack consciousness fails to explain normal human behaviour. As John Searle (1998) put it: 'I do not infer that my dog is conscious, any more than, when I came into this room, I inferred that the people present are conscious. I simply respond to them as is appropriate to conscious beings.' Almost every form of impressive planned behaviour, especially those involving retrieval from memory and piecing them together, requires some degree of conscious effort, perhaps even self-projection (Hills and Butterfill 2015). In fact, following Jane Goodall's pioneering work with chimpanzees (Goodall 1971), it is eminently plausible that animals may even be self-conscious. Following Goodall's anecdotal evidence, the subsequent use of controlled mirror tests, enhanced with red-spot tests, suggests that animals exhibit several forms of self-awareness. Subjects in these tests include primates, elephants, dolphins, even birds (Gallup et al. 2002).

1.2.3 Descartes on thoughts

In more focused research on animal behaviour, psychologists often conduct experiments on animals to elicit structured, discriminatory responses. For example, some authors suggest that monkeys may be viewed as 'reliable reporters of their own visual experience' (Flanagan 1998, 143). Flanagan formed this opinion about monkeys because monkeys have been trained to press a bar depending on whether they see a downward or an upward motion. Then, using the phenomenon of binocular rivalry, downward motion is presented to one eye, while upward motion is presented to the other simultaneously. Apparently, monkeys 'report' just as humans do.

I set aside the issue of whether this sort of example is sufficient to count as structured thought, or whether it is just (stimulus-dependent) bodily response as Descartes would have insisted. In other words, it is unclear if this sort of evidence makes animals more like us as Flanagan apparently wants, or humans more like animals as Descartes thought. The issue is predominantly empirical. My point here is, if Descartes denied that animals lacked pretty systematic conscious responses, he would have been flat wrong. But do these examples of conscious response from animals have any effect on Descartes' basic idea that animal consciousness is essentially thoughtless, that thought is not included in their sensation? Let me try to address this question from another direction involving hierarchies of thoughts.

Contrary to Descartes, suppose that animals are ascribed some restricted range of thoughts such as *Washoe get banana*: just agent-action-object, no tense, no 'mental' predicates. We will examine the issue in detail in the next section to reach the result that *ascription* of thought in such cases does not quite amount to *having* of thought. Pending the negative result, let us grant some thoughts to animals. Can we also grant that animals have the thought of having of thoughts? It is hard to see how to make the further ascription in the absence of speech. In other words, even if animals may on occasion be ascribed the (first-order) thought that *p*, it seems implausible to ascribe the (second-order) thought that they have the thought that *p, Washoe happy Washoe get banana*, even if Washoe evidently looks happy; clearly, we cannot avoid 'mental' predicates for this piece of structured thought. Descartes' *Cogito*-thought is certainly a second-order thought (*I have thoughts, therefore I am*) (Corballis 2011); hence, it is not available to animals, he thought.[3]

In the literature on animal minds, this topic is usually discussed under the title *metacognition*. Defenders of animal mind cite experiments to show that animals sometimes appear to know what they know, want and so on (Andrews 2015, Chapter 4; de Waal 2016, 229–33). These proposals are not only hesitant and inconclusive, but they are also typically based on non-propositional, non-conceptual, imagistic and perceptual information (Bermudez 2003), hence, irrelevant for the issue of thoughts raised previously. In his influential book, Griffin (2001, 2) cites Terrace et al. (1979) to suggest that now that Descartes' denial of thoughts to animals has been strongly disputed, 'we just have to ask how animals do think'. In effect, Griffin (and Terrace) wishes (wish) to contest Descartes without first answering the starting question, 'do animals *have* thoughts?' And the answer they eventually came up with required the notion of 'thought without words' such that, according to the authors, it is not possible for humans to entertain them, yet Griffin and Terrace are able to ascribe them to animals. We just don't know how to characterize what animals know to inquire into whether they know what they know.

Maybe the ability to entertain second-order thoughts cannot function in the absence of consciousness; how can we 'look' at a thought unless we are conscious? So maybe this is one way of denying *both* thinking and consciousness to animals. But there are several problems with this. First, this is *not* the notion of consciousness that Midgley and Singer charge Descartes with. Their charge is that Descartes held that animals cannot even feel (first-order) pain. Second, dreams do not lack 'recursive' mechanisms. It is a common 'experience' after all, that while dreaming, we reflect on the absurdity of what we dream.[4] 'Consciousness' is just too thick and nebulous a concept to make much theoretical mileage with. So Descartes can consistently deny both second-order thoughts and 'reflective' consciousness to animals while granting phenomenal consciousness to them.

As an aside, it is unclear whether it makes sense to ascribe first-order thoughts *without* ascribing second-order thoughts? That is, can we think of a creature which has *only* first-order (structured) thoughts, and no competence for second-order thoughts? What notion of thought will that be? The distinction between first- and second-order thoughts is usually made on the basis of (clausal) hierarchy. Consider a complex thought: *I wonder [if Susan knows [that Fred assured Lois [that Clark would remind Pat [to buy food for dinner]]]]* (Jackendoff 2002, 38–9). It has a lot of hierarchies, but is it a second-order thought? Notice that it is hierarchically built up from *Clark would remind Pat to buy food for dinner*. Is that a first-order thought? It too has a hierarchical structure as shown; so does *Washoe get banana*: [Washoe [get banana]]. So, if we are denying second-order thoughts to animals because they cannot construct/interpret hierarchies, it is hard to see how to ascribe first-order thoughts to them (see Chapter 5 for more). Maybe Descartes' denial of thoughts to animals applies across the board (Arsenijević and Hinzen 2012, 432).

Further, I think Midgley and Singer are confused about the notion of machines/automata as it appears in the Cartesian tradition. Again, there is no doubt that Descartes' distinction between humans and animals did rest upon certain ways of understanding the notion of a machine. We just saw that that understanding could not be based on the idea, as Midgley and Singer held, that animals are non-conscious. As an alternative, one could use *machine* in a more or less derogatory sense to mark non-human. In that sense, animals are machines by definition since they are (obviously) non-human. But that is just a verbal move which assumes, among other things, that humans are non-machines. I think this is the use of *machine* that Midgley and Singer have in mind: machines are bad, lowly things, not suitable for characterizing humans. They assume first that Descartes held a similar view of machines and then they accuse him of using it to characterize animals. According to them, machines are so bad that they should not characterize anything living.

The issue is whether Descartes was making such emotional moves, or whether he had some technical point in mind. As a starter, let us see if there is a convergence between the notions of having thoughts and *not* being a machine – a topic that has consumed a lot of space in contemporary discussion on 'artificial intelligence'. In other words, suppose Descartes had a notion of machines that applies only to systems, including living systems, which cannot have thoughts in the restricted *Cogito* sense that interests Descartes. In fact, Descartes did propose such a notion and applied it to animals almost jovially; for him, 'it seems reasonable that nature should even produce its own automatons, which are much more splendid than artificial ones, namely the animals' (Cottingham et al. 1991, 366). It follows then by definition that humans are non-machines.

All that Descartes needs to do now is to tell us how this notion of machines differs from the ordinary (inanimate) notion of machine which applies to pendulums and gyroscopes. As we framed the issue here, it depends on how we understand the notion of having thoughts in the first place. Gyroscopes certainly don't have thoughts: do animals have thoughts? As we will now see, even this question does not have an easy answer. Later, we will see that by *machine/automata* Descartes was perhaps trying to formulate a conception of *super-body*.

1.3 Ascription of thoughts

Traditionally, the question of whether animals have thoughts has been approached as follows. Taking gyroscopes as paradigmatic examples of what we may call a *physical system*, a contrast is then sought between a physical system and a *mental system*. It is then held, somewhat trivially, that only mental systems are capable of having thoughts. Now Descartes certainly held that animals are just bodies; they do not have a mind. If we now identify bodies with physical systems, then it follows that animals cannot have thoughts. This will mean that animals cannot be interestingly distinguished from gyroscopes even though animals are conscious and gyroscopes aren't. *Prima facie*, such a conclusion is at least uneasy. It seems that there may be some problems in placing the mind/body distinction at par with the mental/physical distinction. Unless the cloud just created is partly cleared, we cannot definitely say whether animals have thoughts.

Jennifer Hornsby (1998, 28) addressed the issue from a somewhat different angle. To 'capture our intuitions' about what might count as mental properties, Hornsby suggests the following interesting list:

Is trying to hit the target
Is intentionally annoying Mary
Is aware of the blackboard
has a headache
knows that grass is green
believes that whales eat people
is cheerful today
is arrogant

These are all properties we commonly ascribe to people to whom we *also* apply properties like height, weight, girth and the ability to move around in space. Hornsby's point is that we do not have a coherent notion of how to apply these mental predicates to things *other than those* to which we, in fact, apply the physical properties: 'we have no idea of what it would be for, say, *is cheerful today* to apply except to something readily visible as it were' (29). From this Hornsby concludes: 'Much of what we regard as mental is not to be accounted for in the Cartesian scheme simply by saying how things are with the soul' (1998). I note that Hornsby's observation is meant to be critical of the ordinary notion of the mental understood as independent of the physical.

In this work I have carefully avoided the notion of soul despite Descartes' elaborate discussion of it. I take Descartes' concept of soul to be one of his scholastic legacies with a significant difference, as he insisted. The difference is that, instead of the same soul having a different distribution across the great chain of being as proclaimed in Aristotelian philosophy, Descartes proposed that there are, in fact, two souls. He says, 'The first is purely mechanical and corporeal, and depends solely on the force of the spirits and the structure of our organs, and can be called the corporeal soul. The other, an incorporeal principle, is mind or that soul which I have defined as a thinking substance' (Cottingham et al. 1991, 365). I fail to see how to distinguish the two souls from the familiar notions of mind and body. So, I set souls aside and keep to mind and body.

Returning to Hornsby's list, if Descartes was asked about how to characterize the items just listed, he would have said that many of them arise 'from the union of mind and body', Hornsby reports (29). Hence, Descartes seems to agree with Hornsby that the application of mental predicates requires both the mind and the body. Therefore, the ordinary notion of the mental, as distinct from the physical, requires both of Descartes' notions of mind and body. So Descartes' notion of the mind can only be understood theoretically. What, then, is the theoretical notion of the mind and did Descartes have the right theory? I return to the question later in this chapter after surveying several disjointed ideas that Descartes held in these matters.

Concerning Hornsby's list, it seems to me obvious – something that Hornsby missed – that the so-called 'mental' predicates listed previously by and large apply to animals as well. *We* may apply these predicates to sundry animal behaviour. Circus animals may well be ascribed the predicate *is trying to hit the target*. Between two domestic dogs, the smaller one often intentionally annoys the bigger one, and so on. Ethnologists and animal behaviourists regularly use such terms to explain complex animal behaviour: X is guarding the territory, Y is encouraging her young ones to explore, Z is counting on W to return and the like. Peter Strawson (1959) called such personal predicates *P-predicates*. If we apply at least some of the p-predicates to animals, then if we are Cartesians, we must hold that animals sometimes display a union of mind and body!

Yet, Descartes consistently held that animals do not have a mind; therefore, they cannot display the union. The only way out of this impasse, as already suggested earlier, is to dissociate the Cartesian conception of mind from the unqualified notion of thoughts. Two related points emerge from this discussion: (a) animals can be ascribed *some* thoughts and (b) unless there is a principled (=theoretical) way of identifying and setting *these* thoughts aside, the Cartesian notion of mind as restricted to humans cannot be captured with the general notion of ascription of thoughts. We already saw that it cannot be captured with the notion of being conscious.

We are also beginning to get a glimpse of where Descartes might have gone wrong. It follows from the preceding discussion that Descartes needs a notion of body that includes (i) the property of being conscious, (ii) the property of being ascribed some thoughts and (iii) the usual physical stuff. This concept Descartes simply did not have. In fact, with all the intervening science, neither do *we* have such a concept of body, the 'splendid artefact of nature'. This is because such a grand concept requires large-scale unification of the sciences which is not even in the horizon. So Descartes cannot really be blamed for not having that concept. Nevertheless, we can see where the problem is. Consider the following oft-cited passage from his *Replies* (Cottingham et al. 1991, 360):

> Nothing at all belongs to the nature of essence of body, except that it is a thing with length, breadth and depth, admitting of various shapes and various motions. Its shapes and motions are only modes, which no power could make to exist apart from it; and on the other hand colours, odorous, savours and the rest of such things, are merely sensations existing in my thought, and differing no less from bodies than pain differs from the shape and motion of the instruments which inflicts it.

Yet, Descartes wanted all of the shapes, motions *and* sensations in the (same) animal body. As many authors have pointed out in various ways, Descartes was stuck with a rather restricted view of what counts as a mechanical explanation, that is, he had a rather limited concept of body, as the preceding citation shows. Restrictions in his concept of mechanical explanation forced Descartes to hold a concept of body which cannot accommodate, say, sensations (note his distinction between pain and the instrument causing pain). This in turn enables authors like Midgley and Singer to pounce upon Descartes regarding his view of animals. However, as I suggested earlier, contra Midgley and Singer, Descartes *did not* deny sensations to animals.

So, even though Descartes did not think that there is anything profoundly human about having sensations, he just didn't have the right categories for the *body-end* of his distinction. Since we do not have a profoundly improved concept either, we may set this issue aside for now and turn to what certainly is Descartes' master contribution, namely, his concept of mind. Maybe a clearer understanding of what is in the mind will pave the way for a better understanding of the body.

1.3.1 Thoughts and expressions

While discussing whether animals have thoughts, I was careful in making rather modest claims on behalf of animals. I said that *some* of the thoughts that we ascribe to people (via p-predicates) maybe *ascribed* to animals as well. I neither said that animals *have these thoughts* nor that they may be ascribed *all* the thoughts that we ascribe to people. Let me explain these qualifications.

In the sense under discussion here, we *ascribe* a concept/predicate to indicate a property of an object basically to display our, for want of a better term, *personal* attitudes towards the objects which fall in the domain of application of the concept: *This painting is frightening*. What attitude we hold towards these objects depends partly on our rational, reflective *needs*, rather than on the internal/intrinsic properties of these objects. In this, ascriptions differ sharply from *descriptions* in which we use some predicates with an intention to pick out genuine properties of objects to which we apply these concepts: *Electrons have half-spin*. Whether we do, in fact, pick out genuine properties is a wholly different matter. One hallmark of the distinction between ascriptions and descriptions is that, in ascribing a predicate to an object, we cheerfully entertain the possibility that someone might withhold the said ascription or ascribe an opposite concept, and that we may *both* be right. Obviously, we do not describe something with the expectation that someone might give an opposite description, and we both come out right; if that puzzling situation arose, we would look for a new concept, a new description (see Mukherji 2017, 7.4 for more).

Lack of attention to this obvious distinction is a common feature of the literature on animal minds. Defenders of animal minds simply grant or assume that animals *have* concepts and suchlike and proceed to structured thoughts from there. Andrews (2015, 95) cites Carruthers (2009, 97) as follows: 'If a creature possesses the concepts F and a (and is capable of thinking *Fa*), then for some other concepts G and b that the creature could possess, it is metaphysically possible for the creature to think *Ga*, and in the same sense possible for it to think *Fb*.' Setting the notion of 'metaphysical possibility' aside, let us adopt this familiar criterion for thoughts, commonly known as the *Generality Constraint* following Evans (1982).

The problem is that this constraint is often invoked by animal defenders like Kristin Andrews (2015) to conclude that animals *have* thoughts, because they already assume that animals have/possess discriminatory concepts. In many cases, Andrews actually writes down the steps of logical inferences to show how animals might have been thinking when they were pondering the best route to food!! Once we make the distinction between ascription and description with the severe restrictions stated previously, it is obvious that the generality constraint cannot even begin to apply to animals because they simply do not *possess* concepts.

With the distinction in hand, and generalizing from predicates to thoughts in obvious ways, how do we decide to ascribe thoughts? There are exactly two ways: either we ascribe thoughts to explain some complex behaviour which otherwise remains unexplained given current science or common knowledge, or we ascribe thoughts *on the basis of* a very specific behaviour, namely, linguistic behaviour. In the second case, we ascribe the thought that p to an organism S just in case, other things being equal, S says *p*. Typically, we expect the two methods to converge; that is, we expect that sufficiently complex behaviour has a linguistic or at least a quasi-linguistic component. This explains the widespread false belief that 'higher' animals, somehow or other, possess linguistic abilities even if unspoken.

Ascribing thoughts without the evidence of linguistic behaviour is a restricted affair anyway. Imagine a silent tribe: what thoughts can be ascribed to them unless we are making huge inferences about their like-mindedness? Do they believe in God, approve of extra-marital affairs, love their children, prefer liberty to equality, and know that it is Sunday? It seems there is hardly any *behavioural* evidence to enable us to ascribe such thoughts to silent tribes: what behaviour counts as Sunday-knowing behaviour without begging the question? Willard Quine (1960) called it the problem of radical translation.

So, the chances are that, in the non-linguistic case, we prefer to restrict ascription of thoughts to only such aspects of behaviour where there is some connection between the behaviour and the immediate environment. In those cases, visual and other cues from the immediate environment partly compensate for the silence. Thus, as the primatologist Frans De Wall has recorded, we do ascribe thoughts like

I hate cucumbers to the chimpanzee when he raises tantrums after being offered cucumber slices, rather than raisins as offered to his neighbour. Beyond that, we prefer to keep ascriptions to ourselves, to creatures like us to whom we have successfully ascribed complex and abstract thoughts before. This is the reason why our ascription of beliefs is restricted to same-sayers (Mukherji 2017, 9.3). Thus, even if we find that, in some species of animals, individuals withdraw their demand when the rest are against it, we are not likely to ascribe some sense of democracy to them; there are not enough cues from the environment for such ascriptions. In any case, the range of our ascriptions falls off sharply as we go down the evolutionary tree. That is Descartes' point about oysters and sponges as we will see.

When thoughts are not *expressed,* it is hard to form the opinion that they are there. As the philosopher Bijoy Boruah (2007, 97) succinctly observes: 'Particular thoughts might be inexpressible, and hence idle. Such thoughts may be *contingently* idle. But it is far from obvious that a creature might harbour thoughts that are, for that creature, *necessarily* idle.' Boruah's thoughtful observation is usually rephrased as, 'if you have it, you flaunt it'. We do talk about unexpressed thoughts in *our* case since we know what it would be to express them. When we know that some creature is incapable of expressing thoughts in principle, then the most we can say about them is that they behave *as if* they have thoughts, that is, their behaviour is in accordance with those thoughts, without explicitly holding that they *have* these thoughts.

We routinely ascribe the thought, 'the master is going for a walk', to the dog. In this case, we might even be willing to hold that the dog knows that the master is going for a walk. Does the dog know that the master is fond of him, the dog? Now, some of the dog's behaviour may lead us to ascribe this last thought to him in the sense that his behaviour seems to be in accordance with this thought. But we are likely to suspend judgement when asked whether the dog has formed the concept of fondness; it seems the concept is too much for the dog to possess, if dogs possessed concepts at all.

The distinction between X's having thoughts and our ascription of thoughts to X is one of grades; the distinction expands as we go down the evolutionary tree. For 'higher' animals, we *grant* them many of the thoughts we ascribe to them; for animals lower down the tree, our ascriptions are more in the nature of expressions of our ignorance of animal behaviour than a genuine understanding of the states that cause such behaviour. In other words, we are compelled to explain complex behaviour of animals in the way in which we would explain *our* behaviour of a similar nature. It does not follow that we therefore think of animals and humans as forming a single 'same-thinking' family in those respects.

Opinion varies widely on this issue (Andrews 2015 for a review). Authors like Donald Davidson take the extreme view that thought is essentially linked to talk (Davidson 1975). Thus, if we find absence of talk in some creature, we ought to infer absence of thought. On the other extreme, there are authors like John Searle who think that identifying thought with talk is an 'anthropocentric dogma' (Searle 1992). Most authors, however, take an intermediate position on the issue; for example, Daniel Dennett holds the curious view that animals entertain beliefs but they have no 'opinion' (Dennett 1991). In more recent work, a range of authors have suggested, on the basis of experimental work with animals, that although non-human primates don't ascribe beliefs, they do attribute knowledge to others (Marticorena et al. 2011; Phillips et al. 2020). I return to the point.

At this point, I need to get clear about what the current discussion is about. The only issue I am interested in here is to see what sense it makes to ascribe structured thoughts to non-linguistic animals. The underlying idea is that, once we are sanguine about such ascriptions, we have two options: either we ascribe mentality to animals to that extent, or we remove such ascriptions from mentality and ascribe it to an enhanced conception of body. While the first option begins to challenge the Cartesian conception of a thoughtful mind restricted to humans, the second option maintains the distinction by shifting the phenomenon to the body side. Needless to say, the choice between these options is a research issue.

The so-called 'Theory of Mind' issue throws some light on the topic. I have no space here to review the extremely complex and fascinating research on this topic. Setting aside problems with the uncritical notions of 'theory', 'mind', 'intentionality', 'understanding' and the like freely used in the literature, some of its basic features seem to relate to the issue of ascription of structured thoughts as follows. In a groundbreaking paper, Premack and Woodruff (1978) asked whether animals, say, chimpanzees can ascribe 'mentality' such as beliefs, desires, expectations to other conspecifics or humans. Premack and Woodruff offered a definite answer to the question they asked. They suggested that chimpanzees, indeed, 'inferred' problems a human was facing, and 'judged' the right solution.

The only thing I wish to point out about the result is that Premack and Woodruff's conclusion was based *entirely* on visual clues such as photographs and videos; not a word was expressed. If such evidence leads Premack and Woodruff, and those who agree with them, to ascribe beliefs and understanding to chimpanzees for making nice inferences about them, fine. If that's what 'mentality' is, that's fine too. But if Premack and Woodruff stepped out of their set-up to claim that the concerned belief and understanding of the chimpanzee consists of the thought *that the man in the cage is in trouble*, the ascription is plainly unwarranted: chimpanzees cannot frame such structured thoughts. It is for Premack and Woodruff to explain what they mean by ascription of belief and understanding in the absence of such thought.

To probe the issue a bit further, consider the human child case for theory of mind studied by Baron-Cohen et al. (1985). In this famous Sally-Anne false belief test, a child Sally is shown that a toy is placed inside one of a number of 'opaque' baskets. Sally is then taken out for a walk. In her absence, the toy is removed and placed in a different basket, and another child is asked what Sally will do when she returns. A range of most interesting responses followed depending on species, age, presence or absence of grades of disability such as autism, and the like. I am setting aside the details.

Again, my interest in this experiment is that it is quite natural that language was used to ask Sally when she returned ('can you find the toy?'), to ask the other child when Sally was away ('which basket will Sally look at?'), and so on. With the competence in language proved, it is feasible to assign structured thoughts in these cases. But very similar false belief tests were subsequently conducted with human infants, chimpanzees, dogs, even birds. Here opinion varies pretty wildly, and no consensus has been reached after several decades of intense research. While Michael Tomasello and his colleagues are confident that chimpanzees have a variegated theory of mind (Krupenye et al. 2016), others such as Penn and Povinelli (2007) and Corballis (2011) are sceptical.

Suppose we conclude that, as with some first-order thoughts, some restricted sort of a theory of mind can, indeed, be ascribed to 'higher' non-linguistic animals. Interestingly, there is some evidence that linguistically unimpaired autistic children fail the Sally-Anne test in some cases. It seems to follow that, despite the mention of 'mind', having 'a theory of mind' – the ability to spot the likely behaviour of others – has little to do with the Cartesian mind. To be endowed with a theory of mind, if at all, is part of the 'splendid design' of the 'artefact of nature'. As some authors have noted, every higher animal with a complex brain needs something like a theory of mind for the purposes of social cohesion and cooperative organization of resources (Butterfill and Apperly 2013). Endowed with this animal spirit, humans just raise it to astonishing heights, such as constructing conspiracy theories, because humans are endowed with language as well.

Almost every general review of animal 'intelligence' and 'mind' begins with or emphasizes animal feats such as elaborate tool-making and use, retrieval of food such as nuts from concealed locations, complicated building of nests, complex social behaviour with conspecifics and humans, and the like (De Wall

2016; Andrews 2015; Griffin 2001; Premack and Premack 2003). Since I do not have the space to review each of these cases in detail, let me just state that it seems eminently plausible to explain them without residue in terms of the following: (i) some built-in low-level neural computation *not* amounting to symbol manipulation, (ii) a highly structured, abundant and robust memory, (iii) acute sensory systems linked to the structured memory for efficient recall and (iv) salient adaptation in the environmental niche.

However, as with the fascinating theory of mind case, it is possible that the mechanisms just suggested are not enough to account for all the intriguing cases; as research proceeds, our conception of animal cognition is likely to get richer. Yet, there is no convincing evidence so far that any of the animal feats suggested in the literature decisively meet the criterion of the Cartesian mind: possession of structured thoughts which are at once novel, free from external stimuli and appropriate to the context. To these Cartesian conditions we now turn.

1.3.2 Signs and thoughts

No one doubts that some thoughts are essentially connected with linguistic ability, so that these thoughts are not available to non-linguistic species. Ray Jackendoff (1990) suggests an interesting yet pretty commonsensical account of language acquisition which we might use here. He asks: How do children come to acquire abstract concepts like state, office, study and honesty? Jackendoff's idea is that children first learn empirical concepts like milk, food, toy, car and pillow. These concepts may be picked up from the environment, perhaps even without assistance from caregivers. The availability of these concepts triggers the linguistic system which has syntactic objects like determiner phrases consisting of a determiner and a noun, for example, *the toy*; also, there are syntax-governed quasi-semantic things like cases and theta roles which are assigned to syntactic objects such as nominals (Mukherji 2010, Chapter 2).

In the toy-example, then, the empirical knowledge of toy and the syntactic knowledge of *toy* inside a certain structure are put together. Now, when the child confronts examples like *the office starts tomorrow*, the child can infer that *office* stands for something since its grammatical function parallels that of *toy*. It follows, therefore, that having office-thoughts is impossible without having a grammatical system. Suppose so. Notice that the child acquires the office-thought by first acquiring the toy-thought in concrete contexts as the linguistic system gets empirically triggered. In the absence of a linguistic system, therefore, it is totally unclear which *form of thought* is made available even in concrete contexts. Although we provisionally ascribed a banana-thought to Washoe the famous chimpanzee earlier, it now becomes unclear what it means to do so.

This brings us directly to Descartes' central idea regarding the mind. He thought of humans as displaying 'natural intelligence' and the prime example of this intelligence is the ability to use language, with its distinctive property of novelty, freedom from control by external stimuli and its capacity to evoke appropriate thoughts in the listener (Descartes, *Meditations,* Part V). Notice that each of these conditions is satisfied in the office-case just discussed. Descartes was convinced that animals do not have this ability and, therefore, they do not have any of the *other abilities* that go with it. As we will see later in Chapter 6, the absence of the required abilities results in very restricted primate talk despite the otherwise impressive complexity in their behaviour.[5] Perhaps chimpanzees do not talk because they cannot form structured thoughts for subsequent articulation; in a sense, chimpanzees keep to themselves because they have nothing to say.

The human case, on the other hand, is dramatically different. First, humans can construct a whole language with very little stimuli and, quite often, from a general absence of them: this observation is often referred to as the 'argument from the poverty of stimulus' (APS). Lila Gleitman and her team (Gleitman et al. 1995) provided one dramatic example. They found three blind and deaf children, who were never taught American Sign Language by expert trainers. These children actually invented their own sign language simply by touching the faces of speakers, a very inadequate source of linguistic information. The grammatical complexity of their language matched those of normal children of their age.

In general, between the ages of two and seven, children routinely pick up close to twenty thousand words (sometimes at the rate of a dozen a day) for regular use independently of gender, socio-economic status, location, peer interaction and the like. These words are put together into sentences of extreme complexity for which, in most cases, no definite or correcting evidence is made available. As we saw, this system in turn is used to learn or form new concepts, resulting in novel thoughts. For all practical purposes, the ability is essentially unbounded.

As we will see in Chapter 5, the basic structural features of this system are the following: (a) there are words organized in an extremely complex lexico-morphological system, and (b) there is a computational system with a built-in *generative mechanism* which can produce novel expressions without any bound. In effect, the human linguistic system is a system of *discrete infinity:* there is no sentence with 3.5 words and no 1.2nd sentence. It is no exaggeration to say that all that is distinctively human is essentially linked to this ability, including not only nice things like religions and philosophy, science, complex social and political systems, literature and the arts, but also terrible things such as fundamentalism, terrorism, fascism and planet-threatening greed and stupidity.

1.4 Mind and super-body

Descartes needed some way of capturing this stark contrast between humans and animals in general categorical terms: making a distinction between, say, linguistic and non-linguistic animals just labels the contrast without suggesting any deeper basis for it. To appreciate Descartes' valiant attempts to this end, let me quickly review the Cartesian moves enumerated earlier.

The first attempt in that direction, as we saw, was to invoke the category of consciousness and explain the contrast with it: humans are conscious, animals are not. There are several problems with this. First, as we saw, the *Cogito* argument does not quite require that the thoughtful subject be conscious; so the argument cannot decisively link what is distinctively human with consciousness. Second, it is plainly false that animals are not conscious unless *to be conscious* is question-beggingly used for *able to use language*. Third, the linguistic ability, on which the central thrust of Descartes' argument depends, is largely unconscious. Language users do not have (theoretical) access to their linguistic ability and what little access they think they have often turns out to be wrong or, at best, totally inadequate for explaining the complexity of the cognitive structures attained in this domain. I conclude that the category of consciousness is largely useless for Descartes' purposes even if Descartes himself might have found it useful.

The second attempt was to use the notion of *having thoughts* to display the contrast: animals do not have thoughts, humans do. We saw that even this will not work since, up to a point, animals might be ascribed thoughts. *Up* the evolutionary tree and, hence, close to the human branch, the distinction between *having thoughts* and merely being *ascribed thoughts* is not exactly perspicuous. Therefore, the notion of *not* having thoughts does not pick out the entire class of animals. As Descartes himself observed in his letter to Henry More, dated 5 February 1649, this problem of generality occupied him: commenting on whether animals have thoughts, he wrote, 'I do not think it can be proved that there is none, since human mind does not reach into their hearts.' Yet, as he wrote to the Marquess of Newcastle, dated 23 November 1646, he stubbornly held that '(t)here is no reason to believe it of some animals without believing it of all, and many of them such as oysters and sponges are too imperfect for this to be credible' (Cottingham 1991, 360–5). Still, Descartes' inability to form a large category, with sponges and chimpanzees included, does not rule out the validity of smaller categories with sufficient neural complexity.

Notice that here I am using a rather rich notion of structured thoughts with, say, the basic argument structure and an array of concepts in place. I am suggesting that it is implausible to deny the entire category of structured thoughts to the entire category of non-linguistic animals. The range of animal thoughts no doubt increases manifold if we include notions such as imagistic thoughts, non-conceptual thoughts, emotive thoughts and other 'natural impulses' as Descartes would have preferred to call them. Common notions of thought and consciousness are too thick to capture the fine distinction Descartes needed, as noted.

I think the problem I am raising in this chapter has been largely missed in the huge literature on Descartes. The problem he basically faced was: How do I capture the central contrast between humans and animals – the ability to use language – in more substantive terms and *keep just to the contrast?* In other words, the tensions (and the attempted convergence) between Descartes' mind/body distinction *and* the fact of language use have not really been appreciated, as Clarke (2003) has also pointed out. Thus, many authors, such as Chomsky (1994a, 1997), have found it convenient to accept his view of language while rejecting Descartes' push towards a principled mind/body distinction, as we saw (but see Chomsky 2015).

This brings us finally to Descartes' third and perhaps the most discussed (and ill-understood) attempt to solve the problem just stated: *a substantive* distinction between mind and body. As noted, the starting point for Descartes, as Margaret Wilson (1978, 183–4) observes after careful internal study, was that Descartes was at once committed to mechanistic explanation in physics, together with the 'perfectly creditable belief that human intelligence could never be accounted for on the available mechanistic models'.

To appreciate Wilson's diagnosis, notice Descartes' historical predicament: (a) he was stuck with scholastic categories of substances and attributes; (b) the dominating scheme of things in his time continued to be the Aristotelian great chain of being which he was trying to get out of; (c) he really did not have a substantive theory of language in hand; (d) there was physics in terms of mechanistic philosophy, and not much else in science to encourage the pluralistic body-of-doctrines view of disciplines; hence, he did not have the resources to pose the problem of unification. Yet, as Wilson pointed out, Descartes was empirically dead right; there is no doubt that the remarkable ability to use language was species-specific. In this, he was centuries ahead of currently prominent animal language advocates.

Hence, Descartes persuaded himself to postulate an altogether separate substance called *mind* (*res cogitans*) to lay a basis for *human intelligence.* In effect, as we saw, this means that the Cartesian mind is needed *solely* to account for the human linguistic ability in the general sense in which Descartes posed the phenomenon. Descartes was pushed to postulating this substance because the available mechanistic models failed to account for this ability. If Descartes' dualism is to be rejected *now, we* must convince ourselves that such a 'scientific' model is finally available. We have to see what this conviction means once the evidence is presented because so far, as we will soon see in the next chapter, current basic sciences, especially the neurosciences, offer no convincing picture. Pending unknown scientific knowledge, some telling form of dualism continues to be the only option for this area.

For example, thought and consciousness, we saw, may be ascribed to animals in some cases. What sort of mechanical explanation is available for that? How many times do we need to recall the embarrassment caused by nematodes? We also saw that Descartes' greatest problem was his restricted conception of body. That conception, as Newton showed, is clearly inadequate even for physical explanation, not to speak of biological explanation. As far as I know, this is Chomsky's basic objection against the Cartesian conception of body, and he extends the objection to reject Descartes' concept of mind as well. This is because, according to Chomsky, the concept of mind makes sense only in association with the concept of body. Nonetheless, it follows that Descartes' alleged mechanistic conception of body is inadequate for physical systems and for animals *even when* the latter are viewed as devoid of (full-blooded) consciousness and thoughts. This conception, then, ought to be rejected straightaway. Where does this take us?

Now suppose we are able to enlarge the concept of body to include non-mechanical physical effects (gravitation, quantum potential and the like), unconscious and thoughtless beastly effects as well as restricted conscious and thoughtful animal effects. Intuitively, there ought to be *some* notion of body that meets these tall demands. Sensations, for example, are clearly bodily processes even if they are conscious processes, as Descartes rightly thought. Suppose all this falls under some fancy conception of basic physical laws (Fodor 1994). Grant all this and nurture a grand unified view of science in the future; call the resulting realm a *super-body.*

Something like the idea of a super-body was, indeed, hinted at by Chomsky while discussing the limits of mechanical philosophy, as noted. According to Chomsky, Descartes held that mechanistic philosophy may explain all of the inorganic world, and much of the organic world, 'including everything about plants and animals and much of the functioning of humans, up to elements of sensation and perception' (Chomsky 1994a, 37). The idea of super-body, however, goes beyond Descartes in including non-mechanical aspects of nature, such as gravitation.

Needless to say, we do not have such a grand conception of body at present. Perhaps some recent attempts in quantum physics to understand certain aspects of consciousness could be a step in that direction (Penrose 1994; Chalmers 1996); however, the conceptual issues about demarcation of realms are far from clear in that area of research (Mukherji 2017, Chapter 4). The crucial point is that the grand picture still *does not* include the Cartesian mind as I fashioned it since the Cartesian mind needs a principled 'substantive' distinction between humans and animals, and animals, with thoughts and all, *are* part of the envisaged super-body. Having thus isolated the Cartesian mind from the rest of nature, we need to find out its properties.

Following the ancient idea that substances have attributes, Descartes needed two distinguishable attributes to ground his concepts of mind and body. Following the mechanical conception of body, it was natural to think of spatiality (= extension) as the attribute of body. Since space can be fragmented, bodies maybe fragmented as well. In order to distinguish the mind sharply from body, Descartes needed a different attribute and called it *thought*. By his definition, thought is non-spatial; hence, it cannot be fragmented, or at least no clear notion of fragmentation applies here. Mind thus is a 'unity'. In my view, the conception basically means that the mind is simple and abstract, and we have no idea what it means for it to be located in space, that is, the brain. To emphasize, the mind is non-spatial primarily because mechanistic philosophy fails to apply to it. As noted, the postulation is as salient as the postulation of a gravitational field.

The mind according to Descartes is an all-at-once godly affair in the heavens. I emphasize that the godly picture arose in Descartes' mind exactly because mind is endowed with the mysterious phenomenon of language; Descartes simply had no means of sketching an earthly picture of mind with language at its centre. In view of the unearthly phenomenon of language, we are compelled to view mind as basically falling from the sky. In the ancient Indian text *Rgveda* (*c.* 1000 BC), the phenomenon of language is once described as a 'spirit descending and embodying itself in phenomena, assuming various guises and disclosing its real nature to the sensitive soul'. It's a humbling proposal.

The mind in cognitive science

A very specific conception of the human mind, the generative mind, appears to have significant historical support from the Cartesian tradition. In this conception, the human mind is viewed as a simple and single – that is, a *unitary* – device that links signs with thoughts in a variety of mental systems, including especially the human languages. Since languages are species-specific, so is the generative mind. Metaphysically, the generative divide between humans and non-humans is conceptualized in terms of a distinction between the mind and the super-body; the divide is christened *doctrinal dualism*, in the suggested reconstruction of Descartes' mind–body dualism.

The proposed framework has two distinct parts: general and specific. In the general part, the mind is viewed as a species-specific unitary system; the system is so radically separated from current conceptions of body, matter, physical stuff and the like that the conception of mind is best understood as enforcing a certain form of dualism. In the specific part, we propose that the mind is characterized by generativity in terms of Principle G. In Part II of the work, we will see how far the concept of the generative mind may be developed and defended in the light of contemporary studies on the relevant phenomena.

As for the general idea of the mind as a unitary concept enforcing dualism, we need to judge the idea in the context of contemporary studies on the mind before we can proceed to the specific part. The issue is that, apart from the time gap of nearly half a millennium, the basic difference between the times of Descartes and ours is that, during the former, the concept of mind was virtually a fresh entry in the zoo of philosophical ideas, as Bertrand Russell (1919) would have put it. Although there is always nuanced historical precedence for such global concepts, it is a safe assumption that Descartes and the Cartesians suggested a radically new concept of mind in terms of the startling mind–body dualism. In that sense, Descartes had no need to weigh his concept of mind in terms of other conceptions of the mind proposed by his contemporaries.

In our times, in contrast, the study of the mind is a massive international enterprise comprising a large variety of influential disciplines. Any fresh proposal on the concept of mind now must take into account existing views on the mind, if any, to determine where the proposal stands with respect to recent views on the mind. Broadly, the discussion on the mind are conducted in two disciplinary domains: philosophy of mind and the cluster of disciplines collectively called *Cognitive Science*, with substantial overlap between the two. Assuming something like a disciplinary divide between philosophy of mind and cognitive science in terms of the topics covered, I will concentrate only on certain developments in cognitive science.

I will basically stay away from the discipline of philosophy of mind because, insofar as it engages with the classical mind–body problem in terms of identity, supervenience and the like (Davidson 1970; Kripke 1980; McLaughlin 2005), it does not throw much light on the concept of mind itself; it does not say what the concept of mind *is*. So we do not know how to judge the idea of a unitary mind with respect to some other conception of the mind. Similarly, although the functionalist literature in the philosophy of mind (Jackson 1998; Putnam 1999) does mention 'mental states' as causal intermediaries between environmental stimuli and behaviour, it seldom explains what these states are states *of*. These 'deflationary' conceptions of mind and mental states are perhaps cautionary measures following Ryle's strictures on the ghost in the machine (Ryle 1949). So, post-Rylean philosophers might have been anxious to address the problem of mind without directly subscribing to the metaphysics of the mind. However, Ryle was primarily objecting to metaphysical dualism in the form of substance dualism.

Once we settled for *doctrinal dualism*, rather than substance dualism, to ground the Cartesian conception of mind in the previous chapter, the issue of identity/supervenience becomes a non-issue. To understand whether the mind is identical with the body or whether the mind supervenes on the body, we need to understand something about alleged mental phenomena and something about related physical phenomena with an eye towards unification of the two directions of inquiry. Before such unification, it is pointless to ask if mind and body are identical and such things. When our understanding of mental and physical phenomena grows to the point of unification, there will be no need to ask about identity either. The hotly debated issue of identity in this branch of philosophy of mind threw no light on the mind at all, in my view. As for philosophical discussion of specific concepts such as consciousness, belief, perception and the like, my view is that either they need the generative mind to be counted as a mental concept or they do not belong to the study of the mind at all. Since I have discussed these topics at length elsewhere (Mukherji 2017), I will not repeat the arguments here.

In contrast, certain approaches in cognitive science are directly relevant for us as they seem to disapprove of the general idea of a human-specific unitary mind; cognitive science postulates an immensely complex mind. Furthermore, although as we have framed the divide, cognitive science is not directly concerned with the philosophical problem of the relation between the mind and body, some of the major programmatic advances in cognitive science may be attributed to an underlying hostility to any form of dualism. Although it is difficult to prove so without a detailed review of various branches of cognitive science, I will suggest that the postulation of complex minds could be an outcome of the methods that may be traced to technological developments.

There are at least two related proposals in cognitive science that challenge the very idea of a human-specific unitary mind; as we will see, these proposals can be discussed without getting into the specific proposal of the generative mind. These challenges take two forms, implicit and explicit. The implicit challenge is that the mind is a cluster concept comprising various processes and events covering many domains; for expository convenience, I call it the *traditional view of the mind*. The explicit challenge is that the mind is viewed as modular in structure such that mind is a complex of largely autonomous units.

I will examine the traditional view carefully to suggest that the specific enumeration of classical domains in contemporary cognitive science did show an early intuitive interest in the unity of the mind, more or less along the Cartesian lines. However, the search for the unified mind was later abandoned as the cognitive sciences grew and diversified. In my view, technological developments, such as computer programming and neural imagery, were largely responsible for the abandonment of the initial project. The adoption of these technologies probably suggests why the cognitive sciences adopted a more heterogeneous view of the mind.

As for the challenge from modularity, I will suggest that even if some notion of modularity applies to the classical domains of higher cognition, there is nothing to prevent the search for some domain-general principles. However, the more technical notion of modularity of informationally encapsulated systems appears to apply only to perceptual systems of both humans and non-human animals; if so, then the concept of the generative mind is not affected since it belongs to the higher cognitive functions of humans.

2.1 Traditional view of the mind

The contemporary field of cognitive science, a purported multidisciplinary science of the mind, emerged in the 1950s during what is sometimes known as the *second cognitive revolution* (Chomsky 1991). As we will see, in its initial phase, cognitive science was largely concerned with the character of the human mind in terms of new tools, ideas and research programmes such as Turing computation, Gestalt psychology, generative linguistics, study of biological forms and the like. In that sense, its goals were not very different from the *first cognitive revolution* often ascribed to the classical Cartesian tradition.

In just over half a century of rapid developments, cognitive science has come to cover a bewildering variety of topics. Given the coverage, it is not possible to summarize all the major developments in the cognitive sciences, with their deep forays into highly technical areas of computational theory and the neurosciences, within the space of a chapter. In fact, not surprisingly, much of it is not really relevant for the project here. Therefore, I will take an aerial view of only those parts of the cognitive sciences that relate to my main interest in developing the conception of the generative mind. I will examine whether the current state of the cognitive sciences in these areas has either developed a coherent concept of the mind that includes the human mind or whether it has furnished any reason to question the concept of the generative mind. I will argue that the cognitive sciences have done neither.

As we saw, the idea of the human-specific unitary mind was basically grounded on the human linguistic ability and the related aspects of human cognition. Hence, it is not surprising that the initial focus in cognitive science also was on the structure and functioning of human language and the role it plays in reasoning. I will argue that this was the primary focus for Alan Turing's ideas on the computational properties of intelligence. Given the range of topics covered by the cognitive sciences even in the restricted areas under study here, it is natural that the initial quest for the restricted notion of the human mind has virtually disappeared from the agenda of cognitive science. A brief look at what is currently published in the leading journals of the cognitive sciences appears to confirm this view; there is very little connection between the formal and empirical studies of human language and related aspects of human cognition and the rest of the topics pursued in cognitive science.[1] It is not unreasonable to conclude that by now a focused study of the human mind is at best a minority concern in the cognitive sciences.

Nonetheless, even if studies on language and the related aspects of the human mind occupy a minor area, surveys of cognitive science do claim to cover the study of the mind. For example, Nadel and Piattelli-Palmarini (2003) hold that 'cognitive science can be defined broadly as the scientific study of minds and brains, be they real, artificial, human or animal'. According to its editors, *The MIT Encyclopaedia of the Cognitive Sciences* is concerned with current 'cognitive science approaches to many questions about mind' (Wilson and Keil 1999, xiii). The influential journal *Cognition* 'serves as a forum for discussion of every aspect of cognitive science as a field' by publishing 'theoretical and experimental papers on the study of mind'. What then is the concept of mind studied by the field of cognitive science?

There seems to be a general agreement in the wide cognitive science community that the question just asked is not very meaningful at the current stage of inquiry. In his introduction to *An Invitation to Cognitive Science*, Daniel Osherson (1995, ix) observes that the topics covered in the four-volume series 'range from muscle movement to human rationality, from acoustic phonetics to mental imagery, from the cerebral locus of language to the categories that people use to organize experience'. Cognitive science, Osherson suggests, is concerned with 'everything we do', where 'we' includes other organisms as well. Osherson concludes that 'topics as diverse as these require distinctive kinds of theories, tested against distinctive kinds of data'. In the absence of any overarching theory that covers all these topics and more, there is likely to be little interest in developing a narrow conception of the generative mind. This is not to suggest that the cognitive sciences refuse to study the mental aspects of language; the suggestion, rather, is that it is just one of the topics falling under the study of 'everything we do'.

Steven Pinker's work provides a good starting point for the inquiry into the current state of the art on the human mind. As noted, the basic interest in this work is to understand the intimate specific-specific connection between language and the human mind; the narrow conception of the human mind ensues from this interest. It seems that Pinker flatly denies that interest. Pinker (1997, 1998) holds that humans think with visual images, concepts, auditory signals and 'truth-bearing propositions': 'Knowing a language, then, is knowing how to translate mentalese into strings of words and vice versa. People without language would still have mentalese, and babies and many nonhuman animals presumably have simpler dialects.'

In this view, there is nothing 'linguistic' about human thought itself. Language is basically needed for articulation of thoughts with 'noises', but not for constitution of thought. Pinker believes that there is growing evidence for this non-linguistic view of thoughts from studies of human infants and non-human animals; in effect, a variety of thoughts can be ascribed to creatures to whom we do not ascribe linguistic competence. I have already examined some of these claims about animal minds in the previous chapter to explain why Descartes thought that the mind was human-specific. I will continue to examine the ideas of non-human and non-linguistic thoughts as we proceed.

For now, Pinker seems to be making two general points. First, language and thought are distinct and largely unrelated components of the human mind. Specifically, the notion of language is restricted to externalization or articulation of thought while thought itself is viewed as having non-linguistic origins. Second, even within the domain of thoughts, mind consists of a variety of disparate elements: visual images, auditory signals, concepts, some notion of belief-structures bearing truth and falsity, and much else. The human mind, according to this picture, is vastly complex with a range of apparently disjointed capacities and systems forming its parts. Since these parts are available in a variety of forms in non-human species as well, the human mind is also viewed as non-species-specific in large measure. The suggested complex, non-unitary and non-species-specific conception of the mind is the rule rather than an exception in the general cognitive science literature.

For example, Noam Chomsky is not likely to agree with Pinker's view that language is basically a device for articulation; in fact, Chomsky holds the exact opposite: language is essentially a device for structuring thought (Chomsky 2015; Berwick and Chomsky 2016). Nonetheless, he explicitly proposes a 'deflationary' view of the mind. By *mind* he means 'the mental aspects of the world, with no concern for defining the notion more closely and no expectation that we will find some interesting kind of unity or boundaries' (Chomsky 2000b, 75; also, Chomsky 1995b). He is using the term 'mental' just to draw attention to 'certain phenomena, events, processes, and states' without suggesting any 'metaphysical divide'.[2]

According to Chomsky, people use terms such as *chemical*, *electrical* and the like, with no intention to 'identify the true criterion or mark' of these things. These are 'bodies of doctrines' which are 'local' attempts to study certain aspects of nature with an 'eye to eventual unification' with the rest of science (Chomsky 2000b, 168). Insofar as cognitive science is concerned, it is an 'empirical study of cognitive capacities' such as 'vision, language, reasoning, etc'. Studies of these capacities are 'components of the science of human nature that may not form a narrow discipline' (Chomsky 2000b, 165). Chomsky is thus explicitly opposing a narrow conception of mind at the current stage of knowledge prior to unification. I assume general agreement with these observations in the cognitive science community.

There are several problems with this non-unitary view of mind. Arguably, when people use terms such as 'physical', 'chemical', *electrical* and the like, some intuitive idea of unity and boundary is often implied, even if no sharp and permanent 'metaphysical divide' is intended. In other words, scientists working in different fields (must) have well-formed intuitions of what does or does not fall within their field at a particular stage. When asked about the possible event of nuclear winter and the extinction of dinosaurs due to the crash of a meteor, the physicist-writer Carl Sagan replied that the physics in the two cases is the same. For Sagan, then, certain events involving very different objects such as nuclear devices and meteors fall under the narrow study of the physical. Unity and boundary of fields may be intuitively entertained along with expectations of broadening of horizons and eventual unification of the sciences. How else do we make sense of the concept of a body of doctrines?

This concept arose as follows (see Mukherji 2010, Chapters 1 and 7 for more). The eighteenth-century English chemist Joseph Black, whose work Chomsky cites, suggested: 'Let chemical affinity be received as a first principle ... till we have established such a body of doctrine as [Newton] has established concerning the laws of gravitation.' The triumphs of chemistry were 'built on no reductionist foundation but rather achieved in isolation from the newly emerging science of physics' (Chomsky 2000b, 166). It follows, from Chomsky's own description of the history of chemistry, that chemistry was regarded as a body of doctrines that simultaneously satisfied two properties: (a) it signalled real understanding, that is, genuine scientific advance in the sharply demarcated study of chemical affinities enshrined in the 'table of affinities', and (b) it continued to be isolated from the rest of science, namely, physics.

The focused, non-reductionist character of chemistry marked its boundary, enabling it to illuminate the chemical aspect of nature. Since the unity and boundary of chemistry was thus *internally* achieved in the course of inquiry itself, there was no need to 'define' or 'mark' it, not to speak of erecting 'metaphysical divides'. This perspective on a body of doctrines is likely to be more cogent for even more focused studies that fall under electrical, optical and genetic. In order to satisfy the analogy between the chemical and the mental, then, we must at least be in a position to outline some coherent phenomena that fall under the study of the mental, just as chemical affinity fell under the study of the chemical. The concept of a body of doctrines, therefore, does not help illuminate Chomsky's deflationary view of mind.

Furthermore, there is a clear tension between Chomsky's claim that the term 'mental' is used without any expectation of an interesting kind of unity or boundaries, and his remark that cognitive science is the study of cognitive capacities such as vision, language, reasoning and the like. Setting *etc.* aside for now, there must be some internal unity in the studies of diverse capacities like language, vision and reasoning for them to fall under the general label 'mental', unless the list is intended to be arbitrary. In particular, how do we know that each of these are *cognitive* capacities rather than something else? Does sexuality or bullfighting fall under the mental?

Chomsky's suggestion is that, keeping to the human mind, these mental capacities fall under something like 'traditional coverage' (2000b, 75). However, at least one traditional coverage along similar lines, namely, the one proposed by René Descartes (1637, 1641) was, in fact, based on a rather sharp metaphysical boundary of the mental. Similar remarks apply to the closely related non-materialist tradition inaugurated by Franz Brentano to identify Intentionality as 'the mark of the mental' (Brentano 1874; Haugeland 1997, 4). Both Descartes and Brentano recommended the coverage mentioned by Chomsky: language, vision, reasoning.

It is no part of my argument at this point that Descartes' and Brentano's metaphysical views are valid. Still, if we wish to hold on to their coverage without accepting the proposed boundaries, we need to find out if there is some independent justification for this particular coverage. Otherwise, it is unclear if analogies from *established* terms like 'chemical', 'physical', 'electrical' and so on are appropriate for evaluating *mental* in the intended *non*-established sense, that is, the sense in which the term is delinked from its traditional, unity-enforcing usage. Cognitive science cannot have it both ways.

More specifically, Chomsky holds that 'the study of language tries to develop bodies of doctrine' whose 'constructs and principles can properly be "termed mental"' (2000b, 168). Following the traditional coverage, if *mental* is to cover vision and reasoning as well, it is natural to ask whether the 'constructs and principles' of *these* studies cohere with the study of language for *all* of them to fall under the mental. In fact, as we will see in some detail later, Chomsky strongly advocates the FLN hypothesis that the structuring principles of the narrow faculty of language are specific to the domain of language. Hence, according to Chomsky, these 'constructs and principles' of language are *not* shared with any other domain. What is the ground then for thinking of each of language, vision and reasoning as falling under 'mental'?

In other words, if it turns out that the individual studies of these capacities do not even cohere in a theoretically interesting way, not to speak of forming a 'unitary discipline', then it will be implausible to apply the concept of mind to cover all of language, vision and reasoning, among others. Chomsky's restricted coverage does not mesh with his deflationary view of mind. I am at pains to point this out from different angles because, in my opinion, Chomsky's own work on language and mind is best viewed as a search for a metaphysical divide, a quest for a real joint of nature (Mukherji 2010, Chapters 1 and 7).

As noted, there is general agreement on Chomsky's deflationary view of mind. Yet, it is therefore a matter of much interest that, in practice, there is wide consensus on the coverage suggested by Chomsky as well. To emphasize, the field appears to advocate both a deflationary view of mind and a restricted coverage. Thus, the noted tension in Chomsky's views on these matters generalizes to most practitioners in the field. For example, recall Osherson's remark about the diversity of topics pursued in cognitive science: acoustic phonetics, cerebral locations, muscle movement and so on. However, in a subsequent remark in the same essay, Osherson observes that 'cognitive science is the study of human intelligence in all its forms, from perception and action to language and reasoning' (Osherson 1995, xi). Thus, Osherson not only suggests a more definite coverage, but he also binds the items of the coverage under a single theme: the study of *human* intelligence.

Ignoring the controversial theme and focusing on the coverage, it seems that Osherson's list essentially converges with that of Chomsky and the tradition Chomsky mentions. Assuming that large parts of the general study of human actions are already covered under the studies of perception, language and reasoning, these three broad topics thus constitute the *least* range of cognitive science as envisaged by Chomsky and Osherson just two decades ago. In practice, as the organization of topics in the series edited by Osherson shows, the study of perception so far is restricted primarily to the study of vision. The series consists of one volume each on language, visual cognition and thinking, while a fourth volume is devoted primarily to methodological issues. The actual coverage thus indicates a sense of unity in the topics even if Osherson's general opening remarks for these volumes deny unity.

In the much broader range of topics listed in the *MIT Encyclopaedia* (Wilson and Keil 1999), there is exactly one short entry each for haptic, taste and smell perceptions. There are four entries on auditory perception itself; the three entries on speech relate more directly to language.[3] The rest of the hundreds of entries basically cover language, vision and reasoning. It appears that, despite deflationary claims, actual research had groped for some form of convergence following some intuitive pull at least in the initial decades of cognitive science. What was that pull?

2.2 Computationalism

It is instructive to note briefly how cognitive science converged on the suggested coverage in the first place. Abstracting away from much internal detail and focusing on one major direction, cognitive science appeared as a distinct body of research in the 1950s largely due to the emergence of the computational view of the mind. Based on some developments in the mathematical theory of computation (Post 1921; Church 1936; Turing 1937), the leading idea towards a computational view of mind was proposed by Alan Turing (1950): Turing conjectured that the general phenomenon of 'intelligence' may be fruitfully investigated in the format of digital computation.

Apparently, for some authors, Turing's proposal was at least indirectly related to the mind–body problem; therefore, it has a bearing on doctrinal dualism. According to John Haugeland (1997, 2), researchers who developed the computational conception of intelligence did not believe in 'anything immaterial or supernatural, such as a vital spirit or an immortal soul'. Haugeland asserts that these researchers firmly believed in materialism such that 'matter, suitably selected and arranged, suffices for intelligence'. Following the assertion, Haugeland suggests that, with Turing's attractive formal ideas in hand, researchers were able to focus more on the *how* rather than the *what*. Haugeland's juxtaposition of his materialistic claim on Turing machines implies that Turing's formal proposals can be viewed materialistically, thereby solving the mind–body problem and dispensing with dualism.

In my view, in the early stages, the researchers did not even ask *where*, even though Turing himself engaged in some marvellous speculation, on the side, about evolution of biological forms: *morphogenesis* (Turing 1952). Insofar as the study of 'intelligence' was concerned, Turing just provided an abstract schematic model derived from the study of the formal foundation of mathematics. The fact that some computational schemes can be implemented on digital computers has no bearing on the mind–body problem. After all, if the Turing computation provided a valid model for human intelligence, it means that the scheme is implemented somewhere in the human body, probably the brain. But we cannot conclude from this obvious fact that the computational scheme itself is material; that'll be too easy a solution for the mind–body problem.

It is interesting that Kurt Gödel, one of the pioneers of computational theory, held that 'there will be scientific disproof of mechanism in biology and of the proposition that there is no mind separate from matter', as reported in Wang (1987, 9–10). Noam Chomsky (1995b, 1–2), one of the leading contributors to computation and automata theory, and the founder of contemporary generative linguistics, held not so long ago that 'one seems not to find anything like the basic properties of human language' in 'the organic world' and that 'biology and the brain sciences, which, as currently understood, do not provide any basis for what appear to be fairly well established conclusions about language' (see also Chomsky et al. 2019).

I think Gödel, Chomsky, Turing and other pioneers of computational theory of that generation understood the neo-Cartesian character of their work.[4] But, of course, the understanding was too subliminal in nature to be proposed in a theoretical gesture. Chomsky himself rejected any notion of dualism, but he rejected the doctrine of materialism as well. But that did not prevent Chomsky from formulating his groundbreaking computational theory of language, roughly along the lines of Turing computationalism.

Therefore, there is no reason to adopt Haugeland's materialist understanding of Turing computation in advance of unforeseen unification of the sciences. The issue is critical for us because, while we advocate doctrinal dualism to capture the distinction between the generative mind and super-body, we basically adopt a Chomskyan computational view of language to form the conception of what the generative mind could be. In my view, Turing's ideas offered a direct and elegant scientific approach for studying the human mind as proposed here.

In his landmark paper, Turing made the direct suggestion that human intelligence – the ability to reason on specific topics such as moves on a chessboard – can be encoded in a system of representations that are governed by formally specified rules (Mukherji 2010, Chapter 7). So the basic lesson from Turing's proposal was that the problematic aspects of classical Cartesianism, as well as those of mind–body identity theories, may be simply set aside until we learn more about the related cognitive systems. Moreover, the very idea of a computational mind was based on formal operations on representations; thus, a computational mind extends as far as such representations are available, as we will see in Part II.

Following Turing's suggestion, the reigning doctrine in much of the cognitive sciences for several decades was that cognitive systems are best viewed as computational systems (Pylyshyn 1984); the broad doctrine could be called *computationalism*. The basic theoretical idea is that any device whose input and output can be effectively characterized by some or other computable function may be viewed as an instance of a Universal Turing Machine, given the Church–Turing thesis. Since brains may be viewed as machines that establish relations between causes and effects (stimulus and behaviour), brains are particular Turing machines; all we need is to find the computable function that effectively relates stimulus and behaviour.

However, as Churchland and Grush (1999, 155) immediately point out, this abstract characterization of brains as computational systems merely by virtue of the existence of some I/O function, holds little conceptual interest. Any system that functions at all could be viewed as a computational system: livers, stomachs, geysers, toasters, earthquakes, continental shifts, solar systems, collapse of massive stars and so on, and of course computers and brains. So we need a more focused understanding of the underlying mechanism, involving rules and representations that typically inhabit the mind, to claim why a *cognitive* system could be viewed as a computational system. Notice that when we strictly observe the constraint just proposed, much work on computational properties of brains, including Churchland's own work (Churchland and Sejnowski 1992), could be viewed as essentially unfounded.

Turing (1950) made an even narrower and more substantive proposal. The proposal was articulated in terms of a thought experiment: the *Turing Test*. The test consists of an interrogator A, a man B and a woman C. On the basis of a question–answer session, A is to find out which one of B and C is the woman. Turing asked: what happens when a Turing machine in the form of a digital computer takes the place of B? Turing's proposal was that if A's rate of success (or failure) in identifying the gender of B remains statistically insignificant when a human is replaced by a computer, we should not hesitate to ascribe thinking to the computer.

The details of Turing's thought experiment clearly suggest that, for computational purposes, Turing identified intelligence with the ability to interpret sentences of a language (Mukherji 2010, Chapter 7; Sheiber 2004). For example, Turing required that the test be conducted in writing – teletyped – so that the effect of voice is factored out. In that sense, language is the hallmark of (human) mentality. In other words, the question of ascribing intelligence to non-linguistic creatures does not arise, even if those creatures otherwise display an impressive range of cognitive capacities. Perhaps the notion of intelligence does not even apply to those 'animal' aspects of humans as well – consciousness, emotions, reflexes, drives and the like – that are not essentially linked to the language faculty.

It is often missed in the literature on the Turing test that it was not proposed as a theory of computational mind, but as a research programme to find out if the human mind is, indeed, computational in the abstract sense in which it was posed by Turing (Chomsky, in Sheiber 2004); Turing was not attempting to answer the essentially meaningless question, 'can machines think?' To develop the research programme, one needs to come up with a detailed description in some tangible and realistic computational format to encode the thoughts in a domain such as playing chess, writing a sonnet or diagnosing a disease. Thus we see the beginning of interest in the generative mind.

Following several decades of research on reasoning and language, some researchers, deeply familiar with this work, thought of extending the computational perspective to the study of vision using the format of rules and representations (Marr 1982; Hoffman 1998). Interestingly, the classical Cartesian tradition also mentioned the 'computational' properties of the human visual system (Chomsky and McGilvray 1966/2009, 3). Thus the received coverage of language, reasoning and vision, discussed in the last section was a historical consequence of one version of the computational conception of the human mind. A 'metaphysical divide' was lurking beneath the disclaimers.

Although the research did not always make it explicit, the underlying intuition throughout was to focus on those domains where it is natural to expect something like a computational explanation to obtain: domains that appeared to naturally constitute rules and representations. The paradigmatic domain, of course, was the species-specific system of human language itself. As noted, Turing himself focused on those aspects of reasoning that may be articulated in terms of a conversation (in language). In other words, the idea of a computational system – a system of explicit rules governing a finite array of representations – representing human reasoning itself leans on a prior conception of human language.

With the computational conception of mind in hand, the 'second cognitive revolution' of the 1950s thus opened up the prospect of reviving the fundamental concerns of the 'first cognitive revolution' inaugurated by classical philosophers, as noted in the Introduction. The basic classical concern was to understand the structure of human cognoscitive powers, with language at the centre, to locate the place of these powers in the rest of nature. As we are beginning to appreciate by now, the concern was shared by ancient philosophers in other traditions such as the classical Indian tradition and the Modistic tradition in classical Europe

(Hinzen et al. 2011; Hinzen and Sheehan 2013), and perhaps others as well. The computational view of the mind appeared to lend a scientific handle for addressing these concerns.

My own view, for what it is worth, is that the focused search for the mind in the early years got subsequently diverted for a combination of three related factors. These factors assumed prominence as the abstract, programmatic character of Turing's work was progressively set aside. I suppose that Turing's use of computational ideas, including the Turing test, was designed to analyse the broad issue of intelligence, which classical philosophers would have called *cognoscitive powers*, in terms of a structure of local steps that can be formally tracked. The fact that these steps can be executed on digital computers certainly endowed the abstract formal project some realistic flavour; beyond this, physical computers were of marginal theoretical value, as noted.

However, one reason why the project got diverted was that these abstract research guidelines were understood as an invitation for displaying engineering feats. With the rapid development of computer technology and the attendant discourse, construction of computational models themselves took a life of their own in place of empirically geared theoretical inquiry: computerism overtook computationalism. Popular adoption of loaded concepts such as 'artificial intelligence' and 'machine learning' infected the otherwise benign enthusiasm for technological inventions to absurd levels. In fact, the enthusiasm reached the point where researchers in artificial intelligence, such as John Anderson, claimed that only ancient Cartesian dogma prevents us from granting the feel of hot and cold to thermometers (Searle 1980). The fact that at least two generations of otherwise competent thinkers debated the issue of whether computers think, feel, get upset and so on is a rather sad comment on the field.

The second reason was that, as John Haugeland (1997) suggested, the excitement about artificial systems soon led to the idea that computerism was leading to a significant realistic understanding of mental phenomena. To press such technological understanding of mental realism further, scientists developed computational architectures far beyond the original idea of 'symbolic' computation suggested by Turing. What I have in mind is the range of 'low level' processing systems variously known as *parallel distributed processors* (PDP), *neural nets*, *connectionist networks* and the like (Rumelhart and McClelland 1986). These 'low-level' processes were meant to be artificial units designed to model the 'actual' organization of the brain consisting of neurons, synapses or whatever.

Notwithstanding the deep philosophical problems with the idea that the mind is nothing but the brain, it was nonetheless thought that a hard-nosed science of the mind cannot be ambiguous about the issue. One evidence that these 'dynamical systems' were designed to mimic the organization of the brain is that these artefacts were viewed as *situated* and *embodied* (Brooks 1991). It is another matter, as Chomsky and others pointed out, that neural net models are as abstract as the 'symbolic' models when it comes to the brain. The basic lesson for our purposes here is that, once we jump into 'lower level' connectivity, the distinction between cognitive and non-cognitive effects of biological systems is lost, not to mention the distinction between the mind and cognition.

The third and the most significant diversion was that, since computational models were invoked without attention to the *what* and *where* questions, the coverage of computational psychology exploded much beyond the original Turing-driven concerns. In time, the point was reached where even insects were viewed as implementing elaborate computational machinery (Gallistel 1998, 2018), birdsong was found to contain elements of syntax and suchlike (Miyagawa et al. 2013; Miyagawa et al. 2014); I discuss some of these cases in Chapter 6. My anxious concern is that, as other organisms and computers with their assorted cognitive domains crowded in, the human mind was pushed to the margins of pen-and-paper linguistic research.

It was evident fairly early that there are problems with the somewhat unprincipled expansion of the domains covered by computational psychology because no unified notion of computation emerged across studies in different domains. Thus, the research on language, vision and thinking did not have anything to say to each other, notwithstanding some feeble attempts to do so (Jackendoff 2002). While research on language (generative grammar) developed by leaps and bounds through a series of progressively unifying theories, the computational theory of vision lacked progress after some initial promise; it could be because vision is not a 'Cartesian' domain at all even if the Cartesians allegedly paid much attention to vision as a 'computational' system (Chomsky and McGilvray 1966/2009, 3). Research on thinking, on the other hand and as noted, took on a purely technological form in the study of artificial intelligence; it had little to do with how thought is structured in nature. Thus, advances in linguistic research did not have any discernible substantive effect in the rest of the cognitive sciences.

With some trepidation, I wish to relate the issue of selection of domains to the research choices made by Turing himself. Recall that Turing directed his computational study to human 'intelligent' reasoning. On hindsight, it is unclear if the extremely complex, multi-layered, context-dependent and pragmatic-semantic nature of human reasoning lends itself to simple computational models at all. In that sense, the theoretical investigation of 'intelligence' proposed by Turing was perhaps doomed from the start. As Jerry Fodor (2000, 2) darkly observed: 'The last forty or fifty years have demonstrated pretty clearly that there are aspects of higher mental processes into which the current armamentarium of computational models, theories, and experimental techniques offers vanishingly little insight.' Even if Fodor's rather sharp remark is only partly true, it suggests severe restrictions on how far computational theories can go (Mukherji 2010, Chapter Four).

Noam Chomsky, in contrast, focused exclusively on the grammatical aspect of the mind, a careful theoretical choice which perhaps explains the vast successes of grammatical theory. Moreover, notwithstanding occasional appeals to familiar computational concepts like push-down automata, post-production systems, recursive functions, generalized transformations and the like (Berwick and Chomsky 2016), Chomsky basically built up the formal theory from scratch to describe the linguistic data in hand. I do not think it is widely appreciated that linguistic theory is essentially independent of advances in computer science, even if computational ideas from Post, Turing and others, including Chomsky's own mathematical work, provided some initial background to the idea of generative grammar.

For example, Chomsky showed how a structural explanation could be given for the so-called *passivization* in which, while the meaning is retained, the verbal form changes when we turn the sentence *Donald Trump defeated Hilary Clinton* into *Hilary Clinton was defeated by Donald Trump*. More famously, he explained the structural difference between *John is easy to please* and *John is eager to please*, or how to give multiple structural representations for *John had a book stolen*. Given the systematicity and universality of such phenomena, a principled structural explanation is needed across thousands of particular human languages.

Chomsky offered that explanation. Chomsky's work marked the restricted and abstract aspects of the computational explanation that is needed for the formal study of human languages. The computational form of explanation in generative grammar opened the investigation into the generative mind. For the first time in the history of thought, we had a glimpse of what it means for language to be a 'mirror of mind' (Chomsky 2006, 67). The insights of generative grammar may now be carefully expanded to reach a fuller description of the human mind.

2.3 Neuroscientism

The suggested restrictions on computational explanations are particularly noteworthy in view of how the cognitive sciences developed beyond classical Turing computationalism. The new computerism, aiming for a 'realistic model' with properties of 'situatedness', 'embodiment' and the like, soon joined hands with neuroscience. It does not require elaborate conspiracy theory to understand why two very influential books in that direction were published almost simultaneously: Churchland (1986) and Rumelhart and McClelland (1986). The effort led to the grand 'unified' discipline boldly called *cognitive neuroscience*, meaning that properties of cognition are to be studied by examining the brain. It is not difficult to see that studies on organic behaviour assumed astronomical proportions.

The brain, of course, is the epicentre of virtually every form of behaviour. There is likely to be some perturbation in the brain or in the nervous system whenever an organism is doing something: reaching for food, reacting to sunlight, exhibiting depth perception, weaving nests, undergoing a headache, watching others eating a banana, meditating, falling in love or humming a tune.[5] So a sample survey can be conducted and brain signals measured for any apparently 'cognitive' behaviour that catches a researcher's fancy. The research effort no doubt generates tons of impressive charts and pictures. But what does it say on the *cognitive* properties of the brain except demonstrating the obvious that some component of the brain is activated when some cognitive behaviour takes place?

It is not difficult to see that the question ultimately goes back to the mind–brain issue which we have decided to set aside after adopting doctrinal dualism. As with computerism, I have no direct issue with cognitive neuroscience as a discipline.[6] Once we detached the enterprise from the mind–body problem, my only concern is whether this new science is able to suggest some novel conception of human cognoscitive powers that goes against the conception of the generative mind. More specifically, the interest is to see if the resources of the new science offer some means of investigating the generative mind that was not available in earlier pen-and-paper studies.

To get some hold on these rather general queries, I propose to use the mental system of human language as a paradigmatic case to see what these developments mean for the conception of the narrow mind. As I have maintained throughout, the structure of human language forms the basis for the more extended conception of the generative mind. Thus, if the neurosciences have anything to say on the narrow mind, it must reflect in the study of human language. There is no doubt that the ground situation for the marketing prospects of pursuing a unified theory of mind worsened as cognitive inquiry progressively shifted to the study of the brain. But did the prospects for the narrow mind worsen in *theoretical* terms such that the tools of the cognitive neurosciences have unearthed or re-explained the principles of the unique species-specific human language?

The topic has two parts: methodological and theoretical. The methodological issue is that the study of human language was the primary focus of the classical computational conception of the mind which viewed human cognoscitive powers as a distinct 'top-down' assembly of rules and representations. So the methodological issue is: does cognitive neuroscience have the resources to cover the computational properties of human language already discovered in terms of rules and representations? The related theoretical issue is: does the 'top-down' theoretical study of human language *need* the 'bottom-up' resources of cognitive neuroscience *prior to unification*? If the answer is negative in both cases, we can simply view cognitive neuroscience as not studying the (narrow, human, generative) mind at all; *if anything*, cognitive neuroscience studies cognition.

To probe the methodological issue, suppose we have an interested audience which agrees with the following claims of the neuroscientist: the neurosciences have advanced far enough to be able to say something, in good detail, about actual behaviour, say, the behaviour of the sea hare and the leech; some of this behaviour may be described not only with the minutest neuronal detail but also with abstract principles such as geometrical models; applied to humans, there is a reasonable expectation that such explanations may be available for much of motor behaviour, for example, reflexes; many psychological disorders, for example, some forms of schizophrenia, may have excellent and adequate neurological explanation; the effect of drugs, with the attendant neurochemical explanations, on various cognitive states are interesting and well documented; the importance of split-brain studies is undeniable.

In particular, the lateralization effects found in various forms of brain conditions do tell us something about the location and distribution of various cognitive functions in the two hemispheres; we will cite some of the interesting results as we proceed (Fedorenko and Varley 2016). Despite problems posed by nematodes and other lowly creatures, our audience will readily agree with each of the listed steps since none of them are particularly surprising and each of these is largely irrelevant for the specific issue that concerns us, namely, whether neuroscience has anything significant to say about human language.

About the only neuroscientific research on language that people commonly cite, however, will not do. Split-brain research and imagery of brain functions,

I have agreed, do say interesting, sometimes even quite dramatic, things on the localization of cognitive abilities. But such research throws hardly any light on the central issue, namely, an *explanation* of such ability. Such research says, at most, things of the following sort: a cognitive capacity C_i is located in the area X_i. Sometimes such descriptions can be finer and more interesting: a sub-capacity S_i of C_i is located in the sub-area Y_i of X_i. Probably one can go finer still. Yet, however fine it goes, it can only keep on describing without explaining the nature of C_i, S_i and so on.

The methodological limitations of neuroscience lead to the theoretical point of whether neuroscientific research on language can be conducted without 'top-down' results in hand. Suppose (incredibly) that a certain area of the brain 'lights up' when Ram hears *Trump defeated Clinton*. Now suppose the same area of Ram's brain 'lights up' again when he hears *Clinton was defeated by Trump*. Will the lighting up explain that these sentences mean the same? In other words, it does not make sense that Ram's linguistic intuitions, which grasp the sameness of meaning, are explained by the successive neural events, although it does show what happens to Ram's brain when Ram displays the intuition. That critical explanatory step requires that the concept of meaning is understood in terms of the concepts used to describe events in the brain. Indeed, there is a severe limit even to its descriptive depth in the absence of a theory of the concerned capacity.

For the explanatory issue under discussion, the limitation of split-brain research is essentially linked to the limitations of the neuroscientist's answer to the question 'what is C_i?' It is very well known that interesting answers to such questions can be reached only if we are able to focus directly on the concerned cognitive behaviour, say speech, to form some idealized, abstract notion of such behaviour. These idealizations are essential if we are to eliminate from the study the effects of other cognitive systems and various factors external to the core competence. Particular proposals for the concerned competence may be suspect, but the preceding general idea must be available for any interesting research to take shape. Thus, the neuroscientist needs the top-down models of competence for his own models, otherwise, there is nothing further for him to look at after his initial cartography (Embick and Poeppel 2015). The neuroscientist needs top-down theories; the converse, however, can well be ignored since no notion of competence will emerge from simply looking at the brain.

As an illustration of these general points, I will now look at some of the key results from the neurosciences concerning the grammatical aspect of human language. There are, in fact, tons of results by now that show neural correlates of various aspects of the language faculty. In an early study, Moro et al. (2001) were able to locate a component in the Broca's area of the brain that is principally dedicated to syntactic and morphological processing. More specifically, Grodzinsky (2000) claimed to have located a system of neurons that execute what is known in linguistics as the *trace deletion hypothesis*. Musso et al. (2003) showed that the relevant component of the Broca's area is activated only when the inputs from a variety of languages followed the principles of universal grammar. Pallier et al. (2011) showed how the hierarchical structure of syntactic processing is represented in the brain (also Nelson et al. 2017). Friederici (2011) presented a comprehensive picture of various components of language processing in the brain (also Berwick et al. 2013).

More recently, Ding et al. (2015) showed how the brain tracks the hierarchies generated by syntactic processing while the acoustic signals are presented in linear order. Berwick and Chomsky (2016) suggest that the lexical system and the phonological systems are located in different areas of the brain, and the computational operation bridges these systems by working from somewhere in between. In interesting recent work pursuing a 'non-cartographical' approach, Murphy (2016), Benítez-Burraco and Murphy (2016) and Murphy (2018) have suggested that there are periodic oscillations in certain areas of the brain that seem to relate to what linguists call *recursive hierarchical phrase structure*.

Thus, in a recent review of the preceding area of neurolinguistic research, Friederici et al. (2017) point out with justified enthusiasm that the study of brain correlates of the language faculty has progressed impressively from listing of brain areas for speech and vocalization to the localization of deeper syntactic principles in the frontotemporal network. The research has revealed that 'adult humans possess a specific network including a functionally specified BA 44 that is structurally and functionally connected to the left pSTC' (719); thus, the study has shown how the truism that 'language is essentially a cognitive computational system' is 'grounded' in the brain (720). Hence, one is perfectly justified to use the *bio* in *biolinguistics*.

Nonetheless, it is totally unclear what 'grounding in the brain' means beyond the trivial observation that certain events of grammatical construction are associated with certain neural events. The notion of 'association' is so weak that, currently, as we will see in Chapter 5, there is nothing in the *formulation* of the computational system of human language that requires that the system cannot be located in the knee joints. The rules of language do not mention anatomical regions, temperature, voltage, neurons, chemicals, fibres or amplitudes of neural oscillations at all. Therefore, even if narrow physical channels have influenced the evolution of the brain as with much else in nature (Cherniak 2005; Carroll 2005), it has not been shown how or whether that influence extends to the design of the language faculty.

There is a vast explanatory gap between properties of language and properties of the brain: the unification problem (Poeppel and Embick 2005, Mukherji 2010, Chapter 7). The problem appears in the other direction also. There is nothing in the description of the brain that tells us anything about linguistic categories. As a result, a new theoretical move in linguistic theory makes no predictions about what differences we might expect in the brain; similarly, new discoveries about properties of the brain make no prediction about what needs to be changed in linguistic theory.

The neurolinguistic research reported earlier just show some activations of the brain that appear to correlate with some of the thick aspects of the language system – hierarchy, distinction between syntax, phonology and semantics, separation of lexicon from the computational system and so on – long known to linguists. In that sense, the neurosciences do not even *confirm* the results of linguistic theory, not to mention making predictions about linguistic behaviour studied by linguistic theory. Neural research throws no additional light on the properties of language at all. For all its fancy technological show, the entire discipline of neurolinguistics is basically an afterthought.

In fact, it is unclear what there is to show: 'What do we mean when we say that the brain really does have rules of grammar in it? We do not think there is a neuron that corresponds to *move alpha*' (Chomsky et al. 1982, 32). Over a decade later, Chomsky observed that 'the belief that neurophysiology is even relevant to the functioning of mind is just a hypothesis' (1994c, 85). Several years later, he continued to hold, after an extensive review of the literature, that 'current understanding falls well short of laying the basis for the unification of the sciences of the brain and higher mental faculties, language among them, and that many surprises may lie along the way to what seems a distant goal' (Chomsky 2002).[7]

In general, the problem of unification between 'psychological studies', such as linguistics and biology, is as unresolved today as it was two centuries ago (Chomsky 2001; Poeppel and Embick 2005). The 'locus' of the problem continues to be on biology and the brain sciences (Chomsky 1995, 2). To insist on some biological 'basis' to the actual operations and principles contained in the human language faculty is to miss the fact that, with or without biological explanation, biolinguistics has already uncovered an aspect of nature in its own terms.[8]

2.4 The modularity issue

So far, I have been talking informally, and somewhat loosely, of modularity, domain-specificity, mental organs, cognitive domains and related concepts. Much of the central thrust of this work depends on settling a possible debate between a modularist and a non-modularist regarding the generative mind, that is, whether the human mind can be viewed as a (non-modular) unity in some interesting sense. I will now try to be a bit more explicit about the issue to relate it to the much-discussed topic of modularity of mind, 'the notion that mental phenomena arise from the operation of multiple distinct processes rather than a single undifferentiated one' (Barrett and Kurzban 2006). In this formulation, the modularity thesis seems to be a direct challenge to the very idea of a unitary generative mind.

Almost anywhere we look in the vast literature covering the cognitive sciences, the organization of mind is taken to be modular in some sense or the other, where each module performs a given task or stores specific representations or has a specific structure. Informally, we may think of modules in terms of cognitive domains such as language, vision, music, emotions and the like; we will discuss more technical notions later. These modules are obviously distinct from each other in terms of their function, organization and the like. In the modular view of mind, then, mind is thought to be a cluster of these cognitive systems satisfying Barrett-Kurzban's definition. It is obvious that this cluster view of mind does not encourage a simple, unified view of mind.

In contrast to the suggested modular view of mind, the concept of narrow mind I have proposed arises as follows. I suppose that a cognitive domain or a module is identified in terms of a system of principles operating in the domain. Some of these cognitive systems constitute mental systems in that each mental system contains Principle G as the generative principle. In our conception, the mind is identified by this single principle, Principle G. The crucial point is that Principle G is viewed as available *across* a number of mental domains. To emphasize, otherwise distinct domains like language, arithmetic, kinship, music and possibly dozens of others are all governed by the same principle! A cluster view of the mind is thus incompatible with the notion of generative mind. The problem with this view is that somehow the idea of a single principle and the idea of multiple domains need to cohere.

The problem may be addressed by viewing each mental system as having two parts: a part that is specific to a domain and a part that is Principle G; the functioning of a domain then consists of Principle G operating on domain-specific parts without Principle G itself being domain-specific. Thus, say, Principle G works with words to generate thoughts in the language system; it works on tones to generate the musical system, on social relations to generate the kinship system and so on. Now suppose that the parts that are specific to a domain are not specific to humans. Suppose further that Principle G is not available to any non-human organism. Principle G, then, will be the exclusive property identifying the species-specific narrow human mind.

Therefore, I do not rule out the possibility that, in some sense of *module*, the cognitive parts that humans share with non-humans could be modular in character (Carruthers 2014). This could be a general design feature of organisms, including humans, for meeting the demands of survival in specific environmental niches. So while non-human organisms are endowed with finite, fixed, autonomous modules as part of their architecture, only humans can extend these otherwise modular resources in novel directions because humans can use Principle G to transform these resources. This explains the array of *mental domains* like language, arithmetic, music and the like only in the case of humans, even if each of them shares a modular part with non-human organisms; for example, there must be aspects of human speech in the domain of language which we share with non-human organisms.

In this picture, then, while a modular architecture is available at some level of biological organization, certain architectural features are *ruled out*: (a) it is ruled out that humans have modules in the required sense which they do not share with animals, and (b) it is also ruled out that there are interesting features of human cognition that are not covered either by what they share with the (modular organization of) non-human organisms or by the sole principle of the mind, Principle G. Thus, to emphasize, the human mind is completely explained under the picture in which humans emerged on the scene as Principle G was inserted on the available non-human architecture. I will now review the current literature on the modularity of mind to see if the suggested picture of the unitary mind, along with the modular organization of cognitive systems, can be sustained. In my view, the picture reinforces the distinction between mind and cognition introduced in the Introduction.

2.4.1 Modularity of domains

Consider some very interesting methodological insights that Chomsky offered nearly half a century ago to challenge the then prevailing behaviourist view that cognitive systems basically consist of 'general learning strategies' (Chomsky 1975,

14–35). Chomsky's incisive criticism of 'general learning strategies' is often thought of as a strong argument for the modular view of the mind. Therefore, I wish to look at Chomsky's classical arguments in some detail. At the outset, I wish to dispel the impression that the non-modular conception of mind sketched earlier advocates anything like general learning strategies for humans. My concern is whether a rejection of general strategies leads to a rejection of some conception of a unitary mind as well. According to the behaviourist, the learning strategies adopted by pigeons and human infants to press a lever or pick a word, respectively, are the same. Chomsky argued against this view as follows.

Suppose a cognitive scientist S is trying to account for different cognitive systems attained by various organisms by way of proposing a learning theory (LT) for a particular cognitive domain (D) of an organism (O). A theory LT (O, D), then, can be viewed as a system of principles embedding a mechanism such that an input to the system is mapped on to an output. The input to the system will be data and its analysis in D by O; the output will be a cognitive representation with an internal structure. Two idealizing assumptions are likely to underlie S's inquiry: (a) S will assume that, other things being equal, the individuals in O under investigation are essentially identical – *homogenous* – with respect to their ability to learn over the domain D, and (b) such learning, other things being equal, is initially conceptualized as an instantaneous process, that is, the final cognitive structure attained is based on a cumulative record of data available to O. The assumptions are obviously false in practice, but that's how science works with frictionless planes and point masses.

Thus, taking O to be rats and D to be maze running, LT(R, M) is the system of principles used by rats in learning how to run mazes. The input to LT(R, M) is whatever preliminary analysis of data – in terms, say, angles, light and shade, curvature and the like – used by rats to accomplish the feat, and the output is the relevant cognitive structure attained to enable rats to run mazes. Or, take O to be humans and D to be concept formation. A theory LT(H, C) then gives an account of the cognitive structures attained by humans in this domain (Keil 1979; Carey 1985; Spelke 2003; Carey 2009, etc.). Given this sketch of a scientific research programme, it is now possible to ask some of the central questions that pertain to the debate between modularity and general strategies of the mind.

First, we can ask: Is it the case that however we select O and D, we find the same LT(O, D)? If the answer is in the positive, we would expect identical structures to govern, for example, humans and rats, in their learning abilities. For example, we will expect that, since humans are superior to rats in language learning, humans are superior in maze running as well. Conversely, since rats are superior to humans in maze-running ability, rats are superior in language learning. Since the consequences are grossly false, we abandon the search for general learning strategies covering all organisms and all domains.

Second, we can ask: Are there significant features common to LT (Oi, D) and LT (Oj, D)? Here we are looking for common strategies *across* organisms for a fixed domain, for example, whether humans and rats use identical cognitive structures for running mazes. It is unclear which ability is under comparison here. It is hard to see the point of comparing the ability to run mazes in burrows between rats and humans. In contrast, suppose the task is to run mazes where the most efficient running requires turning right at every prime numbered option. Now this ability is not available to rats at all. Here we seem to lose control on the notion of a domain.

Next, suppose we ask: Is there some interesting set of domains $D_1, \ldots, D_n$ such that $LT(O, D_i) = LT(O, D_j)$ (i, j < n), or that they are similar in interesting ways? Taking O to be humans, we are asking if there are significant structures common to two or more domains. Again, it is obvious that we do not have a notion of domains which enables us to look in advance for common structures (=general learning strategies) for all human cognitive domains. There are such stark differences between, say human arithmetic competence and sexual competence that it will be a startling result if, in fact, they share significant principles of organization. In fact, in some cases, we know that the general thesis *is* false: there are wide differences in the cognitive principles that enter into human linguistic and visual processing (Chomsky 1980, 1988, 2018). I agree with Chomsky therefore that no theoretically significant notion of general strategies can be upheld.

The only issue of interest at the current stage is to see whether a pair of domains, say, D_i and D_j, among a large array of human cognitive domains, in fact share significant structures. As far as we know, there may be no durable interest in finding out shareable structures between racism and arithmetic, but there are, indeed, interests in locating similarity of principles between mathematics, music and drawing (Hofstadter 1980). Such findings might significantly alter the way we currently think about the organization of human cognitive systems.

Although nothing in the preceding discussion rules out the empirical possibility that two or more apparently disjointed domains of human cognition may, in fact, share significant structuring principles for some choice-set D_i and D_j, Chomsky and other biolinguists are likely to insist that language must be outside the choice-set because linguistic principles are assumed to be specific to the domain. In general, Chomsky (1986, xxvii) has consistently held that, even if the 'approaches' pursued in linguistic theory may be extended to study other cognitive systems, the principles postulated by the theory are likely to be specific to language. In contrast, my claim is that the domains of language, arithmetic, music and many kindred mental systems share the same structuring principles. This is my basic disagreement with Chomsky. The disagreement is purely theoretical and empirical, and nothing in the arguments against general strategies prevents the possibility of a unitary mind (see Mukherji 2000 for more). I will return to the topic of linguistic specificity in Chapter 5.

2.4.2 Modularity of input systems

In his influential book, *The Modularity of Mind*, Jerry Fodor (1983) made very different proposals on modularity than Chomsky. The effect of Fodor's ideas is more difficult to judge for the project of a unitary human mind under discussion here. We recall that the conception of the generative mind requires that some structuring principles are available *across* a certain specific range of cognitive domains. In this proposal, by *cognitive domain* I essentially mean what Chomsky does: classical domains (=modules) like language, music, arithmetic, and the like. Fodor's conception of modules, and thus his conception of mental modularity, are embedded in a very different framework.

Following the practice adopted in the last few sections, I will restrict my attention basically to the domain of human language. How do we place human language as a mental domain in Fodor's framework? I will argue that Fodor's notion of modularity does not apply to the envisaged concept of mind with language at the centre at all. In that sense, Fodor's notion does not apply to the *mental* aspects of higher human cognitive systems. However, Fodor's notion is likely to apply to the *perceptual* aspects of these and other cognitive systems, human and non-human. We thus have the beginning of an explanation of the modular (perceptual) and non-modular (mental) organization of human cognitive systems.

Fodor's conception has two parts: (i) the distinction between central systems and input systems, and (ii) the modular character of input systems. So mind is 'modular' in two ways. As far as I understand, central systems are more 'classical' in the sense that they consist of what have traditionally been called *thought systems* that represent the content of propositional attitudes such as beliefs. These are vast, flexible, open-ended bodies of information which freely interact not only among themselves but also with the rest of the physical and social environments.

In contrast, Fodor views the modules of the mind as 'input systems' which act as bridges between impinging stimuli and the central cognitive systems. The thought is most natural. The impinging stimuli are too 'physical' and their effects too 'biological' in character to carry the thoughtful burden of central systems; Descartes' shadow just won't depart. So the total cognitive architecture needs a 'bridging' system that compulsorily converts the impinging stimuli into small packets of codified representation as input for the central systems which, in turn, convert codified representation into thought.

After two decades of intense debate over the exact features of Fodorian modules (=input systems), Elsabbagh and Karmiloff-Smith (2004) summarize the resulting view succinctly as follows: (1) Modules are *informationally encapsulated*; other parts of the mind/brain cannot interfere with the internal functioning of a module; (2) the operations within a module are *unconscious* and are not available for reflection; (3) modules have *shallow outputs*, that is, the intervening operations that give rise to the output are not apparent from that output; (4) the operation of a module is mandatory – *obligatory firing*; (5) innate modules are *localized* in particular brain areas, common to all individuals; (6) they exhibit *ontogenetic universals*; their development is bound to a given time schedule; (7) there are characteristic ways in which modules break down, giving rise to *pathological universals*; and (8) finally, innate modules are *domain specific*; they operate exclusively on certain types of input: in Fodor's terms, modules have 'proprietary' inputs.

The features of input systems seem to complement each other. For example, if a system is informationally encapsulated – that is, it is immune from information from adjacent systems – then its operations become mandatory with respect to the specific band of information it is dedicated to process. This speeds up the operations of the system since the system blindly processes the information when appropriate stimuli trigger it off, thereby cutting down on the complexity and the length of derivations. Aspects of the visual system illustrate these ideas. For instance, in the Muller-Lyer case, two unequal lines are seen even by those who know that the lines are equal. Once diverging and converging arrows are attached to the two equal lines, respectively, the case can be interpreted only in terms of unequal lines, no matter what else we know about the case.

Elsewhere, Karmiloff-Smith (1992, 2) cited the influential work of Charles Gallistel (1990) to point out that the perceptual systems of non-human species, such as rats, also have this form of information encapsulation. Gallistel showed that although rats can represent non-geometric information such as colour and texture, they cannot use it for determining position; they determine position only from geometric representation. Later Elizabeth Spelke (2000, 2004) used these facts to develop the concept of core knowledge systems that 'show characteristic limits of domain and task specificity: each serves to represent a particular class of entities for a particular set of purposes'. Such observations suggest that the Fodorian form of modularity could be a property of perceptual systems in general.

It is not surprising that such an input system is in operation for the perceptual part of linguistic processing as well, especially in the phonetic part of processing in which certain acoustic signals are compulsorily interpreted as linguistic ones. Berwick and Chomsky (2016, 1) open their book citing evidence that babies apparently begin to internalize aspects of native speech *in utero*, which are then mirrored in their cries when they are born. Elsewhere, Chomsky remarked that, in the case of speech, the perceptual system just 'tunes in'. Fodor himself says rightly that speech is more like 'reflex'. The same could be true of aspects of face recognition, cognition of music and the like, insofar as, to emphasize, these are *perceptual* systems.

Fodor's concept of a module originates from the *character* of the principles; in particular, the principles of a Fodorian module are informationally encapsulated with the consequences, as noted. So if there are operations of the kind Fodor describes, then there ought to be a domain of distal stimuli to which the operations are dedicated. It follows that if a group of these operations are detected *across* classical domains, say, language and music, then we have found a Fodorian module that is dedicated to the common area; it will be modular with respect to the given aspect of the perceptual systems. For example, some rhythmic and prosodic properties of sounds seem to be available for both human speech and human music as well as in a variety of non-human animals (Ramus et al. 2000; Fitch 2006).

However, it is unclear what the effect of this modular analysis is on *mental* systems such as language, music, arithmetic and the like. Are these central systems or input systems? Consider language. As we saw, the linguistic system, especially in the perceptual part, may well have 'reflex'-like components which blindly process impinging stimuli. In fact, according to Chomsky, there are two notions of module involved in the case of language (Chomsky 2018). The first is the organ view of language: language is a *cognitive* system that stores information and is internalized by the speaker to attain *cognitive* states. The second is just the system of parsing of structured sound which is likely to meet most of Fodor's criteria for input systems. So the question is whether the organ/cognitive view of language supports Fodor's conception of a module.

As Chomsky (1986, fn. 10) points out, 'it is too narrow to regard the "language module" as an input system in Fodor's sense, if only because it is used in speaking and thought', where thought, according to Fodor, consists of central systems. The point is, we cannot place the input system of language – speech – separately from the output system of thought, because the architecture of the language system requires that the input and the output systems must be linked, they must talk to each other. This is because 'we do not expect a person to speak only English and understand only Japanese'. In other words, 'the input and output systems must each access a fixed system of knowledge. The latter, however, is a central system, a fact that brings the entire picture into question' (also, Chomsky 2018; Prinz 2006). As a result, the language system turns out to be at once a central system and an input system. It seems to follow, therefore, that it is meaningless to ask whether the language system as a whole is modular or central.[9]

Nonetheless, we can still think of a human high-level cognitive system as consisting of two parts, a modular part and a central part. I am personally attracted to this conception because, as we saw, there are aspects of the human linguistic system where infants just 'tune in'. The phenomenon appears to be even stronger in the case of music. Perhaps that's the reason why pleasing sounds emitted by birds are never viewed as speech, because the perceptual system of language cannot tune in, but the perceptual system of music can, thereby detecting birdsong; whether these are actually songs is an entirely different matter as we will see in Chapter 6. Hopefully, it will be possible to trace every modular part in human mental systems not only to perceptual systems but also to pre-existing non-human sources. By the same token, anything in the human design that cannot be so traced can hopefully be explained in terms of the narrow mind. But life is never easy.

Be that as it may, and keeping to our current interest in the narrow mind, Fodor's notion of a module as an input system seems to have no effect on how the narrow mind is organized across a range of thought systems. Hence, there is no notion of module which prevents the postulation of the narrow generative mind as characterizing the human mental system.[10]

Part II

The proposal

Language as mirror of the mind

Galilean restrictions on an inquiry suggest that we are able to abstract away from the complexity of the phenomena encountered in ordinary experience to reach some deeper principle as a joint of nature. Thus an inquiry into the human mind requires, first, that we are able to make some principled distinction on naturalistic grounds within the complexity of cognitive phenomena to locate an area for focused investigation. Once we locate a theoretically promising area, then, second, we may proceed to identify some core property of the systems inhabiting the area. We expect the property to be simple and unified across the concerned systems, if the property so identified is to meet Galilean standards.

To that end, we proposed a largely intuitive distinction between mind and cognition to carve out a cluster of human-specific mental systems that are characterized by Principle G. So the starting point for a theoretical investigation of the narrow mind is to substantiate the intuitive distinction between mind and cognition such that a distinctive selection of human cognitive behaviour is ascribed to the mind, while the rest continues to be viewed as cognition as shared with animals. However, given the complexity of the phenomena, it is not clear if cognitive behaviour can be so neatly partitioned without some theoretical measure in hand.

Consider a thoughtful list of human cognitive behaviour suggested by Penn et al. (2008) in an influential paper. Penn et al. open with the observation that human animals – and no other – can do the following things:

(1) build fires and wheels
(2) diagnose each other's illnesses
(3) communicate using symbols
(4) navigate with maps
(5) risk their lives for ideals
(6) collaborate with each other
(7) explain the world in terms of hypothetical causes

(8)   punish strangers for breaking rules

(9)   imagine impossible scenarios

(10) teach each other how to do all of the above.

This small list no doubt can be vastly expanded to truly reflect the full range of human ingenuity, as noted earlier. Still, even this limited sample is thick with a variety of abilities, cognitive capacities and rich forms of living. The authors observe: 'At first blush, it might appear obvious that human minds are qualitatively different from those of every other animal on the planet.' So the authors invoke the concept of the human mind to articulate the suggested discontinuity between humans and non-human animals: human minds are viewed as 'qualitatively different'.

However, it is unclear if the list does establish the required radical discontinuity between humans and non-humans. Consider items (3), (6) and (8). For (3), depending on what one means by *symbols*, many existing non-human animals certainly communicate the presence of food, danger, mate, change in weather and the like by using sounds and gestures that seem to have a conventional relationship with the stimuli, a hallmark of symbols (Hauser 1996). As for (6), a variety of animals such as wild dogs, hyenas, lions, beavers and birds exhibit pretty remarkable cooperative behaviour during hunting, nest-building and sharing of food between parents and their offspring. For (8), depending on how we understand 'rules' and 'strangers', there is interesting recorded evidence that a young chimpanzee, about to mate with the chief's favourite female, attempted to hide his intention by covering his erect penis with his hands, when the chief happened to pass by suddenly (Hauser 1999). It is natural to interpret the action in terms of the young chimpanzee's awareness of the rule that a subordinate male will be punished if he makes advances towards the chief's chosen female. In the literature, there are many recorded cases exhibiting similar phenomena (De Wal 2016).

3.1 The onset of language

So what makes Penn et al.'s complex behavioural data uniquely applicable to humans? Following Newell and Simon (1976), Penn et al. hold that the entire spectrum of qualitative differences can be accounted for by the 'higher-order, systematic, relational capabilities of a physical symbol system' only humans are endowed with. Thus, 'only humans appear capable of reinterpreting the higher-order relation between these perceptual relations in a structurally systematic and inferentially productive fashion.'[1] Since this characterization resembles the idea of the generative mind, suppose we hold on to the notion of a physical symbol system as marking the distinction between humans and non-humans, provided, of course, we understand the notion of a 'physical system' in terms of doctrinal dualism.

Although the appeal to a 'symbol system' with 'systematic, relational capabilities' seems broadly to point to the unique presence of language in the species, Penn et al. hold that the suggested human-specific system 'runs much deeper than even the spectacular scaffolding provided by language or culture alone can explain'. The suggestion appears to indicate that, although the listed abilities seem to be intuitively related to the endowment of human language, the presence of language by itself does not explain the range of abilities involved; according to the authors, something 'deeper' is needed.

The need for a deeper factor arises because it is not immediately clear how the language factor explains the uniqueness of each of the items in the list: for example, what has language to do with building fires and wheels or collaboration with each other? Furthermore, earlier we saw many apparently unique human phenomena – music, arithmetic, cooking, knitting and the like – that seem to be only indirectly related to human language. Nevertheless, an informal notion of language does bring some clarity in the list offered by Penn et al. because language after all is a human-specific endowment that is central to our conception of a generative mind.

Pending details about which aspect(s) of the language factor suggests the conception of the mind, the language factor as a whole suggests the following thought experiment to explain the human–non-human divide. Apart from the unclarity already noted, a significant limitation with Penn's data is that it is based on a contrast between modern humans and, primarily, chimpanzees. Even though chimpanzees are the most advanced and 'human-like' of the existing non-human species, we know that chimpanzees branched off the hominid line several million years before the emergence of modern humans whose abilities are described in (1) to (10). So chimpanzees do not quite belong to the relevant comparison class of our closest ancestors.

The literature is pretty inaccurate on this issue. In their very influential paper, Hauser et al. (2002), the authors repeatedly compare humans with chimpanzees to show aspects of human uniqueness. For example, they hold that humans represent various novel capacities such as imitation that 'evolved in our recent evolutionary history, sometime after the divergence from our chimpanzee-like ancestors'. Even in the evolutionary scale, six million years is not just 'sometime'. Also, we do not have a convincing record of the cognitive abilities of the long list of pre-human species in the hominid line. The palaeo-anthropological evidence from fossils and terrains collected so far appears to be too indirect and uncertain for the problem in hand (Berwick et al. 2013; Hauser et al. 2014). We examine some of the evidence in Chapter 4.

To circumvent the problem of missing ancestors, let us postulate a hypothetical individual, *Proto*, as the *last of the pre-human* series in the hominid line (see Figure 3.1); under this imagination, Proto was the founding mother of all humanity – the penultimate human. Following Chomsky (2000a), suppose some physical event happened, such as a lightning strike, which rewired Proto's brain to insert human language; with the lightning strike, Proto turned into a human. Our conception of Proto will keep changing as we know more about the properties of human language. As of now, Proto *just* represents an immediate pre-human ancestor to whom the faculty of language was made instantly available.

With Proto in mind, we can now suggest a more accurate picture of the distinctive human abilities between early Proto and later Proto, rather than with chimpanzees; the additional cognitive power of humans, if any, can now be traced to the language factor. Given nearly six million years of hominid evolution since the chimpanzees, it is natural to assume that even early Proto's cognitive abilities

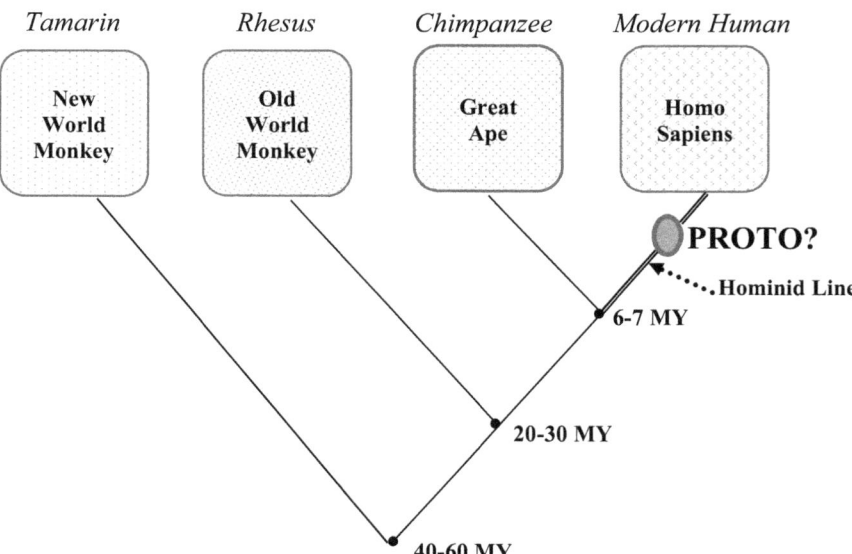

Figure 3.1 A section of the primate line. © N. Mukherji

before the lightning strike went far beyond those of chimpanzees. Under this assumption, it is most likely that not only cases (3) (symbolic communication), (6) (cooperative behaviour) and (8) (obeying rules), mentioned earlier, were more firmly and widely established for the early Proto but also that several other items of Penn's data – such as (1) (build fires), (2) (diagnose illness) and (5) (risk lives for ideals such as motherhood) – extend to early Proto as well. Suppose so.

Nonetheless, there are some items in Penn's list that do not extend to early Proto since these need an additional ability. Consider (7) and (9): explanation of the world in terms of hypothetical causes and imagining impossible scenarios, respectively. Both the abilities require the prior ability to entertain abstract thoughts whose constituents (hypothetical causes, impossible scenarios) are essentially free from direct stimulus-information; the first requires the additional ability to articulate such thoughts in language. The cases thus require the presence of at least an 'inner' language (Chomsky 2000b). Let us assume, for now, that this 'inner' language is nothing but *un*articulated human language itself. Once we see the unique presence of language as the crucial element for some cognitive abilities, the phenomenon begins to cover the other cases as well. Earlier we did allow that a variety of non-human organisms may be endowed with some of the abilities listed by Penn et al. Yet, once we link up such abilities with the availability of human language, these abilities take up such vastly different forms as to suggest a difference in quality.

Thus, consider (3) (symbol use), (6) (collaboration) and (8) (obeying rules) once again, this time for the human (= later Proto) case. With the use of language, humans can not only communicate the presence of food and danger but also abstract thoughts of hypothetical causes and impossible scenarios, as noted. For (6), human cooperative behaviour extends from surgical procedures to the building of pyramids and linear accelerators. For (8), when rules are stated in a language, such as *smoking is prohibited*, the rule enforces obedience not only in the immediate community of conspecifics as in the chimpanzee case, but also in any English-speaking 'stranger', as Penn et al. note. Hence, the notion of a 'community' itself is linguistically organized in such cases.

Needless to say, this perspective extends to the rest of the five cases listed by the authors; for example, we can appreciate why building fires and risking lives for an ideal require the ability to entertain complex thoughts; the making of wheels, for instance, requires the combination of ideas of a rotating circle and ease of locomotion. Broadly then, all the ten cases listed by Penn et al. suggest species-specific abilities when these cases are understood in terms of uses of human language. That is the crucial difference between Proto and humans.

The unique role of human language for characterizing the species comes out even more perspicuously in the list of abilities noted by the neurobiologist George Streidter (2004, 297). After mentioning that non-human animals such as birds and chimpanzees exhibit impressive abilities for manufacturing tools and remembering past episodes, Streidter observes that 'one is tempted to conclude' that there is no 'qualitative discontinuity between people and animals'. 'However', he continues, 'no other animal writes books, lectures on history, or tells stories around a fireplace.' To make his point, Streidter naturally lists uniquely human abilities – writing books, telling stories – each of which involves explicit use of language.

The Khoi and San (Khoisan) people of South Africa are considered to be a unique relic of the hunter-gatherer lifestyle; they carry paternal and maternal lineages belonging to the deepest clades known among modern humans (Behar et al. 2008). As Premack and Premack (2003, 121) report, the San tribe of Kalahari narrate their recent hunt in great detail in the evening: 'Hunter-gatherers hunt twice: once in the field and a second time around the campfire.' Premack and Premack contend that 'chimpanzees, having caught a monkey and eaten it, simply digest their meal'. It is unlikely that early Proto, devoid of the lightning strike, would have done any better.

It is not surprising, therefore, that language is viewed as a natural cause whenever we see humans engaged in species-specific behaviour over a vast range. Citing the Stanford archaeologist Richard Klein, Holden (1998) observes that the so-called 'Upper Palaeolithic explosion' occurred 'when tools, burials, living sites, and occasional hints of art and personal adornment reveal beings capable of planning and foresight, social organization and mutual assistance, a sense of aesthetics, and a grasp of symbols'. On that basis, 'everybody would accept that by 40 KY, language is everywhere', Holden remarks. Recent work suggests that the more accurate date for emergence of language preceded the migration out of Africa which occurred at least 80 KY ago, if not earlier (Behar 2008; Huybregts 2017). Later, I will object to the very idea of a consolidated cultural explosion exclusively around the phenomenon of language as language bias (Chapter 7), but right now my purpose is to show the significance of the emergence of language for the mental identity of humans.

There is then a marked phenomenon, with effects in a wide variety of directions, in which human cognitive abilities are crucially linked to linguistic endowment. The presence of language is not restricted to the making of 'noise' to convey thoughts obtained independently; language enters into thinking, planning and foresight, social organization, mutual assistance and much more.

Hence, these abilities are strictly restricted to the human species. As Penn et al. observe, there is not only absence of evidence of these abilities in non-human organisms, but there is also evidence of absence. We will explore these themes in more detail as we proceed.

I have so far urged the case for the language-centred mind without really clarifying the notion of language at issue. I will discuss the issue in some detail later in the work in Chapter 5 when we review the basic properties of the human language system. However, some idea of which aspects or components of human language inspire the notion of the human mind is appropriate at this point to form a preliminary understanding of which conception of mind I am arguing for. It is needed here because, without setting theoretical priorities, it is easy to view human language as an immensely complex phenomenon.

Recall the methodological guideline that genuine theoretical understanding seems to be restricted to the study of simple systems; the quality of explanation falls off rapidly as inquiry turns to more complex systems. The history of the more established sciences also suggests that once some observed complexity has been successfully analysed into parts, a study of the original complexity often drops out of that line of research, perhaps forever. Hence, just as the singular phenomenon of language provided the guide through the complexity of cognitive phenomena, we need some singular guidance through the complexity of human language itself. Human languages, as we observe them in the world, have many components. Even a cursory look at the phenomena suggests at least the following parts.

A storage of morphemes consisting of phonemic units, a class of words constituting morphemes held together by morphophonemic rules, a finite system of formal categories that classifies these words, rules of combining these words into phrases, rules for combining phrases into (single) sentences and more complex objects, rules for reordering these complex objects into other complex objects, rules of pronunciation of individual morphemes, syllabic rules governing pronunciation of words, rhythmic and prosodic structures governing pronunciation of complex objects, meaning rules for individual words, rules for combining those meanings for computation of truth conditions, pragmatic rules governing discourse contexts, rules of conversational and conventional implicature, inventory of proverbs and idioms, mapping rules from vision and other non-linguistic domains for interpreting metaphors, structure of speaker's beliefs including beliefs about the hearer's beliefs, the empirical contexts of utterance, cultural-specific beliefs shared by large linguistic communities, clan-specific beliefs including idiosyncrasies shared by small groups of interlocutors and so on.

It is unlikely that such complexity can be harnessed in a single 'Galilean' form of explanation. In fact, it is doubtful if the phenomena just partially listed belong to an identifiable joint of nature at all. According to Chomsky (1991a), it is possible that 'there is nothing in the real world corresponding to language. In fact, it could very well turn out that there is no intelligible notion of language.' Apart from unmanageable complexity, there are several other problems with the phenomenal picture of language in view of the project under consideration here. As explained in the Introduction, we seek a conception of language that is not only simple and species-specific but also one that has components or properties which are not linguistically specific such that we may view that component as covering not just human language, but the human mind itself.

In the light of these restrictions, many parts of the informal phenomenal picture of language fall out of the search for mind. For example, phonemic units of languages are arguably not even species-specific since a variety of non-human species can identify them (Hauser 2001). Similarly, not only human infants but also some species of monkeys can identify and respond to the rhythmic and prosodic contours of human speech (Ramus et al. 2000). In contrast, the lexicon of human languages, such as words and the categories to which they belong, are certainly specific to human languages: we don't expect split infinitives, anaphora and ergative markers in music or stone stool-making; they are not even there in arithmetic which is supposed to be an 'offshoot' of language. Other factors, such as the incorporation of visual information in metaphors and idioms like *needle in a haystack* obviously borrow from visual images; thus, they do not strictly belong to the language faculty itself.

Further, though components such as word meanings and truth conditions arguably belong to the broad language faculty, it is unclear if they can be harnessed theoretically (Mukherji 2010). Other factors such as pragmatic rules and implicatures appear to be too dense and unstructured as phenomena to fall under a formal theory; we will survey some of these problems in Chapter 4. In any case, many of these factors such as truth conditions, pragmatics, idioms and proverbs, and the like do not seem to belong to the category of language per se, but, rather, to a thicker and uncertain category of language use. We cannot study language use, of course, unless we have studied language itself which remains invariant across a diversity of uses. As Ludwig Wittgenstein (1953) remarked, a screwdriver continues to be a screwdriver even if it is primarily used for gardening.

The task, then, is to somehow conceptualize, from the complex spread of human language, that singular element, if any, which, in a strong evolutionary sense, marked the onset of language; *if any*, because our ability to identify the singular element depends on how we are describing languages. In the Introduction, we expressed the hope that there is a simple generative operation, Principle G, that meets *all* the conditions needed for a conception of narrow mind: it is simple, species-specific, necessary for generativity, yet not linguistically specific.

Once the (linguistic) generative mind is so identified, we proceed from there to see if the single operation extends to other mental systems. An explanatory advantage with this strategy is that, since language is known to be species-specific in its generative capacity (Berwick and Chomsky 2016), the strategy is likely to ensure the species-specific character of Principle G. Needless to say, how the promise is to be fulfilled depends entirely on what lessons we have learned from the study of language so far.

3.2 Language and thought

Languages are systems of sound–meaning correlations without bound. So, the required notion of language not only incorporates some notion of mind, but it also somehow incorporates aspects of sound and meaning systems to be able to generate sound–meaning correlations. For now, I am setting the sound and gesture systems aside because in some influential recent literature (Chomsky 2015; Berwick and Chomsky 2016), sound and gesture are viewed as mere instruments of externalization and are thus 'ancillary' for the core language system. On this view, the core language system is primarily geared to generate structured thought; we recall the rationalist dictum that 'language is a vehicle of thought'.

Although I will be beginning to raise doubts about the 'sound is ancillary' hypothesis – especially in the next chapter in connection with Charles Darwin's ideas on the origins of language – a refutation of the hypothesis is not my goal in this work (see Mukherji 2021). This is because I am not primarily concerned with internal disputes on the design of the language system as long as we can locate the aspects of the design that show the incorporation of the mind. As we will see, a close study of the part of the system that generates structured thoughts is sufficient for that purpose (but see Section 8.4).

In any case, it is obvious that the study of aspects of sound systems such as vocalization, structure of vocal chords, the hearing system, properties of sound and the like belong to physics, anatomy and acoustic phonetics rather than to the study of core language. As such, much of these are likely to be shared with non-human species. Although aspects of the sound system such as phonology and morphology do belong to our basic conception of language, there is no abiding intuition that these are involved in our conception of the mind. Hence, we may set them aside without any loss.

The situation with thought systems is very different. Thought systems are essentially involved even in the narrow core conception of language that views language as a generative procedure for thoughts. This is because, if language is a system of sound–meaning correlations, and sounds are ancillary, the conception of language with its meaning-part can be understood only in terms of the thought systems. Moreover, if we are to extract some conception of mind from a conception of language, as desired, we need to accommodate the intuition that the concept of mind involves notions such as thinking, reasoning, imagining, reflecting, pondering, contemplating and the like; all these aspects of thinking are dependent on the broad category of thought. So some notion of thought as contributing to the meaning-part of language is required for the concept of mind as well.

However, as with mind and language, one may doubt if the concepts of language and thought have the same coverage. It raises the possibility that there could be some realm of thought that is not covered by language. If the concept of mind is to cover *all* realms of thought, which seems to be an intuitive requirement for the concept of mind, we face the possibility that some realm of thought will be left out if we approach the concept of mind exclusively from the architecture of language alone. It appears that there are three ways in which language and thought may have different coverage.

First, a reason for separating thought and language is that perhaps the notion of thought could be extended to some human-specific non-linguistic domains such as music, arithmetic, arts, kinship and suchlike. There is no obvious reason why we should reject notions such as musical thought, mathematical thought, artistic thought and the like. These domains of thought are genuinely distinct from language because, in each case, it may be futile to ask if there is a linguistic rendition of such thoughts. As Wittgenstein (1931/1958, 178) remarked for music: 'it is a "strange illusion" that possesses us when we say "This tune says *something*", and it is as though I have to find *what* it says.' Nevertheless, Wittgenstein also held that 'understanding a sentence lies nearer than one thinks to what is ordinarily called understanding a musical theme' (1953, 527; Mukherji 2010, Chapter Six). When we put these ideas together, it follows that there is a genuine notion of non-linguistic musical thought on a par with linguistic thought.

However, this form of separation between language and thought poses no problem for the project in hand since the concept of structured thoughts, and hence the concept of mind, extends to a class of language-like mental systems such as the mentioned non-linguistic domains (Mukherji 2010; Hauser and Watumull 2017; Miyagawa et al. 2018). In fact, the extension to music, arithmetic and so on is most welcome if the concept of mind is to have a wider coverage, as desired, than just human language. As we repeatedly urge in this work, the proposed concept of mind requires that there are different domains of information, such as words, tones and numbers, where the same concept of mind works in terms of the shared generative principle. Naturally, then, these differing domains generate varying forms of non-linguistic thought. It all depends on where the *structuring* of thoughts, linguistic or non-linguistic, is coming from.

A second reason for separating language and thought is that most authors in the relevant literature believe that some concepts and thoughts are prior to and progenitive of language. Notice that here we are only concerned with thoughts that are expressed in language; so non-linguistic thoughts, such as musical thoughts, arithmetical thoughts and so on, are not at issue, not to mention imagistic and non-conceptual thoughts, if any. The point is, a large number of authors think that conceptual thoughts exist independently of language even if they may be expressed in a language (Hinzen 2014b). This view is most predominantly ascribed to the classical rationalists because of their suggestions about innate, clear and distinct ideas. However, as Gleitman and Papafragou (2005) contend with rich documentation, this view of concepts as prior to and progenitive of language is 'not proprietary to the rationalist position'.

The progenitive view is deeply problematic. How do these progenitive thoughts, including their *atomic* constituents, which are known as concepts, *look like* without the presence of language? Do these thoughts have a symbolic form? If yes, then what does it mean to have a symbolic form without language? If not, then how and what do those thoughts say and convey in the absence of symbols? These questions concern both the atomic constituents of thought and structured thought. We recall Boruah's scepticism about the possibility of creatures who 'harbour thoughts that are *necessarily* idle'. So it is possible to hold a strong view in which both concepts and structured thoughts are products of language. There are two reasons for setting aside the strong view, which includes concepts, for now.

One, we need to be clear in advance about the notion of language at issue to avoid the view, known as the Whorf hypothesis, that concepts are specific to the individual languages in which they are spoken (Hinzen 2014b). On the one hand, the language-relative notion of concepts is difficult to make sense of (Davidson 1974); there is simply no denying that most concepts are universally available *across* thousands of languages. However, on the other hand, as we will soon see, we are yet to reach an understanding of the conceptual system related to languages that accommodates this fact.

Two, as we are beginning to realize, our real interest is in the generative aspect of human language that produces structured thought. To look for the notion of structure, we need to assume the prior existence of some of the fragments/units of thought as contributing to the overall design of language. Once we settle for the overall design, we may then seriously examine where the units came from (Mukherji 2019, 2021). Therefore, we will assume that a handful of unstructured 'atomic' thoughts are already available prior to the construction of structured thoughts.

As for the weaker progenitive view of prior existence of structured thoughts, a brief look at Jerry Fodor's idea of 'language of thought' (Fodor 1975, 2008; Fodor and Pylyshyn 2015) may be instructive. I must clarify just which aspect of Fodor's complex work interests me here. As against various behaviourist doctrines, Fodor's basic goal in the cited work was to argue for an internalist – and thus psychological – view of thoughts: essentially, Fodor upheld the Cartesian assertion that thoughts *are* there, perhaps 'hidden' in the body. According to Fodor, items of thought, such as beliefs, desires and other propositional attitudes, are codified structures in this 'mentalese' somehow instantiated in the brain. Fodor's impressive contribution was to use the idea of inner codes – the language of thought – to argue that the rich structure of mental representations so encoded in structured codes may be processed by Turing computation to establish the causal link between propositional attitudes and behaviour: the computational-representational theory of mind.

Here, in view of the issues raised earlier regarding a possible separation between language and thought, my only interest is in Fodor's idea of inner codes for thought. Did Fodor succeed in explaining how thoughts by *themselves* are structured to display what they say? If he did, we would have known how a structured thought could have a life of its own without the resources of human language. Even a cursory look at Fodor's work brings out the obvious fact that Fodor failed to perform the miracle. The few examples of 'codes' he discussed were invariably either simple sequences in the notation of predicate logic or English sentences, with elementary syntactic organization displayed in some cases. Since predicate logic is an offshoot of small fragments of human languages such as English (Russell and Whitehead) or German (Frege), it is obvious that the only 'language of thought' we have is the human language itself (Mukherji 2010, Chapter Two). In that sense, the idea of structured thoughts cannot be separated from human language, notwithstanding the postulation of mythical mentalese.

A third and more serious issue, concerning the separation between language and thought, is that, even when we keep to structured thoughts that are expressed in human language, it is unclear how to describe those thoughts for the meaning-part of an intelligible theory of language. It appears that some separation between language and thought is, indeed, motivated here not because there is a divide in human nature, but because much of the thought systems appear to fall beyond explanatory control. As Chomsky (2002) pointed out, 'nobody really has much of an idea about the computational processes right outside the language faculty. One could say there is a language of thought, there are concepts, etc., but there has never been any structure to the system outside the language faculty.' More recently, Berwick and Chomsky (2016, 71) contended that there is a lack of evidence about the systems of thought and action with which the language system is linked.

Thus, Chomsky (1980, 54–5) suggested a distinction between the computational and the conceptual aspects of language. According to Chomsky (1980, 54–5), the computational system of language includes the syntactic and the semantic components which together provide the 'rich expressive power of human language'. In contrast, Chomsky viewed the conceptual system as not belonging to the language faculty at all but to some other faculty that provides a 'common sense understanding' of the world (CSU). There is no *a priori* restriction on how much of the broad thought systems may be progressively incorporated within the theory of language itself; for example, conceptual features such as +/− animate or pragmatic features such as +/− definiteness may play a role in linguistic computation (Ormazabal 2000; Diesing 1992). Nevertheless, from what we can guess, the chances are that the human cognitive capacities that are involved in CSU are likely to remain outside the scope of the core conception of language.[2]

Chomsky's distinction between the computational system of language and the conceptual systems for CSU basically recommends a principled partition between thought systems that enter into language to enforce sound–meaning correlation, and the rest of the apparently unmanageable thought systems. The partition results in a largely 'concept-free' notion of language with minimal engagement with thought systems. Chomsky's distinction is clearly programmatic for the putative theory of language in pursuance of the Galilean style at the current state of knowledge to reduce the 'noise' of the surrounding systems and enhance explanatory control. However, we need to convince ourselves why the distinction is needed even for a theory of mind.

The scepticism about the theoretical understanding of the human conceptual systems raises an interesting dilemma for the project on the concept of mind. It is hard to deny that our intuitions about the concept of mind involve the conceptual systems in a significant way. Insofar as our intuitive concept of mind includes processes such as thinking, pondering, reasoning, reflecting, doubting, questioning and the like, the mind is viewed as acting on ideas and images rooted in our conceptual system. If, following Chomsky, we need to set them aside due to our lack of theoretical understanding of them, we are asked to ignore an apparently significant part of our mental realm. Therefore, we need to understand why a general theory of ideas and concepts is currently unavailable.

From one direction, the problem of lack of explanatory control arises for semantic theories that attempt to describe the organization of thought systems with notions such as semantic markers, semantic features, exemplars, conceptual spaces, basic concepts, semantic primitives, semantic networks and the like (Fodor 2000; Mukherji 2010, Chapter Four). Pretty early in the enterprise, Norbert Hornstein (1989, 36) explained the general problem thus: 'postulating semantic markers only pushed the problem back one step. Instead of explaining what it was for a word to have a content, the problem was to explain what it was for a marker in mentalese to have a content.'

These theories may satisfy a part of the descriptive task of systematic arrangement of various fragments of languages; but they explain nothing about the meaning system. To take a celebrated case, suppose the meaning of the term *bachelor* is given by a sequence of semantic markers ADULT, MALE, HUMAN, UNMARRIED and so on, in that order. Suppose the sequence captures the similarities in meaning between *bachelor* and *spinster* thus showing some of the uses of markerese descriptions. But as Hornstein pointed out, such descriptions require that we already know the content of ADULT, MALE and the like; but to know such content is to know what the words *adult*, *male* and the like mean. The net result is that even if we enlarge the scope of semantics in many dimensions to include the origin, material constitution, layout, function and future course of things as well as social expectations, conventions and psychological needs, it is unclear how these additional dimensions fit the organization of semantic intuitions (Mukherji 2010, Chapter Four).

From another direction, insofar as psychological studies on human concepts are concerned, it continues to be a mystery how children generalize from watching Fido and Rover to form the concept DOG to subsequently apply it to previously unseen dogs (Gleitman and Bloom 1998). As Chomsky (2000b) observed, it is totally unclear how to specify the meanings of even mundane words such as *book, London, river, house, climb* and the like that enter in CSU beyond incomplete lists of features and shades (Mukherji 2010; Chomsky 2020). However, although there is lack of theoretical understanding of the conceptual systems themselves, studies on concepts acquired by human children suggest an astonishingly rich capacity. As Landau and Gleitman (1985) showed in a classic study, blind children rapidly and effortlessly learn visual concepts associated with words such as *look, red, picture*. Children learn over a dozen words a day with their meanings to assemble tens of thousands of words in the lexicon within a few years.

So the intriguing situation is that, although there is an absence of theoretical understanding of the conceptual systems, its robust presence cannot be denied. In that sense, the human conceptual systems may be viewed on analogy with *dark matter* in physics. Dark matter is usually viewed in physics as matter that current physics cannot really give an account of. Yet, as with the conceptual systems, there is strong evidence that dark matter is there; in fact, according to some estimates, dark matter and dark energy fill almost 90 per cent of the physical universe. Valiant attempts over several decades to account for the widespread dark matter in terms of familiar objects such as white dwarfs, dead stars, black holes, residue of big bang and the like have failed to explain the estimated amounts. Yet, neither are current physical theories abandoned nor dark matter declared as a non-issue in physics. We just await further developments, including perhaps a revision of some of the fundamental theories of physics. Given the striking points of analogy, I suggest that the human conceptual system be viewed as 'dark matter' for the emerging theory of mind.

So, for the project in hand, the issue is that if a clarification of the classical idea that 'language is a vehicle of thought' requires a prior characterization of (the entirety of) human thought, the project may not be theoretically viable. It follows that, if the task is to construct a theory of language that provides the window for a theoretical conception of the mind, it is prudent to set much of the thought systems aside from that inquiry, while keeping to a narrow version of the classical idea that language is a system of sound–meaning correlations. Preferably, the system of core language is so organized as to leave room for the progressive incorporation of the conceptual system as the theory develops.

The largely practical decision to set aside the conceptual system from the narrow study of human sound–meaning correlations may, in fact, turn out to be a virtue. There is a growing understanding that much of the rich lexical and conceptual capacity displayed by children is human-specific and is developmentally linked to the scaffolding offered by human language (Spelke 2003; Carey 2009). This picture suggests that the language system must be independently available so that the initial rudimentary conceptual repertoire can be assembled to generate the rich resources of the conceptual system. In the last chapter, we will indicate how the core mind, when extracted from the core language, may be viewed as setting up the conditions for generating the rich complexity of the conceptual system.

In the contemporary biolinguistic framework, it has been possible to skirt around CSU to show systematically how structured thoughts are generated with minimal assumptions about the structure and content of the broad thought systems. In other words, once legible linguistic objects are generated in tandem with minimal computational constraints on interpretation, the language system can ignore the rest of the thought systems. This was the point of Chomsky's famous example, *colourless green ideas sleep furiously*, which is a perfectly legitimate linguistic object even if it fails to satisfy common sense understanding. The fact that people strain to assign some interpretation to this sequence shows that it has some 'internal significance' (Mukherji 2010 for details). I will say more on internal significance as we proceed.

To emphasize, structured linguistic objects must be made available by the language system for the thought systems to read them in the first place for any subsequent assignment of more semantic and conceptual content to them beyond internal significance; for example, conceptual systems governing CSU may declare that the terms *colourless* and *green* are in conflict. In other words, even if we wish to eventually reach something like a wide or broad conception of language that includes an account of CSU, the core conception of language will be needed at the heart of the wider conception for generating the required structured thoughts. Thus, once the core language system is found, we may look for a concept of mind in terms of that core system.

Otherwise, what does it mean to look for a coherent concept of mind in terms of the wider notion of language that includes CSU? Consider, for instance, Daniel Osherson's contention that the cognitive sciences are concerned with 'everything we do' (1995, ix). For Osherson, what we do includes 'recognizing a friend's voice over the telephone, reading a novel, jumping from stone to stone in a creek', and so on. Suppose these are some of the things we do for which CSU guides us. The point of interest here is that CSU is formed with the help of capacities and processes such as perception, consciousness, thinking, beliefs, introspection, emotions, social interactions, intentionality and the like, as noted. These capacities must be working in tandem with the broad language system to produce the vastly complex conceptual schemes and the attendant referential apparatus with which we form an understanding of the world.

As the citation from Osherson suggests, CSU is the preferred domain for the application of traditional notions of mind, mentality, mental states, cognition and the like. Thus, something like CSU appears to be the common ground for wider conceptions of language and the traditional broad conception of mental systems as an array of a variety of cognitive systems. As we saw, the problem is that the putative wide notion of language – which includes conceptual semantics, intentionality, referentiality and the like – is surrounded by dark matter. According to Chomsky, such a notion of language is unhelpful for 'determining the real properties of the natural world'; in fact, Chomsky doubts if this notion of language is even 'intelligible' (1991). If the rationalist idea 'language is mirror of mind' is applied to this wide conception of language, it is likely to reflect a blurred and broken image of mind.

3.3 Principle G

We have been trying to conceptualize the relationship between language and thought from various angles. It seems that, if anything at all, only some rudimentary aspects of basically *un*structured thought – perhaps just some *atomic constituents* of thought – were progenitive for language, because structured thought simply does not make sense without language. Assume so. Language in the form of a (complex) system of sound–meaning correlation emerged when a critical resource was somehow made available to put the rudimentary aspects of thought together, resulting in genuine structured thoughts. Obviously, some generative mechanism is needed as the critical resource. Suppose the mechanism constitutes a basic principle; call it Principle G.

The suggestion means that a set of rudimentary pre-linguistic thoughts is viewed as the 'input' to the linguistic system. When it is fed into the language system that includes Principle G, it generates the rich complexity of structured thoughts that characterizes human languages. Suppose that is the resolution of the issue of the relation of language and thought on the 'input' side. What should be the prescribed relation between language and thought on the 'output' side and how is language related to the rest of the thought systems? Recall that here we faced the problem that the thought systems are unmanageably too complex, perhaps beyond human theoretical scrutiny.

With the distinction between the computational and conceptual aspects of language in hand, we think of much of the semantic and conceptual components as falling in the 'external' conceptual-intentional (CI) systems, not in the language system per se. All we need the language system for is to supply structured expressions to the CI systems, and similarly, for the otherwise highly complex sensorimotor (SM) systems. The structured expressions of the language system – the output of the system – meet the demands of SM and CI systems at the two *interfaces*. The language system itself does not access the rest of the SM and CI systems. No doubt, in order for the expressions of the language system to supply legible information to the CI system at the interface, the expressions must satisfy some of the structural semantic conditions imposed by the external systems at the interfaces. For example, keeping to the CI systems, the structured expressions must meet the constraint of Full Interpretation: all elements in a structure must be interpretable by the CI systems; there cannot be any vacuous terms in a linguistic expression, such as the vacuous quantifiers in an artificial logical expression. That is all the 'semantics' we need (Mukherji 2010).

In effect, we hold on to the impressive development that, in focusing on the grammatical aspects of language, the discipline of biolinguistics has been able to maintain some distance from topics that are traditionally thought to be central to the study of language: meaning, denotation, concepts, truth conditions and communication. The conception of language as a system of sound–meaning correlation is now more narrowly captured in terms of correlations between representations of sound and a thin grammatical conception of *internal significance* for satisfying interface conditions (Mukherji 2010); we saw that the expression *colourless green ideas sleep furiously* satisfies internal significance in this thin or minimal sense. We will see more theoretical examples of internal significance as we narrate some aspects of the biolinguistic programme in Chapter 5.

This is not to suggest that what currently falls under the non-grammatical aspects of language will never be a part of grammatical theory. We saw that some elements from the conceptual system may influence grammatical computation. But, as with the matured sciences, the chances are that each such incorporation will be hard-fought, since it will have to be formulated, not due to pressures from 'outside', but from within the evolving framework of biolinguistics; that is why each of the very few incorporations from the conceptual system, such as features like animate, artefact and the like, are hotly debated. Nevertheless, more theoretically motivated incorporations from the 'outside' of narrow syntax do take place.

A recent fairly dramatic example is the explanation of some of the principles of argument binding covering pronouns, reflexives and the like; for example, in the structure *John shaves himself*, *John* must bind *himself*, but in *John shaved him*, *John* cannot bind *him*. In an earlier theory called 'Government-Binding Theory' (Chomsky 1981), these principles were viewed as constituting one 'module' of the grammatical theory itself. In the earlier version of the minimalist programme (Chomsky 1995a), these were viewed as located at the front part of the CI system outside narrow syntax. In more recent work (Chomsky 2008), some of them are now explained in terms of purely grammatical principles such as minimal search; thus, those conditions of argument binding take place *inside* grammar.

To review, we reached the preceding complex yet narrow view of language in order to satisfy the Galilean requirement for the thought part. The narrow (minimal) complexity of language in the suggested picture consists of a collection of what may be informally called *words* containing 'atomic' thoughts, a computational system with Principle G, and two interfaces for SM and CI systems; to emphasize, the SM and CI systems themselves are external to the language system. With this characterization of the core language system, let us return to the desired notion of mind as somehow reflected in language.

As discussed earlier in the Introduction to this work, it is an open research question what else, apart from language, falls under the conception of mind viewed as covering the class of 'language-like' kindred systems. There is a strong intuition that humans do not lose the mind, including the capacity to think, even if they lose the language faculty in important respects; for example, patients appear to retain arithmetical competence (Varley et al. 2005) and musical competence (Peretz et al. 2015; Faroqi-Shah et al. 2019) despite severe language impairment.

At the moment, it seems that, for the mind to be a broader notion than language as indicated, the most coherent way to think of the organization of the mind and language is to view the mind as a primaeval system that gave rise to a range of more complex closely related systems, one of which is language. As proposed, the mind is to be viewed as 'installed' in each of these language-like systems. In order for the mind to be a part of language, we need language to be complex. We have reached the minimally complex notion of language two paragraphs ago. The suggested picture of language is complex because it has several components, it is minimal because it will cease to be a system of language if any of the components is taken away from it.[3] Which part of the language system may now be genuinely designated as the mind?

Words constitute the human lexicon for language, so they are specific to the language system; in fact, insofar as words also include information about how they sound, they belong to particular languages like Warlpiri, Navajo and Pashto. By the same token, the structured expressions at the interfaces are linguistically specific because they are organizations of lexical information. This follows from what is known as the *Inclusiveness Condition* in generative grammar which states that no new objects are added during computation apart from rearrangement of lexical properties (Chomsky 1995a). Words and structured expressions at the interfaces then cannot be viewed as the mind because they are linguistically specific.

This leaves Principle G as the only candidate for the mind. As we proceed, we will see that that is exactly the concept of mind we want. The rest is super-body. In this picture, the mind is thought of as a generative resource that conjoins the existing resources of sound and thought from elsewhere in nature, including other parts of human nature, to give rise to the complex phenomenon of language with its rich expressive power exclusively for humans. The aspects of sound and meaning/thought are what endow the concept of language with its specificity as a cognoscitive power. The generative part, in contrast, is *just there* to endow the total system with generative power. In that sense, the concept of mind is at once separated from the concept of language as well as implicated in it, as desired.

The picture appears to assume that the mind emerged first to cause language and other cognoscitive powers to develop in due course. When I say that the mind emerged *first*, it is natural to think of a temporal order between the emergence of mind and, say, the arrival of human language, especially if we are thinking of some order of evolution. However, I don't see any conceptual requirement for a time gap: it could be that all the conditions for languagehood appeared simultaneously as things magically fell in place. The conceptual requirement is that the components of language must have been separately available for the magic to be triggered; the mind is one such component.

So, the picture at least has the merit of locating each of the mind, language and thought in something of a natural order such that empirical issues, including evolutionary issues, may now be raised without making the category mistakes that Gilbert Ryle warned us about. The rest of this work may be viewed as a detailed examination of this picture. We will soon see that roughly similar evolutionary pictures of the organization of human cognoscitive powers were often mooted in the literature, notwithstanding differences in how each of these powers was labelled. In particular, we will see that the evolutionary evidence offered so far is consistent with the hypothesis that Principle G was available before the emergence of human language. Once a general evolutionary picture emerges around the emerging concept of mind, we will be in a position to examine its theoretical validity and the empirical support that may be harnessed. We will engage in that task from the next chapter onwards.

3.4 Boundaries of the mind

It is worthwhile to quickly review what has been accomplished so far in our search for the narrow mind. In pursuance of Galilean restrictions, recall that the task for this chapter was to first suggest some measure to mark the divide between mind and cognition. It was achieved in terms of the emergence of language in organic evolution. Once we formed some idea of the concept of mind so reached, we proceeded to impose further Galilean abstractions for forming an even narrower conception of mind in terms of a more restrictive understanding of language. This led to the conception of mind as a generative device, Principle G. What does this notion of mind mean in the overall organization of cognoscitive powers of organisms?

Consider the familiar cognitive capacities of consciousness, vision and emotions, to name a few. It is fruitless to deny that humans share them with animals. Even earthworms seem to have consciousness and vision; I do not know if they are endowed with emotions as well. But chimpanzees, along with Descartes' dog, certainly have all of these and more. At the same time, it is questionable if these capacities are intrinsically related to the linguistic capacity at all, 'computational' accounts of them notwithstanding. After losing the linguistic capacity due to severe impairment of the brain, humans with a 'shattered mind' do not always lose the mentioned cognitive capacities (Gardner 1975); thus, language appears to be disassociated from vision, consciousness and the like.

So, there seems to be an intimate connection between what we share with animals and the absence of linguistic capacity in them. This is not to deny that humans can form judgements that result from an *interaction* of these capacities with the linguistic capacity; humans can talk and think about virtually anything, and behave accordingly. For example, many animals certainly experience pain and can 'express' pain by shrieking, as Descartes noted; humans do the same, but they can also *report* pain to seek medical attention. Since it is implausible that the mentioned capacities – the capacity to feel pain, for example – are themselves human-specific, we need to make theoretical decisions about the scope of the human mind.

From what we saw so far, the human mind is *not* postulated to cover the entirety of the human cognitive architecture; it covers only those parts or aspects of the total architecture that are specifically enriched by generative endowment. In this sense, the human mind is an abstract, theoretical postulate. It is not immediately discernible by looking at what organisms do. Failure to grasp the abstract character of the ascription of the mind leads people to ascribe a human-like mind to gullible parrots or singing birds or even to chattering insects, just because some structured sounds are emitted by them. I think it is this theoretical sense in which classical philosophers viewed language as a 'mirror of mind'. So, the central question for this work is: 'which mind is reflected in the mirror of language'?

We have already decided to set aside consciousness, vision, emotion, attention and a host of other phenomena from the scope of a narrow conception of the mind because these can be robustly ascribed to animals as well, unless, of course, human language is necessarily implicated in them.[4] However, there are some boundary-line cases that demand closer inspection. According to the terms of the thought experiment so far pursued, it is plausible to assume that early Proto already had (some of the relevant) sound and thought systems in place. These systems are commonly viewed as falling under the concept of mind as they belong to a comprehensive notion of language. In that sense, Proto already had at least that part of mind. Insofar as humans are descendants of Proto, humans also must have been broadly endowed with these systems; after all, what is language without sound and meaning?

But such a wide notion of mind, that includes the original sound and thought systems, misses the novel conception of mind that arises with the unique aspects of language. That is why we made much effort to suggest that both the broad sound and thought systems fell outside the scope of the mind because they are external to language. However, I am not denying that there is some conceptual tension here. As some authors have pointed out, aspects of human sound and thought that enter into human language themselves contain apparently human-specific elements that are hard to explain as borrowed from pre-existing systems (Pinker and Jackendoff 2005; see also Fitch et al. 2005). I will keep addressing this issue as we proceed.

In this connection, I emphasize that the event of a lightning strike only means that a computational system constituting Principle G was inserted. It does not necessarily mean that human *language* also emerged simultaneously with the strike. I will discuss the possible separation between the mind and language in terms of the time of insertion of Principle G with more detail in Chapters 4 and 8. If the separation is credible, then it opens up the prospect of using the human mind (=Principle G) to explain some of the human-specific initial conditions of human language. In any case, a language-independent presence of Principle G helps explain the formation of various non-linguistic mental systems.

The postulation of Principle G places several empirical and methodological constraints on the concept of mind. To emphasize, a single operation, Principle G, was inserted to give rise to the human mind. Thus, strictly speaking, any mental aspect in the current state of humans is a computational consequence of Principle G; there is simply no other option. As a result, even within the species-specific domains of human cognition, the proposed concept of mind may not at once extend to the rich and complex ways in which we like to describe our mental lives. For example, the suggested explanatory restrictions raise the prospect that not all the aspects of perception, emotion, consciousness, scientific beliefs, religiosity, sexual preferences, moral, political and aesthetic intuitions, anxiety and depression, and the like, fall under the narrow concept of mind even if some of these may have exclusive human content. This may happen in at least three ways.

First, it may turn out that some of the listed phenomena – such as the perceptual systems –were inherited from early Proto and have been retained as such without computational modification. Second, the listed aspects, even when they are human-specific, such as reported spiritual experiences, may not be susceptible to the chosen computational account. Ideally, we would expect the first and the second ways to coincide; that is, we will expect that the cognitive systems we inherited from early Proto are exactly those that resist computational explanation. But life is never easy: knowledge of those cognitive aspects may influence what computational explanation we are seeking and *vice versa*.

For example, even if we are able to determine, following some discussion in Chapter 6, that computational explanations do not extend to some non-human animals, we may not be able to determine that the cognitive systems we inherited from non-human animals are also non-computational. The human visual system is a dramatic case in point. As the Cartesians pointed out, arguably, the human visual system is also a computational system without being an exclusively human system (Chomsky 1966). However, in such cases, it is likely that there is a crucial distinction between the notion of computation that applies to human mental systems (I-computation) and the notions of computation applicable to the rest of nature (N-computation); see Chapter 6.[5]

Third, the phenomena may be too ambiguous, complex and open-ended to lend themselves to focused computational inquiry; for example, as we saw, not everything that is covered by the common thick notion of language, especially in the thought part, falls under the computational/grammatical enterprise (Chomsky 1986, 2013; Mukherji 2010). It is likely, then, that most parts of these broad domains – such as religiosity, morality and scientific beliefs – will continue to be explored in philosophy, arts and literature, in anthropology and the study of human history, but not in the science of the mind; perhaps forever. The resulting proliferation of diverse human inquiries should not be either surprising or disappointing because the quest for simplicity in scientific inquiry typically works in severely restricted domains (Mukherji 2017).

Studies on human cognition face the additional problem that, since human cognition is used to study itself, there ought to be severe restrictions on how far humans can theorize upon the mental life of the species (Mukherji 2010, Chapter One). We are thus led to a lingering intuition that our ability to have a theoretical grasp of ourselves must be severely restricted somewhere. As Thomas Nagel (1997, 76) observed, 'there are inevitably going to be limits on the closure achievable by turning our procedures of understanding on themselves.' It is likely that when we approach that limiting point, our theoretical tools begin to lose their edge and the enterprise simply drifts into banalities since our resources of inquiry and the objects of inquiry begin to get hopelessly mixed up from that point on. So the prospect is that even when we reach some understanding of apparently well-bounded cognitive domains such as language, the understanding is likely to be restricted to small and simple parts of the domain such as grammar.

This is not to deny that many of the listed mental aspects, such as concepts (especially abstract and theoretical concepts), visual imagery, formation of beliefs including causal and moral beliefs, emotions and other affects, grades of consciousness and the like, may have taken on uniquely human forms precisely due to the effects of the generative machinery of the human mind. If so, then these aspects of the otherwise broad mind certainly fall under the narrow concept of mind. There is no *a priori* limit on what constitutes the generative mind. In general, it is eminently possible that much of the broad mental aspects of humans, in contrast to those of non-human animals, are themselves historical products of the human mind.

But then the immense explanatory burden, rarely met, is to isolate exactly those aspects of the broad mind to show how they might have developed in a historical chain via the computational resources of human language embedded in the narrow conception of mind. The postulation of Proto marks the boundary for such explanations. For example, as noted, researchers in anthropology and developmental psychology often allude to the influence of 'language' in the acquisition of concepts by human children (Gentner and Goldwin-Meadow 2003; Spelke 2003; Carey 2009). Even though these studies do throw light on where human children differ from, say, rats, chickens, dogs and chimpanzees, it is unclear whether the proposed human-specific properties were missing in early Proto as well. That stronger conclusion can be reached only by showing that the suggested differences can be traced to the computational resources embedded in human language in the form of Principle G. Pending such advances, if at all, the concept of the generative mind may not extend to the desired notion of a broad mind.

To my knowledge, most of these issues of demarcation between the human mind and the rest of the organic world remain unaddressed even though the computational approach to mind and language is one of the central features of what has come to be known as the cognitive sciences. In the vast body of research that has ensued in a fascinating variety of directions, it remains unclear how the twin notions of language and mind inform each other. In fact, across the literature in the cognitive sciences, some notion of the mind or cognition or mental capacities, even when computationally construed, seems to span the entire range from insect navigation and storing of food by birds to political choices and sexual preferences in humans. In my view, such over-application of computational explanations happened because insufficient attention was paid to the rationalist proposal that language is the mirror of mind.

4

Redesigning Proto

The picture of the generative mind sketched so far seems to encourage something like a model where we might be able to place the components of cognoscitive powers in some order to study their interaction in a freeze, so to speak. The postulation in the last chapter of a pre-linguistic hominid, called *Proto*, was designed in part to serve that purpose. Recall that Proto was imagined to be a pretty advanced hominid individual just prior to the emergence of modern humans; by postulation, Proto was endowed with most of the relevant cognoscitive powers *except* language.

How realistic is the postulation of Proto and what notion of language is involved in making the critical distinction between Proto and humans? More significantly, exactly which cognoscitive powers to endow Proto with such that the very next step leads to language? In effect, we are using the idea of the hypothetical Proto as a thought experiment to test the conceptual picture of mental organization reached in the last chapter. We will see that somewhat similar pictures are proposed in the thought experiments narrated by Charles Darwin and Noam Chomsky with interesting differences between them. In effect, therefore, we are trying to make sense of the origin and relation of the mind and language in terms of a comparative study of thought experiments in the light of whatever we know of human evolution. That is my only interest here; I am not particularly interested in forming an opinion on research on evolution of language and mind. That is why I will restrict the discussion to various conceptions of Proto.

4.1 Aspects of language evolution

The palaeo-anthropologist Ian Tattersall (1995, 29) reports that the great nineteenth-century zoologist Ernst Haeckel conjectured about a Proto-like creature in some detail. Haeckel's 'hypothetical primaeval man' possibly developed out of 'the anthropoid apes', and had a very long skull with slanting teeth and with hair covering the whole body. Its arms were comparatively longer and stronger; its legs, on the other hand, were 'knock-kneed, shorter and thinner' making 'its walk but half erect'. Setting more such anatomical details aside, Haeckel's central conjecture was that this creature lacked the crucial feature that marked the onset of humanity: *articulate speech*. Haeckel called this creature 'speechless ape-man' or *pithecanthropus alalus*.

In the 150 years or so that have elapsed since Haeckel's conjecture, our knowledge of the hominin species has advanced significantly to raise doubts about the suggested morphology of Haeckel's hypothetical creature (Tattersall 1995, 2012; Streidter 2004). Haeckel probably relied heavily on his extrapolations from rather fragmentary fossil evidence of the Neanderthal skull. Following Haeckel's nomenclature, Eugene Dubois called his 'Java Man' *pithecanthropus* – now known to belong to the species *Homo erectus* (Stringer 2011).

Controversies remain (Johansson 2013; Dediu and Levinson 2013; Leiberman 2016; Tattersall 2019), but by now there is some reason to believe that even the Neanderthals, one of our closest extinct ancestors, did not display language in the strict sense (Stringer 2011). Tattersall (2012, xiv) points out that 'not only is the ability for symbolic reasoning lacking among our closest living relatives, the great apes; such reasoning was apparently also absent from our closest extinct relatives – and even from the earliest humans who looked exactly like us'. Later in the book (p. 208), Tattersall includes the 'non-symbolic' Neanderthals as one of those 'extinct relatives' (see also Pearce et al. 2013). Thus, Tattersall appears to favour a 'saltational' explanation of evolution of language which holds that language emerged suddenly only with modern humans. The explanation is, of course, hotly disputed by theorists who, in contrast, favour a 'gradualist' explanation of the phenomenon by citing tools and dedicated sites from earlier hominids such as *Homo erectus* onwards. As we will see, the comparative study of thought experiments throws interesting light on the debate.

My understanding is that, at the current state of knowledge, we may safely set aside the archaeological details offered to pursue the debate between saltation and gradualism. As many authors have pointed out, most of the palaeo-anthropological narratives have the form of 'just so stories'. In an important review of the literature on evolution of language, Hauser et al. (2014) observe, among other things, that 'the fossil and archaeological evidence does not inform our understanding of the computations and representations of our earliest ancestors, leaving details of origins and selective pressure unresolved'. Berwick et al. (2013)

suggest that the language system consists of internal 'phonological, syntactic and semantic representations'; however, fossil records are not likely to show 'what those representations were like' and 'whether the human brain had yet formed the necessary connections' between the required representations.

For example, no direct evidence is provided by either side of the dispute for what would count as 'symbolic reasoning', and how fossils record such facts. All we are offered are discoveries of 'cultural' effects such as tool-making, sites for burial and other rituals, locations for workshops and so on. Even if these discoveries are more or less accurately dated and assigned to specific species, no causal reasoning is offered as to how and which aspects of language and symbolic reasoning are involved; in any case, calling some locations 'workshop' or 'burial site' on the basis of scattered evidence appears to be an act of over-interpretation. It is never made clear how an uncomfortably large number of alternative explanations are to be ruled out.

To have a feel of the problem of how alternative explanations for discovery of 'cultural' objects are addressed and ruled out in human evolution, consider the fascinating study of human bone-flute in Kunej and Turk (2000). Even though music, like language, itself does not fossilize, musical instruments sometimes do. The study by Kunej and Turk concerned a fairly well-preserved bone specimen from the Middle Palaeolithic era and was examined from a variety of directions to rule out the alternative that the holes in the bone were due to animal bites. Although I have used the study as strong evidence for early musical ability (Mukherji 2010), there is much opposition to the credibility of the evidence by leading anthropologists such as Stringer (2011); the issue continues to be inconclusive. In the case of language and thought, there are no 'material' specimens for the concerned period in the first place. It is no wonder therefore that even a rough identification of the 'speechless ape-man' remains elusive.

The problem is compounded by the requirement that, other things being equal, we are looking for a creature in whose brain the fine-grained unique property of a theoretically motivated notion of mind/language – namely, a grammatical system with Principle G at the core – was inserted. There is some recent evidence of how grammatical structure may be represented in the cortical structure of current humans (Moro et al. 2001; Musso et al. 2003; Berwick et al. 2013; Pallier et al. 2011; Nelson et al. 2017, etc.), as noted in Chapter 2. So there is neural confirmation of the obvious fact that *now* it is there. However, at the current state of knowledge, we do not really know what it means for an organic system to have this property (Mukherji 2010, Chapters One and Seven; Poeppel 2012; Bennett and Hacker 2003); in that sense, we do not know *how* it was made available to early humans, not to mention *when*. Unsurprisingly, current appeals to broad morphological features from fossil studies, or even to neural and genetic features, are not likely to unearth the specific (state of the) species in which the computational system of language was initially inserted (Berwick et al. 2013; Hauser et al. 2014).

As we saw, these problems arise basically because language and thought do not fossilize. The already intractable problem is compounded by the recent proposal by Chomsky and others that the sound part is not the primary aspect of the linguistic system, 'sound is ancillary'; according to these authors, perhaps the sound system is an evolutionary afterthought (Chomsky 2006; Chomsky and McGilvray 2012; Chomsky 2015; Berwick and Chomsky 2016; Huybregts 2017). The human linguistic system, on this view, is essentially designed for formation of thought, as some of the classical philosophers apparently held.[1] The sound-is-ancillary hypothesis, if valid, casts doubt on the linguistic significance of much evolutionary evidence focused on the anatomy of speech. Speech is something that can be proxy studied by fossil evidence of growth in anatomical structures related to vocal abilities, as well as by direct behavioural evidence of vocalization in extant species (Tattersall 2019). Perhaps this is the reason why, as we will see, Darwin the scientist urged and made an attempt to derive as much as he could from such slender and indirect physical evidence.

It is hard to find such evidence for the presence of (abstract) structured thoughts. The absence of direct evidence for thought is the reason why the current state of the topic of how language and the mind are related must lean heavily on thought experiments rather than on recorded behavioural properties of chimpanzees and fossil records of extinct creatures in the hominid line. These thought experiments can plausibly be constructed because, even if there is no direct evidence of specific abilities as noted, there are, indeed, some broad facts which furnish some relatively stable perspectives to the thought experiments.

The attested evolution of the human brain is one such fact. After the hominid line departed from chimpanzees, there was little increase in the brain size for about the next five to six million years. While chimpanzees have brains of about 400 cc, the various ape-like species, such as the *Australopithecus* family that followed for several million years, could reach only about 500 cc. There is strong evidence that there was a sharp increase in the growth of both absolute and relative brain sizes of the earliest hominid (*Homo habilis*) around two million years ago. By the *Homo erectus* phase about one million years ago, the brain size had climbed to over thrice that of chimpanzees (Streidter 2004, 314; Bolhuis et al. 2014). So, there was a sudden explosion in brain size somewhere between

Homo habilis and *Homo erectus*, perhaps nearer to the *erectus*-end. Raichlen and Polk (2013) report that the major increase occurred during the early evolution of the genus *Homo*, becoming especially pronounced during the evolution of *Homo erectus* (see Figure 4.1).[2]

As the figure shows, the sharp rate of growth attained thereof continued until the emergence of *Homo sapiens* when the human brain resulted in approximately three times larger than expected for our body size, due to increases in several brain components, including the frontal lobe, temporal lobe and cerebellum, Raichlen and Polk report. However, Tattersall (2018) raises a variety of objections regarding inferences from brain size to various cognitive abilities. As several species of the same genus/clade typically cohabited at about the same time, it is difficult to determine direct links between increase in brain sizes and increasing abilities, cognitive or otherwise. Moreover, it is unclear, until very recent phases of hominid evolution, how development of various non-linguistic abilities, such as increase in memory, relate to the development of language. We need to keep these cautionary factors in mind.

Returning to the evolution of brain size, it is beginning to get established that modern humans emerged only about 150 to 200 KY due to another 'burst' in increase in brain size and other structural modifications in the brain (Crow 2010), but the rate of change of brain size during this period via a series of hominin species was somewhat less dramatic. Also, a number of closely related hominid species – that sometimes cohabited and interbred – shared roughly

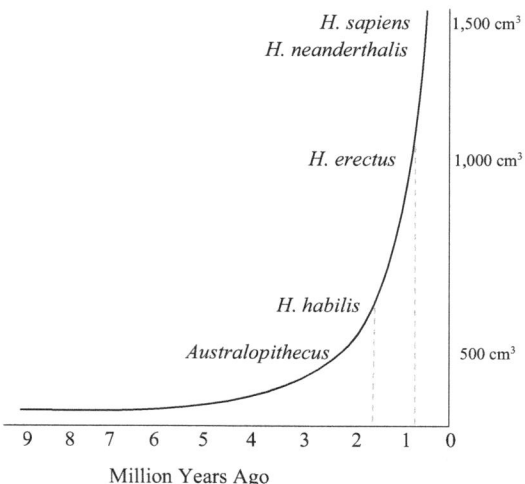

Figure 4.1 Evolution of hominid brain size. © N. Mukherji.

similar brain sizes during that penultimate period just before the emergence of modern humans; apart from humans, perhaps the species most talked about in the folklore is *Homo neanderthalis*.

Despite the clustering of hominid species, there is substantial agreement that only one species, *Homo sapiens*, also known as *Anatomically Modern Humans*, developed the language ability. Ian Tattersall (2016) points out that modern humans display two fundamentally novel abilities in connection with the general ability to use language: the ability to 'process information symbolically' and the ability to express ideas by 'using structured articulate language'. As noted, Tattersall (2012) held that symbolic reasoning and articulate structuring were absent even in the species that 'looked exactly like us'. In what follows, I will mention repeatedly the twin abilities that mark language: *symbols* and (articulated) *structures*. The present point is that, as Tattersall emphasizes, *no* other creature, past or present, ever did *either* of these things.

Although the origin of human language is hotly debated (Behar 2008; Fitch 2010; Johansson 2013), (full) human language possibly emerged at a later date. Although some authors hold that language emerged as late as 50 KY (Holden 1998; Klein 2008; Berwick and Chomsky 2011), current estimates suggest an earlier date, perhaps preceding the migration out of Africa which happened around 80 KY (Mcbrearty and Brooks 2000; Behar 2008; Huybregts 2017). Although some evidence of stone tools, burial sites and suchlike have been found for earlier hominids during the Lower Palaeolithic era, it appears that most of the complex cultural objects consisting of artworks, ornaments, clothing, weapons, shelters and the like abound during the later Middle to the Upper Palaeolithic period, about 40,000–100,000 years ago. This is where most of the convincing examples of 'symbolic reasoning' are found, according to many authors (Tattersall 2019; Sahle and Brooks 2019). The more we recede from this period, the more uncertain it is to align evidence of language with whatever scattered and scanty material evidence, including genetic information, is currently available. This is where 'just so stories' prominently take over the narrative.

So what perspective for setting up thought experiments can we achieve for understanding the evolution of language and thought from the robust fact of a sudden and rapid increase in brain size? As Liberman (2016) and many others point out, the fact of the sudden increase around *Homo erectus* nearly a million years ago does project something like a starting date for postulating the remarkable and unique ability that finally resulted in human language. The continuity and the rapidity of the increase in brain size also suggests that some processes were certainly speeded up far beyond the apes.

However, from the fact of the rapid increase in relative brain size we need not jump to the conclusion that most of the increased brain was devoted to cognitive features such as language and thought. As Raichlen and Polk (2013) suggest, 'a significant portion of human neurobiology evolved due to selection acting on features unrelated to cognitive performance.' These features include rapid developments in physical prowess and activity which were probably critical for increasingly better nutrition leading to more effective hunting skills, reproductive efficiency and the like. Since several proximate hominid species developed similar or better 'brawn' than humans, it is unclear how much these features contributed to the astonishing development of language and the mind rather selectively in a single species.[3] With the cautionary note in mind, nonetheless, it is plausible to assume that both the remarkable growth in brain size and the attendant physical developments could have necessarily contributed to, and gained from, the emergence of unique mentality. However, since a range of species benefitted from these developments, it is unlikely that they provided for the sufficient condition for unique mentality as well.

In this connection, Ian Tattersall (2017) suggests, 'the biology underwriting our unusual cognitive and linguistic systems was acquired in the major developmental reorganization that gave rise to our anatomically distinctive species around 200 KY in Africa'. It is unclear to me which timing Tattersall has in mind regarding the emergence of linguistic and related systems to the general fact of 'biology': the period *since Homo erectus* leading up to events around 200 KY, or specifically to some 'reorganization' only *at* about 200 KY. As Tattersall (2018) is generally sceptical about drawing lessons for human language from hominid brain size, I assume that the 'major developmental reorganization' he is talking about occurred around 200 KY itself. The suggested reorganization, then, could be viewed as the sufficient condition for the striking development of human-specific systems that led to much 'selectional advantage' to the species, as Chomsky and others suggest. However, Tattersall also suggests that 'the material record indicates that this new potential lay fallow for around 100 KY'. I return to this interesting suggestion (see Figure 4.2).

Regarding the features of major reorganization at about 200 KY, to my knowledge Tattersall mentions only the well-known archaeological evidences from sites in Kibbish, Ethiopia, that are widely taken to be specimens of first modern humans (McDougall et al. 2005); perhaps this is what Tattersall means by 'anatomically distinctive species'. Just this much is not entirely convincing since, as noted, Tattersall (2012) also held that the distinctively unique cognitive features were not shared even by the species who looked 'exactly like us'.

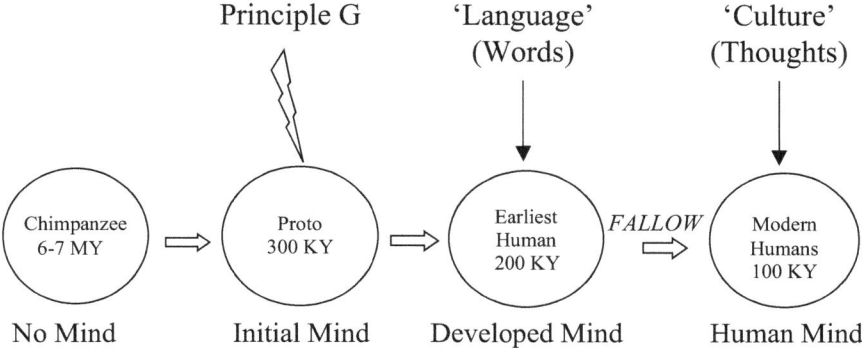

Figure 4.2 Modelling mental powers. © N. Mukherji.

Timothy Crow (2010) offers a more fine-grained explanation. After a detailed review of recent schizophrenia research across human populations with respect to time of onset and gender variation, Crow (2008) traced the psychosis 'precisely to the genetic mechanism that distinguishes the species *Homo sapiens* from its precursor'. According to Crow, the gene pair Protocadherin XY was probably involved in a discrete speciation event that took place about 160 KY. Following this suggestion, Crow (2010) argued that the said speciation event created the modern human brain which is distinguished from that of all other mammals by having four quadrants of association cortex marked with asymmetries, called 'torques'. These torques are apparently absent in chimpanzees (Li et al. 2017), which gives some reason to suppose that these were absent in most hominids as well. According to Crow, the compartments of the human brain are associated sequentially with speech perception, meaning, thought and speech production, or more technically, with perceptual, conceptual, intentional and articulatory capacities (Hinzen et al. 2011). In the case of schizophrenia, the distinctions between compartments break down.

From the discussion on the rapid growth of brain size and the structural changes that occurred, it appears that, while constructing any thought experiment on the evolution of language and mind, we might hold on to the following relatively uncontroversial facts. (1) There was a sudden and rapid increase in hominid brain size at least from *Homo erectus* onwards roughly a million years ago, (2) there was another milder spurt in size and restructuring of the brain perhaps at 200 KY or less, (3) the increased brain size and restructuring could have substantially contributed to the unique emergence of the mind and language only in humans and (4) the uniqueness consisted of two basic features: symbolic reasoning and structured expressions. While (1) and (2) suggest something about where in time it is plausible to place various fables on Proto, (3) and (4) suggest something about what features to endow Proto with. Let us now see how some famous thought experiments in the literature fare with respect to these constraints.

4.2 Two thought experiments

In a famous passage in his *Descent of Man*, Charles Darwin (1871, 57) conjectured about an 'early progenitor of man' as follows:

> As the voice was used more and more, the vocal organs would have been strengthened and perfected through the principle of the inherited effects of use; and this would have reacted on the power of speech. But the relation between the continued use of language and the development of the brain has no doubt been far more important. The mental powers in some early *progenitor of man* must have been more *highly developed than in any existing ape, before even the most imperfect form of speech* have come into use; but we may confidently believe that the continued use and advancement of this power would have reacted on mind itself, by enabling and encouraging it to carry on long trains of thought. A long and complex train of thought can no more be carried on without the aid of words, whether spoken or silent, than a long calculation without the use of figures or algebra. (Emphasis added)

In what follows, this long citation will serve as something like a text. I will not be much concerned with exegetical details about what Darwin himself might have meant by these remarks; nor am I concerned with what may be called 'Darwinian theory of language evolution', if any.[4] The wording of the citation itself will be used to draw lessons on how the 'progenitor of man' was designed. This caveat is needed for the following reason.

There is much discussion of this passage in the recent literature on evolution of language. For example, Fitch (2010, 472–4) also engages in a detailed analysis of this seminal passage. However, Fitch interposes the ideas mooted in the passage with whatever else Darwin says elsewhere about vocalization of animals, sexual selection of traits in species, properties of music and so on. Moreover, Fitch also adds sundry recent ideas on vocal learning in animals such as songbirds, gestures of apes, phonological properties of speech, cultural distribution of music and the like. Fitch needs all this to prepare the basis for his theory of 'musical protolanguage'. In my view, in doing so, he missed Darwin's sharp and focused narrative in the passage.

Berwick and Chomsky (2016, 3) also cite this passage at length. From the context of their discussion, it appears that they basically agree with Fitch's questionable interpretation of the passage. Insofar as the sound side of human language is concerned, Berwick and Chomsky seem to approve of what Fitch takes to be Darwin's idea that human language co-opted resources from non-human sources; however, Berwick and Chomsky seem sceptical of the idea that human language originated from music: namely, *Caruso* theory (Studdert-Kennedy and Terrace 2017).

As noted, there is nothing in the cited passage itself for drawing such a conclusion; I will discuss later why Darwin might have stressed the strengthening of vocal chords in the evolution of language. In contrast to Fitch and others, my sole interest is in the thought experiment of the progenitor of man. Also, as with the earlier discussion on Descartes, my goal is to form a convincing narrative on language and mind from some of Darwin's ideas, without any claim that the narrative is what Darwin intended. All we need the narrative for is to see whether we can find a conceptual story for the human mind that fits the evolutionary steps in hand.

In this very carefully thought-out passage, Darwin attempted a thought experiment on how the different elements that are needed for the eventual emergence of language might have been harnessed. More specifically, Darwin adopts something like the familiar Aristotelian view of language as a system of sound–meaning correlations to show how the elements of speech and thought get correlated in a hypothetical evolutionary narrative. Before I proceed, I must note that this otherwise careful passage contains a variety of familiar conundrums on language, mind, speech, thought and the like. Instead of indulging in complicated philosophical analysis to disentangle these things from each other, let me simply adopt some dictionary conventions to interpret the passage: language = (power of) speech, mind = mental power, thought = language + mind. Darwin's goal is to show how 'long trains of thought' developed when language and mind began to act on each other.

The first step of the narrative raises the obvious need for postulating some *post-ape but pre-linguistic mental powers* for explaining the evolution of thought; human language and thought could not have directly emerged from the chimpanzee brain. It needed a much larger brain size and significant evolutionary time to attain the powers of a species that eventually spawned structured thought. A significant property of the initial mental power was that it was independent of and perhaps prior to speech. Beyond this, Darwin did not say what constitutes these powers. However, his subsequent use of the expressions *mind* and *long train of thought* suggests that he viewed these mental powers as closely related to thought. In the last chapter, I discussed the widespread belief that concepts were available prior to language; it is plausible to assume that Darwin also thought so. Suppose by *mental powers* Darwin meant a rich conceptual repertoire that must have been vastly more developed than in the last apes to provide for 'words', as we will see.

The second step of the narrative suggests that speech (=language) was already developing independently of mental powers as a result of the strengthening of vocal chords. It is obvious that, since mental powers were thought to be already in place outside the realm of speech, Darwin could not have thought of the strengthened vocal chords as *mental* power. His only requirement was that strong vocal chords laid the basis for the continued use of speech with subsequent effects on the mind. Needless to say, the continued use of speech required strong vocal chords, just as the ability to play cricket requires strong arms, but having strong arms does not guarantee a cricketing mind. Unfortunately, in the passage, Darwin did not say where speech came from; he only said that the vocal chords grew stronger over time due to singing. Obviously, he assumed that singing (=music) was already in place; in fact, for Darwin music must have been going on for a while independently of both speech and mental powers. The assumption might have led recent authors to launch their own narratives about musical protolanguage and Caruso theories.

Anyhow, in the third step of the narrative, Darwin stated that, at some point during the growth of the brain accompanied by the continued use of speech that 'acted' on mental powers, 'words' occurred, both spoken and silent. The mention of 'silent' words suggests that Darwin did not identify speech entirely with articulation, or what is now called 'externalization'. In that, his idea of speech was akin to Descartes' idea of sign which Descartes thought may occur in humans even without the 'organ' of speech. It is plausible to suppose that both Descartes and Darwin wished to emphasize the *symbolic* character of words. In due course, these words contributed to long trains of thought just as long calculations require the aid of figures and algebra. Except for saying that somehow words resulted out of interaction between speech and mental powers, Darwin did not elaborate on what constituted the interaction. He also did not give any hint of how the 'algebra' for 'long trains of thought' evolved when the words became available. There are other infirmities in the narrative to which I return.

So the narrative is that a progenitor of man started out with richer conceptual resources than the apes due to his larger brain size. The progenitor was also endowed with strong vocal tracts that grew out of prolonged singing over generations, an 'inherited trait' according to Darwin. The strong vocal chords led to speech, which also grew as the brain grew. As speech grew, conceptual growth and growth of speech converged to give rise to words which eventually contributed to the construction of long trains of thought 'algebraically', so to speak. Thus, Darwin's progenitor appears to have had mind and language in separate locations; when mind and language converged in due course, thought emerged.

Darwin's narrative needs at least two distinct phases, perhaps separated by evolutionary time, for distinct operations: speech acting on mind to form words, and algebraic construction of trains of thoughts. After narrating a general growth of the hominid brain for over a million years, the archaeological record we looked at earlier also suggests two distinct phases at about 200 KY and 100 KY, respectively. Whether the two narratives – archaeological and Darwin's – match is an empirical issue concerning how the distribution of cognoscitive powers was laid out. I will return to a cumulative view of all the narratives after visiting another related model suggested recently.

Chomsky also proposed a similar progenitor; however, Chomsky's narrative is simpler than Darwin's, and more dramatic. Calling it a 'fairy tale', Chomsky suggests that 'there were primates with pretty much our sensorimotor (SM) and conceptual-intentional (CI) systems, but no language faculty, and some natural event took place that brought about a mutation that installed a language faculty' (Chomsky and McGilvray 2012, 14–15). Earlier, Chomsky suggested that the language faculty was inserted in the brain of a wandering hominid with a lightning strike or a cosmic ray shower, and the hominid's brain got rewired (Chomsky 2000a). So Chomsky has narrated this thought experiment consistently for several decades.

Since the progenitor imagined by Chomsky was endowed with 'pretty much' our SM and CI systems, this hominid also must have been far more advanced than the apes who got delinked from the hominid line about six to seven million years ago. Recall from Chapter 3 that in Hauser et al. (2002), Chomsky et al. suggested that human language evolved in our recent evolutionary history 'sometime after the divergence from our chimpanzee-like ancestors'. In that picture, it was unclear how much time was 'sometime'. In the narrative just sketched, Chomsky explicitly suggests that the progenitor had reached pretty close to modern SM and CI systems; so the difference of several million years is acknowledged.

Chomsky's picture is in sharp contrast with Darwin's with respect to the SM and CI systems. Darwin made no assumptions about SM and CI systems except for some initial store of 'mental power'. In Darwin's narrative, these systems got progressively filled up over time as the mental powers interacted with speech. In this sense, Darwin's basic goal was to suggest a dynamic picture for the prolonged growth of conceptual and speech systems to get them ready for long trains of thought inside what Eric Lenneberg called the 'language-ready brain'. In this dynamic picture, the conceptual and speech systems grew together to prepare for even more complex structures. In contrast, Chomsky offers a largely synchronic picture in which SM and CI systems were already in place largely separately before they were put together by the 'language faculty'.

No doubt, Chomsky intended to emphasize the absolutely critical and fundamental aspect of the unbounded productivity of human language to explain the novelty of language use. To that specific end, other things being equal, all that was needed was the insertion of the 'language faculty' in the form of a computational system which operated on 'word-like' units to progressively generate the complex expressions of language (Studdert-Kennedy and Terrace 2017). In effect, Chomsky essentially provides for a mechanism for generating structured expressions – the 'long trains of thought' – once Darwinian resources were in place; Chomsky calls this mechanism itself the 'language faculty'. According to Chomsky, the emergence of the language system signalled a 'Great Leap Forward'.

I wish to emphasize that, since according to the narrative the SM and CI systems were already located in the progenitor, by *language-faculty* Chomsky means basically the computational system with resources to *interface* with the SM and CI systems. The interaction of the computational system with the SM and CI systems enabled the formulation of the 'basic property' of human language in terms of the Strong Minimalist Thesis (SMT): human language is a computational system that constructs structured expressions without bound for the SM and CI interfaces (Chomsky 2008, 2015; Berwick and Chomsky 2016). We will review the operation of this system in the next chapter.

At this point, it is instructive to point out what appears to be an apparent ambiguity in Chomsky's conception of language; the task is relevant for deciding what relation, if any, Chomsky is proposing between the mind, language and thought. The prior existence of SM and CI systems clearly suggests that they are not parts of language – they are 'external' to the language faculty, as noted in the last chapter. But the formulation of SMT, which describes the basic property of language, requires a mention of SM and CI systems such that the computational system may interface with them. So, which is the faculty of language? Just the bare computational system inserted at the last moment when everything else was ready, or the entire complex system consisting of the computational system and the interfaces with SM and CI? In fact, there is more to the complex system.

Chomsky's narrative requires that the interfaces become active just in case linguistic information contained in the human lexicon, 'words', are linked to the computational system; hence, words are also part of the same faculty. As we saw in Darwin's narrative, the notion of a word refers to the conceptual and signing systems: a word is a composite unit which combines units from both systems; let us hold on to this familiar idea. In that sense, it is natural to think of the entire complex required for SMT – words, computational system and interfaces – as constituting the language faculty. The computational system is just a part of the complex; SMT will not apply until (a) the words are there and (b) the computational system is inserted in the existing SM-CI environment: *that* is the Great Leap Forward.

This way of looking at SMT and the language faculty seems to cohere well with the conceptual picture reached in the last chapter. *This* picture requires that Darwinian conditions for word formation must be achieved first before SMT applies. In that sense, we can think of Darwin and Chomsky as complementing each other to satisfy the composite conditions for the origin of language suggested by Tattersall (2019) from archaeological records.

Let us recall that the picture sketched earlier on purely conceptual grounds viewed the mind as consisting *solely* of some generative operation, called Principle G, while language was viewed as a complex system with the mind embedded in an organization of SM and CI interfaces; this is how the mind was supposed to be both distinct and 'reflected' in language. It appears that Chomsky's linguistic programme matches the purely conceptual picture almost point by point if we think of Chomsky's 'language faculty' as the mind. Curiously, in the later part of the citation, Darwin held a similar view of the mind itself carrying on long trains of thought once words were available due to interaction with speech. In that sense, Darwin placed within his conception of *mind* what Chomsky considers to be the expressive power of *language*.

Returning to Chomsky's thought experiment, it seems to have approval from leading palaeo-anthropologists. Thus, Ian Tattersall (2019) recommends the view of language as 'underpinned by an algorithmically simple interface between sensorimotor and conceptual-intentional systems that were co-opted from pre-existing functions or potentials'. According to Tattersall, this view of language 'predicts' that 'language as we recognize it today originated suddenly, at some definable point in the human past'. The proposed saltational picture is supposed to be a contrast to the view that language 'evolved gradually and incrementally over the eons'; the latter 'gradualist' view is often ascribed to Darwin. I will return to these remarks about 'gradualism' later in the chapter.

It is obvious that at least one 'pre-existing' function could not have been directly 'co-opted' from our last non-hominid ancestor, the chimpanzee, because these great apes are strikingly silent creatures (Fitch 2010). Indeed, the absence of the sound system in our closest living relative is a serious problem. Chimpanzees appear to have a moderately rich conceptual repertoire without having much of a sound system and with a pretty moderate gesture system; in contrast, some species of birds and insects, far away from the primate line, are full of sound with very little conceptual resources.

Somehow this deep evolutionary asymmetry was resolved in the human case as the sound and the thought systems were located in the species to be put together subsequently by the generative operation of the mind/language. So, the evolutionary issue is: How did both sound and thought systems occur simultaneously for humans? More importantly, what does this joint endowment of sound and thought mean for the succeeding emergence of language? Darwin and Chomsky approached this problem very differently.

As we saw, Darwin was perhaps trying to make both the speech and the thought systems available to the evolving language system from within the hominid line. For the SM systems, Darwin assumed the prior existence of music in the hominid line which led to the strengthening of vocal chords over generations. Strong vocal chords somehow gave rise to speech; in that sense, SM systems developed from within the (musical) resources of the species. For the CI systems, Darwin assumed a minimal conceptual repertoire available in advance after several million years of growth of the brain; the rest of the CI systems developed as the speech systems 'acted' on the growing conceptual repertoire in some feedback mechanism. It is another matter that the narrative has gaping holes with respect to the initial conditions and one power acting on another.

What Chomsky is assuming, in contrast, is that the required sound and thought systems were simply available in one member of a pre-linguistic species. For the sound part, Chomsky holds that a 'deep convergence' somehow transmitted the properties of vocal learning to the human system via a few hundred genes borrowed from songbirds (Berwick and Chomsky 2016). In any case, insofar as the sound side of the asymmetry problem is concerned, Chomsky's response is to set the problem aside for explaining the origin of language. As Hauser (2009) puts it, 'language evolved for internal thought and planning and only later was co-opted for communication.' Suppose Hauser's claim means that the sound system was no part of the initial emergence of language. Setting the evidence for this startling evolutionary story aside (Huybregts 2017), the point here is that, since the sound system was plugged in later in this view, words as units of sound–meaning correlations emerged much later than the emergence of language. So Darwin's dynamic view of evolution of language is not available to Chomsky.

A different problem arises for the CI system: In which format were such rich systems of concept and intention displayed without the resources of the language faculty? Consider a proposal by the leading linguist Tanya Reinhardt (2006). Following Chomsky, Reinhardt imagined a pre-linguistic creature who was endowed with all of the following components: a system of concepts similar to that of humans, a sensorimotor system for perceiving and coding information in sounds, an innate system of logic, an abstract formal system, an inventory of abstract symbols, and connectives, functions, and definitions necessary for language. Setting the sensorimotor systems aside, I presume that it is totally implausible to endow the chimpanzee with these things since chimpanzees don't even understand what *apple* means even when they are provided with the chimpanzee-equivalent of the symbol (Petitto 2005); we will study this example with more detail in Chapter 6. So, how did the conceptual system and the related CI resources arise for Reinhardt's pre-linguistic hominid?

Indeed, one wonders what it means for an organism to acquire such rich internal systems of thought without the resources of language at all. According to John Bolender (2007), the cultural explosion in the Upper Palaeolithic era, at about 40 KY, may be traced to the human ability to use something like a system of Russellian quantified logic that also includes the basic inferential resources mentioned by Reinhardt. Bolender reminds us that by that time, human language was already firmly in place for several tens of thousands of years. Apparently, exactly the same problem arises for Berwick and Chomsky's claim that the CI system contains resources for 'a conceptual system for inference, interpretation, planning, and the organization of action – what is informally called "thought"' (2016, 11); I said 'apparently' because, unlike Reinhardt, Berwick and Chomsky do not specify what resources enable inference, planning and so on without the resources of language.[5]

4.3 Generative operations

Let us review some of the salient points that have emerged from the preceding survey of thought experiments. The thought experiments were supposed to provide some schematic idea of how all the human-specific cognoscitive conditions fell in place for the emergence of human language. The point is worth insisting on because there is a growing sense that as our knowledge of cognitive systems across species increased, almost everything that specifically goes into the making of human language, apart from general environmental and organic conditions (Hauser et al. 2002), is due to developments in the hominid line itself (Berwick et al. 2013).

As we saw, according to Tattersall (2016) and common sense, human beings process information symbolically to form ideas which are then used to form structured articulate language: 'no other living creature does either of these things.' Tattersall (2019) explains how these two conditions are related: 'the elements of symbolic thought map closely onto the vocabularies of words' to form 'linguistic building-blocks' that enter into 'symbolic mental operations'. Since these conditions are absolutely basic to any conception of language, let us see what narrative is needed to install these conditions. I wish to emphasize that what follows is basically some plausibility considerations based on virtual conceptual necessity; no substantive proposals about mental mechanisms should be read in it. Once a suggestive conceptual picture is in hand, I examine its theoretical and empirical viability in the chapters that follow.

For the first condition of the origin of symbols, Darwin did not explicitly mention CI systems, but he did require that some mental powers had developed much beyond the apes. Needless to say, everyone needs to explain how, beginning with the limited conceptual repertoire of chimpanzees (Petitto 2005), the mental powers of Proto reached near-human proportions. So what did Darwin assume when he remarked that several million years after departure from the primate line, his progenitor of man had rich mental powers? Suppose, with advanced sensory systems, increased memory, emergence of digital manipulation involving demonstration, ability for imitation, vocal learning and the like, some of the growth in mental powers amounted to growth in individual stock of concepts: RED, WOOD, RIPE, BANANA, HOLE, WATER and so on. Of course, someone who deals only in concepts under the sound-is-ancillary hypothesis needs to explain how the concept of banana, namely BANANA, gets to have the shape *banana*; I am just assuming that it happens. In the beginning, it was also a problem for Darwin because we have not yet got to the point where the power of speech started acting on mental powers.

In principle, the growth of concepts can accelerate if individual concepts can be combined and stored in some hierarchies: RED-WOOD, WATER-HOLE, RED-WATER-HOLE and the like. This requires some form of combinatorial operation acting directly on individual concepts; suppose so.[6] In that sense, it is possible to have a concept-only conception of language based on generative operations of the kind indicated. I do not know how far such generative operations may capture the relevant properties of human languages, but, as noted, I will stay away from a comparative study of language with and without the involvement of sound.

In this connection, consider the topic of 'core knowledge' discussed by Elizabeth Spelke (2003). The suggestion of 'core knowledge' is that conceptual knowledge is organized in terms of domain- and task-specific concepts: colour, geometry, material object, number, social relation and the like. Spelke (2000) suggests that humans and non-human animals share roughly the same system of core knowledge. From what we have seen, this suggestion itself could be problematic because these systems of core knowledge consist of concepts, but, according to Petitto (2005), even chimpanzees are unable to form concepts as humans do; Spelke, nonetheless, thinks that even rats are endowed with core knowledge.

Be that as it may, Spelke argues that only humans can combine concepts *across* core domains: for example, humans can combine colour and spatial concepts, such as RED-CORNER. As Spelke puts it, by 'combining representations from these systems, human cognition may achieve extraordinary flexibility'. Spelke (2003) traces the development of cross-combination of concepts to the 'generative properties of language' (296). By *language*, Spelke appears to mean the unbounded system of word combination, but never clarifies how the resources of language led to concept combination across domains of core knowledge. The point is that a combinatorial operation is needed to combine concepts across domains.

However, instead of appealing directly to combination of concepts, Darwin seems to have used the idea of concept combination in terms of symbols with his suggestion that the power of speech 'acted' on the mental power to create 'words'. Suppose this simply means that the sound /banana/ was linked up with the concept BANANA. In effect, it means that a generative operation forms a pair-list (/banana/, BANANA), represented by the word *banana*. In other words, the generative operation enables humans, and *only* humans, to symbolize a concept with the mark of a sound; needless to say, sound is not the only marker. In this way, the 'sign' signals the presence of 'hidden' thought, as Descartes put it. I wish to stress the point that symbolization (=marking) in terms of words requires a generative operation which is a uniquely human endowment since no other animal displays such symbols, as Tattersall emphasized. I will discuss the topic of symbols in more detail as we proceed, especially in Section 8.4.

With the introduction of words, Darwin's narrative satisfied the condition of availability of symbols because one of the ways of marshalling a symbol is to form words. Once words are available, initial 'algebraic' operations can take place arguably far more efficiently and productively between words themselves, rather than between individual concepts: *red-wood, water-hole, red-wood-water-hole* and so on. It is plausible to suppose that the mechanism would have had a significant effect on the growth of mental powers as Darwin indicated: more sound, more meaning; more meaning, more sound. The shift to words endowed the species with radically enhanced mental powers.

However, having said that the power of speech grew with continued use, Darwin never explained where the system of speech came from except for suggesting that strong vocal chords were already available from singing. So, Darwin assumed that singing (= music) was already available prior to words. Even a rudimentary form of singing requires putting together individual units of sound in some order, thus requiring another generative operation. Further, it is implausible that units of music – tones/notes – directly go into the making of speech except in a very limited way in rare cases. Therefore, the units of speech – phonemes – must have been picked up from some other resource, and put together to form signs that entered into the formation of words: *ba-na-na, ri-pe*; this requires another generative operation.

As generative operations are beginning to come out of our ears, let us suppose that eventually these operations also cover the formation of inflected words such as *un-ripe, banana-s*. Given an existing stock of morphemes, such a finite stock of inflections enables further 'extraordinary flexibility' in human mental powers. For example, for English speakers, a single inflection -*s* for pluralization classifies all countable objects into individuals and collections, while the lexical store remains virtually unchanged (Chomsky et al. 2002). Once words were available, Darwin simply assumed that they helped in forming long trains of thought in an 'algebraic' fashion. Darwin never told us what that critical algebra was.

As we will see in some detail in the next chapter, Noam Chomsky's fundamental contribution to our understanding of human language concerns precisely the required generative operation that explained where the unbounded structure of human thought came from. In his narrative, Chomsky simply assumed that some forms of symbols were already available (Studdert-Kennedy and Terrace 2017), in the form of either sound–concept combinations or, more recently, just concepts as atoms of thought (Chomsky 2015); in the latter case, it is not immediately obvious which notion of symbol is involved since nothing seems to be marking these concepts.

Returning to Tattersall's two broad conditions – symbol and structure – that made human language unique in nature, we can now see that the species-specificity of the human language faculty required generative operations throughout its prominent stages of development: Darwin's idea of enhanced mental powers, Darwin's assumption about the expressive power of music, Darwin's suggestion that speech was linked to mental powers to form words, mechanisms for forming words, mechanisms for combining concepts and, of course, Chomsky's fundamental claim about the rich expressive power of human language. Following Tattersall, perhaps two of the most prominent operations are (1) combination of sound and meaning to produce words, and (2) combination of words/morphemes to produce structured thought. How many generative operations were needed to fully develop the faculty of human language?

Keeping just to virtual conceptual necessity and cutting through a very large number of alternative narratives in the literature, I wish to raise the following issue. We saw that no description of the language faculty is credible without the powerful unbounded generative operation that distinguishes humans from the rest of nature. We called it Principle G. The issue I wish to raise is this: will Principle G suffice as the *only* generative principle for describing *all* unique aspects of human language? Notice that if Principle G does suffice, the issue of uniqueness is settled once and for all because, by hypothesis, Principle G is unique to the species. Once Principle G is inserted in human anatomy, all stories of purely gradual evolution, protolanguages and so on appear to drop out of the picture.

Interestingly, the proposal just mooted is not entirely heretical to my knowledge. We know that linguists explain structural ambiguities such as *birds that fly instinctively swim* in computational terms (Berwick and Chomsky 2016). It is of much interest, as Hauser et al. (2014) report, that linguists also use the notion of computation to describe word formation for 'flatter' ambiguous structures such as *un-lock-able*. So what is the notion of computation here? As we will see in the next chapter, the relevant notion of computation may be identified with the unbounded operation of language, that is Principle G. Unless Hauser et al. are thinking of (at least) two distinct notions of computation – one for *unlockable*, and the other for *birds that fly instinctively swim* – Principle G appears to be active throughout. Having come thus far, I wonder if they will insist on a third notion of combination/computation for inflected words such as *un-ripe* and *table-s*.

I am aware that some of the generative examples just listed may be viewed as superficial or rudimentary; for example, it is said that morphological rules for structures such as *un-ripe* are shallow (Chomsky et al. 1982). It could be that different generative mechanisms are responsible for satisfying varying generative tasks: some may require very restricted operations, others perhaps demand unrestricted procedures. Yet, for achieving something like a Galilean simplicity of the linguistic system, can we think of a single unbounded operation, Principle G, as operating in each of the cases just discussed, and unleashing its generative powers selectively as the case demands?[7] The chef's knife that cuts meat also slices ginger, and you don't want two doors for a small dog and a big dog in the same doghouse.[8] I will return to this topic from a different direction in Chapter 8.

As mentioned in the Introduction in connection with the variety of generative operations of the mind, a more substantive point now is that each of the generative operations for the origin of language, superficial or otherwise, is novel for the species, since it cannot be drawn from pre-existing resources (Miyagawa 2021). Therefore, it can enter the hominid system only by saltation, raising the explanatory problem that the evolutionary process will require a large number of saltations. Further, we already have a saltational operation in the unbounded generative mechanism of language, as Tattersall (2019) pointed out. A natural solution to the explanatory problem, then, is to restrict saltation to the generative principle of language. An evolutionarily plausible explanation of combinatorial operations in language thus coincides with the requirement that Principle G covers all generative operations of the human mind.

Before I consider some objections to this picture, notice that I have not proposed that Principle G covers the generative effects needed for the *externalization* of the structured thought generated by the principle. No doubt, one of the most difficult problems in current linguistic theory is to explain how the hierarchical structure of thought is transferred for the linear structure of utterances (Uriagereka 2008; Berwick and Chomsky 2016). This problem of transfer is faced by any linguistic theory in any case.[9] A plausible scenario is that the articulatory system with linear ordering was probably in place independently of Principle G, perhaps co-opted from non-human sources (Berwick and Chomsky 2016). In any case, we know that the human brain is capable of simultaneous processing of hierarchical and linear orders (Ding et al. 2015). So, whatever be the generative system for externalization of thought, it appears to be independent of Principle G.

Two objections, among others, need to be discussed at this point regarding the postulation of Principle G. First, suppose there are two creatures who are both engaged in some restricted task such as piling ten bricks in some order. How do we know if one of them is endowed with a restricted finite operation and the other an unbounded one but using a finite part of it? The simple answer is we don't. Such problems of distinguishing between finite and infinite abilities can always be raised. For example, one cannot directly find evidence of unbounded principles of language in children's use of telegraphic speech containing two-word or three-word sequences; yet, telegraphic and caretaker speech are exactly the right kind of examples of bounded use of unbounded principles. Telegraphic speech is *not* a protolanguage (Gentner 1982; Gleitman et al. 1984; Gleitman and Bloom 1998; Gillette et al. 1999). So the structuring principles of telegraphic speech cannot be different from structuring principles in general, even if only a bounded use of some unbounded principle is in operation.

Second, a somewhat more serious objection is that, if Principle G itself creates the symbolic character of language with sound–meaning correlations, how does Principle G operate as a symbol manipulator? The issue is, if Principle G is an operation of the form $C(x, y)$ then x, y need to be symbols themselves to execute the generative effect. A quick response is that this is precisely the reason why Principle G must be viewed as an abstract domain-independent operation; hence, as in logical theory, Principle G needs to be formulated in terms of abstract symbols which take specific values when applied in a domain.

Symbols are representations; they 'stand for' something. Thus, /banana/ is a phonological representation of the sound, BANANA is a representation of a (hidden) concept probably associated with a mental image of some sort; each of them is a symbol in its respective domain. In the domain of language, the terms of Principle G pick units of sound and units of thought as values to generate *linguistic* symbols, words; thus the word *banana* consists of the structure (/banana/, BANANA). In effect, in the word case, Principle G generates symbols of symbols; perhaps that is why the emergence of words is so late and unique in organic evolution.

4.4 Proto and Principle G

Earlier we postulated, on purely conceptual grounds, that the human mind is constituted of a generative principle which acts as a primaeval system for developing a variety of cognoscitive systems, language being one of them.

I have just suggested that, more specifically, the generative Principle G could be viewed as the only device involved for a variety of generative requirements in human cognoscitive systems. We also saw that the human language faculty is best viewed as a complex system consisting of Principle G, among other things. Can we now view Principle G as the human mind itself which is embedded in language and other mental systems?

There are at least three interesting aspects of Principle G. First, it is needed in any case to account for the unbounded generative power of human language. Second, since it is the most powerful generative principle in hand, it may satisfy all other generative requirements of the total system. Third, as described in terms of narratives so far, the principle appears to be operating in a flexible manner in various ways. For example, as noted, within the domain of concepts, it not only combines concepts within a core domain, but it also combines concepts *across* such domains. Further, as we saw, lexicalization itself – perhaps the most fascinating aspect of human language – requires a pretty remarkable generative operation involving concepts and speech sounds. Concepts and speech sounds belong to two entirely distinct domains.

The idea that Principle G puts items from such disparate domains together means that the principle is *domain-free*; it operates abstractly regardless of which domain it is operating in. If we now think of Darwin's suggestion that the generative system of music was already in operation prior to human language, then it follows that the principle could have been operating on musical sounds as well. Finally, Principle G enforces the real generative power of human language by putting lexical items together in an unbounded fashion; in effect, it means that the principle is combining units that are themselves effects of previous generative operations.

The preceding description of Principle G raises the prospect that the principle does not belong exclusively to the domain of human language if this domain is to be viewed in terms of sound–meaning correlations; that is just one of the effects of Principle G, in accordance with the Strong Minimalist Thesis (SMT). Moreover, in terms of conceptual necessity, Principle G must have been available in advance to initiate the sequence of processes that finally led to structured thoughts in human language. Therefore, Principle G must be invoked to explain (a) lexicalization or linguistic symbolization, and (b) satisfaction of SMT; in other words, Principle G satisfies both the conceptually necessary conditions of symbol and structure for the emergence of human language. In that sense, the human mind is embedded in the complex phenomenon of human language.

Since we now have a complete description of the generative principles of human language, it is useful to see how they may be embedded in the conception of Proto. We saw that the postulation of (early) Proto, while allowing us to sidestep the noted uncertainties of evolutionary timing, enables us to assume much evolutionary progress, *sans* language, up to the point when the primary structural condition for the subsequent emergence of language as a 'long train of thought' had been attained. Conceptually, as noted, all the preparatory steps for language could have happened at the same time. Yet, given the significant difference in time – which Tattersall described as a prolonged 'fallow' – between the emergence of early humans (about 200 KY) and full human language (about 100 KY), it is methodologically unsafe to infer that human language emerged just as the lightning struck.[10]

In that light, it is reasonable to conjecture that the immense complexity of linguistic phenomena – with their lexicon, syntax and semantics, not to mention morphology, phonology and pragmatics – must have required considerable time to fall in place bit by bit. Considerations of timing suggest that the mind emerged first essentially in the form of a generative principle. Among other things in a narrow generative space, human language *followed* in due course. So the initial intuition is that the emerged (computational) mind prepared the basis for the eventual great leap forward in which sound and concepts were combined to give rise to linguistic symbols.

Once a sufficient stock of symbols developed and finer mechanisms of combination, such as the inflection and agreement systems, emerged and stabilized, the full human language with its phasal structure emerged gradually which, in turn, shaped much of human history. The suggested picture may be schematically represented as in Figure 4.2. Several interesting consequences seem to follow once we adopt the picture.

As a starter, two heated debates concerning evolution of human language seem to lose considerable ground. For one, since Principle G as the most powerful computational principle is postulated to be the only generative principle in human evolution for all levels of generative need, the distinct linguistic course of human evolution may be identified with this principle. Hence, contrary to Boeckx (2017), Martin and Boeckx (2019) and many others, any notion of 'lower' principles in the hominid line preceding human language becomes conceptually unnecessary. For another, the heated debate on gradual versus sudden evolution of language begins to lose appeal. It is most likely that any plausible picture of the evolution of language required both saltational and gradualist steps (Clark 2013). The picture suggests that the required mind of the progenitor emerged suddenly due to a radical mutation such that the (full) language system, facilitated by enriched sound and conceptual systems, then developed gradually. The picture of gradual development of human language becomes even more plausible if we agree, as suggested earlier, that the human lexicon constituting sound–meaning correlations is itself a generative product of Principle G.

Another consequence is that, since Principle G was available prior to language, it might have left its mark elsewhere in hominid evolution between (later) Proto and humans with a variety of generative effects unrelated to the human faculty of language. Music could be one such effect as Darwin imagined, but it is hard to find archaeological evidence for music for such an early period. In contrast, evidence of tool-making from bone and stone are growing for the relevant period (Stout 2011; Uomini and Mayer 2013; Joordens et al. 2015; Brooks et al. 2018); these discoveries seem to be supported by the recent discovery of humanoid facial fossils from Jebel Irhoud in Morocco (Hublin et al. 2017). Other hominid populations could have developed early architecture, complex social relations and certain initial art forms (Hauser and Watumull 2017; Miyagawa et al. 2018). Music and other art forms are particularly interesting in the suggested category of pre-linguistic effects of Principle G because they are 'ineffable'; they are symbolic but 'wordless', and as such they can emerge and develop without the scaffolding of language if Principle G is available. We will study some of these cases in Chapters 7 and 8.

Theoretically, therefore, the preceding speculation regarding non-linguistic domains seems to motivate a generalization from language to the human mind, albeit within a narrow generative space, for the contemporary state of the species as well. Suppose we identify another cognitive domain X in humans, say knitting, which is also species-specific and which appears to fall within the available generative space in terms of, say, unbounded productivity. It is natural to expect, other things being equal, that X as well was the result of the same lightning strike or grand mutation that inserted a computational system in Proto. Human abilities such as arithmetic and music immediately come to mind (Mukherji 2010). In this sense, the postulation of Proto leads to a search for human mental systems beyond language to consolidate a human-specific notion of mind.

Furthermore, according to the narrative, human language emerged only when the principle was applied to the specific multi-domain environment of SM and CI in a given population. Given the immense complexity of human language, it is possible that not all progenies of this lucky population could develop the rich resources that the human language system can potentially harness. Only a few 'smart' individuals could have thus developed full human languages and carved the delicate path that ultimately led to human culture. We thus have a route to a natural explanation of why human language resulted very selectively in just one species. Needless to say, some of these consequences are potentially testable.

So, the prediction is that (i) there were some humanoids without language/words who were endowed with the computational procedure, and (ii) there were some early humans with words but without (full) word combinations. In this picture, the essence of mentality emerged with Proto when the computational procedure of Principle G was inserted. However, the essence of human language, as we know it today, emerged much later and has remained largely unchanged since. Whether we wish to view Proto's mind as the human mind is a matter of taste. My sense is that when Bertrand Russell instructed his children to announce that their neighbours originated from monkeys, Russell really had Proto in mind.

The suggested conception of the mind in human beings thus requires locating a principle in human languages that accounts for the unbounded productivity of linguistic expressions in a domain-free way, that is, without being tied to the domain-specific features of human language. Once we find it, we can then go on to ask if the linguistic principle so discovered in fact matches the required properties of Principle G such that all and only kindred cognoscitive powers are also covered. This is the task for the rest of the work.

Merge and linguistic specificity

In this chapter, my task is to display some of the central features of contemporary linguistic theory to ultimately show that, even if the theory is exclusively geared to the study of human languages, the computational principles invoked in the theory need not be thought of as linguistically specific. As enunciated near the end of the last chapter, the task of showing that the structuring principles invoked in linguistic theory are not linguistically specific is the first step for showing that principles of linguistic theory satisfy the requirements of Principle G.

This is not how linguists generally look at their work. My sense is that most linguists continue to agree with the following picture of their enterprise.

> The theory of language is that part of linguistics that is concerned with one specific mental organ, human language. It appears quite likely that the system of mechanisms and principles put to work in the acquisition of the knowledge of language will turn out to be a highly specific 'language faculty'. Stimulated by appropriate and continuing experience, the language faculty creates a grammar that determines the formal and semantic properties of sentences.
>
> (*Glow Manifesto*, Koster et al. 1978)

More recently, the *GLOW*-view has been more sharply expressed in terms of the FLN/FLB distinction: *FLN* for 'Faculty of Language Narrow', *FLB* for 'Faculty of Language Broad' (Hauser et al. 2002). On this view, FLN consists of the core grammatical property of human language in the form of a recursive mechanism that belongs only to the faculty of language; FLB consists of broader aspects of human language that are shared with other human and non-human domains. The FLN hypothesis still reigns in top scholarly circles (Watumull et al. 2014; Hauser et al. 2014).

In Hauser et al. 2014, the distinction is restated as follows: 'FLB designates processes that are shared with other animals, and thus, are involved in language and other sensory-motor and conceptual-intentional processes. FLN, in contrast, describes processes that are uniquely human and unique to language.'

Even more explicitly, Chomsky (2014, 4) approves of the recent 'formulation' by Susan Curtiss (2013): 'language represents a domain-specific mental faculty, one that rests on *structural organizing principles and constraints* not shared in large part by other mental faculties, and in its processing and computation is automatic and mandatory' (emphasis added).

In contrast, I wish to show that the computational principles invoked in the theory of language need not be thought of as linguistically specific (Mukherji 2003). Therefore, if the goal of inquiry proposed here turns out to be correct, the FLN/FLB distinction will collapse insofar as the 'structural organizing principles' involved in 'computation' are concerned. However, just the failure of FLN will be a moderately significant result; it will signify a major result if it leads to a coherent concept of mind along the lines suggested in the last chapter. With that goal in mind, I will describe the relevant aspects of current linguistic theory.

I have reviewed the short history of linguistic theory twice before (Mukherji 2000, Chapter 3; Mukherji 2010, Chapters 2 and 5). I do not wish to repeat that effort, but I understand the need of the general audience that at least some of the basic theoretical ideas are made available right here to avoid frequent reference to the formidable technical literature. I will restrict myself to only those aspects of the theoretical framework that are directly related to the issue under discussion: is the computational system of human language linguistically specific? In particular, borrowing from earlier work when needed and skipping many technical details, I will mostly discuss the phrase structure component of the theory that describes how syntactic units are put together to form complex structures.

5.1 Principles and parameters

We know, among other things, that (a) language acquisition takes place under conditions of severe impoverishment of stimuli, and (b) children are not born with a specific choice of language since, given the right environment, they can pick up any of the innumerable human languages. What then is the organization of language that enables children to learn languages – sometimes a large number of them simultaneously – under the impoverished conditions available to them? We may view the discipline of linguistic theory as providing a uniform and universal answer to this question.

It follows from the two stated facts about acquisition of language that humans must be endowed with some universal linguistic principles as part of their genetic make-up. A linguistic theory thus gives a systematic account of what these principles are, and how they generate the specific sound–meaning correlations of each sequence when triggered with limited information from the environment. Moreover, the structures generated by the language faculty are essentially unbounded; this property of language is often called *discrete infinity*, as noted. Hence, the theory of language gives an account of unbounded structures of sound–meaning correlations for all possible human languages within a single scheme of explanation.

In linguistic theory, the generation of linguistic expressions is explained by postulating a computational system that works on representations. Unbounded hierarchical operations of the computational system generate the discrete infinity of human languages. The study of language thus falls under what came to be known as the computational-representational theory of mind, which we discussed in Chapter 2. We will study the basic contours of linguistic theory under the computational framework of rules and representations.

The design problem that the computational system of language faces is the satisfaction of legibility conditions at the interfaces where language interacts with other cognitive systems external to language to generate sound–meaning correlations. Roughly, the sensorimotor systems (SM) access linguistic representations of sound, and conceptual-intentional systems (CI) access linguistic representations of meaning. Chomsky (2000a, 17) phrases the design problem as follows: 'To be usable, the expressions of the language faculty have to be legible by the outside systems. So, the sensorimotor system and the conceptual-intentional system have to be able to access, to "read" the expressions; otherwise the systems wouldn't even know it's there.' It follows that the expressions at the interfaces must carry information in a way such that they satisfy the readability conditions of SM and CI systems.

The stated aspects of the language system were encapsulated as properties of the *Single Computational System of human language* (C_{HL}). According to Chomsky (2000b), Universal Grammar (UG) postulates the following provisions of the faculty of language (FL) that enter into the acquisition of language:

A. A set of features
B. Principles for assembling features into lexical items
C. Operations that apply successively to form syntactic objects of greater complexity.

Provisions A and B are met as follows. The representations that enter into the computational system are symbolic forms composed of syntactic objects called *features*. These feature clusters, called *words*, enter into the computation. These features are listed in the lexical database: the word *book* consists of syntactic feature noun, semantic feature inanimate, phonological feature / buk/ and so on.

C_{HL} incorporates C in that it integrates lexical information to form linguistic expressions at the interfaces where language interacts with the other cognitive systems, SM and CI. Although there has been significant progress in recent decades on principles of lexical organization, linguistic theory has been primarily concerned with the properties of the computational component C. This is where biolinguistic research attained the high standards comparable to those of the basic sciences. In that sense, the mental aspect of the world uncovered by biolinguistics essentially consists of the properties of C. Hence, by C_{HL} I will basically mean the computational provision C.

It is interesting that Chomsky used the term *syntax* in the titles of his works in the first decade or so (Chomsky 1957, 1965); after that period, he simply started using the term *language* (Chomsky 1972a, 1986, 1993, 1995 etc.) when he was essentially concerned with grammar. As discussed in Chapter 3, a computational conception of language does not include the thick conceptual aspects of language. In that sense, although the computational system does generate sound–meaning correlations, the conception of meaning involved in such computation is severely restricted by design. It is therefore important to be clear at the outset about the conception of meaning involved in a theoretically salient theory of language.

Since about the mid-1970s it was held that the sound part of a string of words correlates with *Logical Form* (LF) in which various intra-sentential facts of interpretation are encoded. In the current minimalist programme, there is no level of representation called 'LF'; as Chomsky (2004, 152) asserts, 'LF doesn't exist.' At some stage of minimalism, linguists used the notion of SEM (for 'semantic') as the bridging level between narrow syntax and the external systems. As far as I know, even that was given up in the current formulation. All we have is the output of narrow syntax which is directly fed into the semantic interface.

A semantic representation of a string in grammar tells whether a string is structurally ambiguous, how the formal features of lexical elements are structurally related to each other for interpretation, and so on. For example, differences in semantic representation exhibit why the string *birds that fly instinctively swim* is semantically ambiguous; *instinctively* can modify either *fly* or *swim*: birds either fly instinctively or swim instinctively (Berwick and Chomsky 2016, 8). The significant difference in meaning in such cases is explained in terms of syntactic principles that show that *instinctively* occupies the same hierarchy with respect to *fly* and *swim* (Berwick and Chomsky 2016, 117).

However, in an important sense, a semantic representation *does not* tell what the specific referential and conceptual meaning of the string is. The semantic analysis for *birds that fly instinctively swim* also applies to *mickwits that foddle glidily zim*: mickwits either foddle glidily or zim glidily. Also, the computational system will generate essentially identical semantic representations for the strings *John tried to attend college* and *John decided to attend church* (Mukherji 2010, Chapter 4); this is because the conceptual difference between *college* and *church* makes no difference in grammar unless it is shown that they differ in some structural properties that contribute to the computation. In that sense, as delineated in Chapter 3, the *linguistic* notion of semantic representation captures the proposed idea of internal significance *within* the grammatical system to adhere to the traditional notion of language as a device for sound–meaning correlation.

The linguistic information represented at the interfaces flows from the lexicon itself, including information regarding how syntactic objects are to move to occupy designated positions in a structure. For example, the fact that *wh-* items (*which, what, when, who* etc.) move for English-like languages to occupy the clause-front position in some cases can be traced basically to some lexical features of these items. At the semantic interface, the grammar displays the correlation between a *wh-* expression and its semantic interpretation as a quantifier, which is the internal significance of the expression. In this sense, the lexical items of language determine the internal significance of linguistic objects; *provision C doesn't*. This feature of grammatical organization has much significance for our project.

Although linguistic theory went through several phases after it was initiated in the 1950s, I will describe some aspects of only the *Principles and Parameters Framework*; there is general acknowledgement that the advent of this framework in the mid-1980s was a fundamental break from past linguistic research. The basic features of the principles and parameters framework may be brought out as follows. We may think of four kinds of rules and principles that a linguistic theory may postulate.

First, the formulation of some rules may be tied to specific languages; call them 'language-specific rules' (LSR): relative clauses in Japanese, passives in Hindi and so on. Second, some rules may refer to specific constructions without referring to specific languages; call them 'construction-specific rules' (CSR): NP preposing, VP $\Rightarrow$ V NP and the like; these rules will include construction-specific rules for particular languages: *wh-* fronting in English. Third, we may have rules which refer neither to specific languages nor to specific constructions, but to general linguistic categories; call them 'general linguistic principles' (GLP): an anaphora such as *himself* must be bound in a local domain, lexical information must be reflected in syntax and the like. However, rule systems must reflect the fact that there are thousands of languages. This is done by attaching parametric choices (values) to some principles. For example, the GLP about the orientation of structures comes with the choice of head-first for English and head-last for Japanese. Finally, we may have rules that simply signal generative principles and general principles of interpretation without any specific mention of linguistic categories; call them 'purely computational principles' (PCP): all elements in a structure must be interpretable, the shorter of two converging derivations is valid, Merge generates a set of syntactic units and the like. It is obvious that, for the issue of linguistic specificity, our focus will be on PCPs.

The remarkable thing about current linguistic theory is that there is a real possibility that rules of the first two kinds, namely, LSR and CSR, may be totally absent from linguistic theory. The principles and parameters framework (P–P) made this vast abstraction possible. According to Chomsky (1991, 23–4), a P–P theory contains only general principles of language, GLPs in our terms. Traditional grammatical constructions such as active–passive, interrogative and the like are 'on a par with such notions as terrestrial animal or large molecule, but are not natural kinds'. Once the parameters are set to mark off a particular language, the rest of the properties of the expressions of this language follow from the interaction of language invariant principles.

In the early phases of sentence grammar, the basic syntactic structure of sentences of a language was described in terms of a system of rewriting rules called 'phrase structure rules', a sample of which is presented in what follows. The fact that such friendly and familiar rule systems were eliminated in favour of deeper principles nearly five decades ago is not yet fully recognized outside linguistic circles. Hence it will be worthwhile to spend some time on this development to appreciate one significant point of departure for the P–P framework.

$$S \Rightarrow NP\ VP$$
$$VP \Rightarrow V\ NP$$
$$NP \Rightarrow DET\ N$$
$$NP \Rightarrow N$$

Here the basic syntactic units are: S, V, N, DET for sentence, verb, noun and determiner, respectively. Notice that these are *linguistic* categories which classify the words of a language in grammatical terms. Also, the rules stated in terms of these categories cover linguistic constructions such as sentence, noun phrase, verb phrase and so on. Hence, these are construction-specific rules, CSRs, as defined earlier. In some cases, the rules are also *language*-specific, LSRs, in that a rule like S $\Rightarrow$ NP VP will be valid only for languages which obey the mentioned order or orientation of VP following an NP.

These rules will analyse a sentence (S) down to the basic syntactic categories at which point lexical items may be suitably 'inserted' to generate an initial (phrase marker) representation. For example, the sentence *Bill read the book* has a structure which may be displayed either as a labelled bracketing, or, equivalently, as a tree diagram.

$$[_S [_{NP} [_N \text{Bill}]] [_{VP} [_V \text{read}] [_{NP} [_{DET} \text{the}] [_N \text{book}]]]]$$

The system can be given infinite capacity by adding a recursive clause and modifying some of the rules accordingly: NP $\Rightarrow$ DET N′, N′ $\Rightarrow$ N, N′ $\Rightarrow$ N S. With the proper addition of lexical items, this system will now have infinite generative capacity. For example, with the addition of lexical items *belief* and *that*, the rule system will generate a structure description for *the belief that Bill read the book*. With a few more additions to the lexicon, this system will generate sentences such as *John's finding that the belief that Bill read the book surprised Tom interested John*. The system will also be observationally adequate in the sense that it can be used to represent all and only expressions of English.[1]

There are a variety of problems with this rule system. The system plainly has an ad hoc, taxonomic character in the sense that it is basically a list of categorial relationships of a preliminary sort. For example, a preliminary analysis suggests that *the book* is a part of speech consisting of two sub-parts *the* and *book* in that order. Rule NP $\Rightarrow$ DET N simply states this observation in categorial terms. Thus, the system, though observationally correct, is likely to have missed underlying uniformities and generalizations. Two of these underlying uniformities, among others, deserve immediate mention.

First, the lexicon, which the child has to acquire in any case, is richly structured (Chomsky 1965, 164–70). As we saw for the noun *book*, each lexical item has three categories of information in a full dictionary: phonetic (how it is pronounced), semantic (what it means) and categorial or syntactic (how it is structurally characterized). For verbs, consider *read*. On acquiring the verb, the child knows that it has the structure 'x(*read*)y' whereas *die* has the structure 'x(*die*)', that is, *read* is transitive and *die* intransitive. The child also knows that transitivity comes in different forms: *read a book* (NP), *made me angry* (NP, AP), *went out of the room* (PP) and so on.

Notice also that each of the examples just listed are VPs such that we get full sentences if we attach a subject, say, *Jones* (NP) in front of them. So, in effect, in learning a verb, the child has learned the categorial information encoded in a VP involving that verb. Let us say that a verb phrase has two major parts: a *head* and a *complement*. The head of a phrase is the most prominent element of the phrase in the sense that the head is what the phrase essentially is: *the old man* is a man, *read a book* is a reading, *told Mary that John is sick* is a telling and so on. A complement is what the head categorially selects: *c-selects*. So various head-complement relationships that constitute VPs are listed, among other things, in the verbal part of the lexicon. To that extent, the phrase structure rule [VP ⇒ V NP] is compositionally redundant.

Second, there are uniformities in the head-complement relationships across categories that phrase structure rules miss. Generalizing from the VP case, we can say that a noun phrase (NP) consists of a head noun followed by a complement. Now, notice the striking similarities between:

Bill [$_{VP}$ observed [$_S$ that Jamie was still awake]]
the [$_{N'}$ observation [$_S$ that Jamie was still awake]]
Bill's [$_{N'}$ observation [$_S$ that Jamie was still awake]]

The noun *observation* which heads the structure [*observation* [$_S$ *that Jamie was still awake*]], and which is the nominal form of the verb *observe*, has the same complement throughout. So the property of c-selecting a (finite) clausal complement really belongs to the word *observe* and its derivatives such that the forms such as those listed previously are largely predictable from lexical information alone. This generalization across phrasal categories is missed in the relevant phrase structure rules. Now if we simply adopt a global principle that links lexical information to syntactic constituency, then phrase structure rules are not needed to that extent. This is achieved by the *Projection Principle*: Lexical structure must be fully represented categorially at every syntactic level. The principle enables us to view syntactic structures as 'projections' from the lexicon. Notice how the information is flowing from the lexical item to the syntactic structures.

The structures mentioned earlier have another interest that, apart from the head-complement structure, each structure is fronted by an element which in the second case is the familiar determiner (DET) *the*. The examples suggest that DET belongs to a category more abstract than the standard category of articles and that the category is available across phrases. Let us call this category 'Specifier' (SPEC) which in English occurs to the front of a phrase. Thus the examples have the structure [SPEC [$_{XP}$ . . .]] where 'XP' is either an N' or VP. Extending the idea, the element *very* in *very confident of his ideas* may now be viewed as the SPEC of an adjectival phrase headed by the adjective *confident*.

The preceding generalizations suggest that, instead of a large number of rewriting rules, phrase structure can be basically captured compactly in a single framework or template, called *X-bar Theory*. In this scheme, the heads N, V, P and A project four categories of phrases, namely, NP, VP, PP and AP. Each of these will obey the general scheme spec-head-complement suggested previously. The important point to note is that a head X projects a category X-bar consisting of X and its complement while a further projection of X belongs to the category X-bar-bar (= XP, a phrase) consisting of the specifier and X-bar; hence, the SPEC belongs to a level 'higher' than the level of X and its complement.

This hierarchy is of much use in defining various structural relationships between categories. For two mutually exclusive elements α and β, we may say, 'α c-commands β' just in case every maximal projection dominating α dominates β. The X-bar scheme can be easily generalized for a full clause when we add the head INFL for inflection which typically marks the tense of a sentence. Taking the complement of V to be NP, we can state the general representation for a tensed clause such as *that English is a language* as well as for an untensed clause like *for John to visit the hospital*; for a detailed elaboration and diagram, see Mukherji (2010, Chapter Two).

Notice that X-bar theory is language-independent though it is associated with a few (probably just two) options: the scheme could be left-ordered, head-first as mentioned above for languages such as English, French and so on, or, it could be right-ordered, head-final, as in Japanese. The interesting fact is that *all* categories of phrases in a given language (typically) obey identical orientation. The child can fix the value of the orientation parameter for his/her language from very simple data such as *drink milk*. Thus, for English, c-selection in combination with X-bar theory now requires that the complement(s) be located to the right of the head. A large part of the computational system becomes operative just as minimal data trigger off the categorial and the inflectional systems and determine one of the binary choices of the X-bar template; this data the child must seek in any case.

Despite its attractive features, X-bar theory faced a range of problems. I will very briefly mention just a few of them to set the stage for the next phase of linguistic theory. First, it became clear that the orientation parameter attached to the X-bar template may not have a clean binary division across languages. For example, languages with supposedly subject-object-verb (SOV) structures also contained subject-verb-object structures. The striking example of polysynthetic languages suggests that X-bar may not even be true for all languages (Baker 2001). In a polysynthetic language, a single long word may carry sentential information in terms of many morphemes glued together: a standard example is the Yupik word *tuntussuqatarniksaitengqiggtuq* which means 'He had not yet said again that he was going to hunt reindeer'.

Second, it seems, with wide support from cross-linguistic studies, that the distinction between head-last and head-initial languages may not be 'a primitive of syntactic theory' (Kayne 1994; Jenkins 2004, xviii). A closer look at syntactic heads across many languages, including languages such as Warlpiri (Legate 2003), suggests more fine-grained 'micro-structures'. Third, Chomsky (1994b, 1995a) pointed out that the crucial bar-level of the theory just carries theoretical convenience since the external systems of language do not access them; as such, this part of linguistic theory is cognitively superfluous, suggesting inelegant design.[2]

5.2 Minimalism

In the early phase of the P–P framework just reviewed, each of the principles and operations in the computational system was universal; that is, the principles themselves did not vary across languages. But most of the principles came with parametric choices such that particular languages could not be described in this system until the parameters were given specific values. Given problems with the parametric character of general syntactic principles such as we saw for the X-bar theory, along with other problems of design and access, a very different conception of the organization of the language faculty emerged as follows.

Adopting a suggestion by Hagit Borer, Chomsky proposed that 'parameters of UG relate, not to the computational system, but only to the lexicon' (Chomsky 1991). Notice the further disassociation of linguistic information from the computational system. Parameters, if any, are removed from the computational system such that the system now becomes uniform for all languages. If this proposal is valid, then 'there is only one human language, apart from the lexicon, and language acquisition is in essence a matter of determining lexical idiosyncrasies'. The 'lexical idiosyncrasies' are viewed as restricted to the morphological part of the lexicon; the rest of the lexicon is also viewed as universal.

In that sense, Chomsky (1993) held that 'there is only one computational system and one lexicon'. Finally, in Chomsky (1994b), this computational system was given a name, 'there is a single computational system C_{HL} for human language and only limited lexical variety'. 'C_{HL}' was used extensively in Chomsky (1995a).

Linguistic theory, therefore, should be guided by the *Uniformity Principle*: in the absence of compelling evidence to the contrary, assume languages to be uniform, with variety restricted to easily detectable properties of utterances. Assuming the detectable properties to reside (essentially) in the morphological part of the lexicon, the conception of a single computational system for (all) human languages follows. The Minimalist Program (MP) for linguistic theory attempts to articulate this conception. Although MP is also viewed as falling under the P–P framework, I will discuss it separately because the notion of parameters plays a less significant role, if at all, in syntax, as noted.

We saw earlier when conceptualizing the notion of C_{HL} that language is viewed as having two parts: a computational system and a lexicon. That has been the guiding idea in linguistic theory at least since the advent of the P–P framework, if not before (Chomsky 1972b). The computational system is viewed as a formal device, a function, that takes items from the lexicon as input and generates complex structures as output. In that sense, linguistic theory appears to fall under some or other version of Turing-machine functionalism. Yet, the distinction between the parts was not clearly 'visible' in the earlier frameworks. In both phrase structure rules and X-bar, lexical information and computational structure were kind of mixed up. Now, in MP, the distinction between the parts is used to formulate the more radical claim that there is one language consisting of one computational system and one lexicon.

The idea of 'one lexicon' (Chomsky 1993) is not immediately obvious. Perhaps Chomsky's thought is that human languages carry essentially the same range of thoughts constituted of units of thought (concepts) which vary, in easily learnable ways, only in how they are articulated. So once we eliminate the morphological elements from the lexicon, we are left with basically a single lexicon for all languages, conceptually speaking. I suppose every aspect of the claim may be questioned. In a revival of the Whorf–Sapir hypothesis, many linguists and psychologists now believe that concepts vary as words vary across languages (Gentner and Goldin-Meadow 2003, but see Gleitman and Papafragou 2005). The topic is interesting but not terribly critical for our purposes for we all agree that the lexical part of language is linguistically specific. So even if there is a single lexicon contained in every human language, the categories in which such a lexicon is organized continue to be linguistic categories.

It is interesting that Gleitman and Papafragou (2005, 635) cite at length from Chomsky (1975, chapter 1) to refute the Whorf hypothesis that thoughts vary as languages vary. Their citation from Chomsky is as follows: 'By studying the properties of natural languages, their structure, organization, and use, we may hope to learn something about human nature; something significant, if it is true that human cognitive capacity is the truly distinctive and most remarkable characteristic of the species.' In this work, as noted repeatedly, I have been following Chomsky on this project as well: which mind is reflected in the mirror of language? But Gleitman and Papafragou seem to have a different interpretation of the rationalist project from what I ascribe to Chomsky.

From the cited words from Chomsky, the authors conclude that 'this view of concepts as prior to and progenitive of language is not proprietary to the rationalist position for which Chomsky is speaking here'. Thus, according to them, Chomsky approves of the view, held by the rationalists, among others, that concepts basically exist prior to the origin of individual languages; hence, human conceptual systems cannot vary as languages vary. Whatever be the evidence for this view of concepts (see Chapter 3), I do not think that 'this view of concepts' follows from Chomsky's cited words at all.

In fact, at about the same place, Chomsky (1975) clearly denies that the 'view of concepts' is his primary interest; he is more intrigued by the possibility that the study of language may lead to discoveries about 'abstract principles'. Later in Chomsky (1980), Chomsky suggested a sharp distinction between the computational and the conceptual aspects of language as we saw, and restricted his notion of language to the former. In that sense, the properties of language under study could be safely restricted to grammatical properties alone, as repeatedly noted. That is why I am setting the debate on the Whorf hypothesis aside without bypassing the rationalist programme of studying language as a 'mirror of mind'.

Given the strict separation between the lexicon and the computational system, it is not obvious that disputes concerning oneness of the lexicon affect the singleness of the computational system. Once the lexicon is strictly separated from the computational system and language variation is restricted to the lexicon, it is hard to conceptualize multiple computational systems. The basic reason is that, as emphasized earlier, language variation is *detectable* with the morphological properties of the lexicon. There is much evidence that the human ear is sharply tuned for linguistic sounds; not only babies just a few hours old, but even babies *in utero* seem to just tune in (Berwick and Chomsky 2016). There are no comparable detectable properties for the computational system, and for the 'semantic' component for that matter.[3] Grammar and 'thought' are, therefore, viewed as basically fixed for the species.

That is why claims regarding language-specific differences in grammar sound incredible. For example, Everett (2005) claimed that the Piraha grammatical system differs fundamentally from, say, Portuguese in that the former does not contain a recursive mechanism; there is no mechanism for, say, embedding relative clauses. Subsequent research showed that Piraha does have recursion in the stated sense (Nevin et al. 2009). The present conceptual point, due to Chomsky, is that Piraha speakers also learn Portuguese which has clausal embeddings. Therefore, the claim that the faculty of language – that is, the basic computational system – varies between Piraha and Portuguese must be false. The issue is crucial for us because only the computational system for human language may turn out to be mentally uniform across kindred domains, if at all; it is obvious that the lexicon cannot be so. Hence, to look for nouns, verbs, complementizers and ergatives in arithmetic, music and kinship is to climb the wrong part of the grammatical tree.

In MP, several aspects of language design were invoked to sharpen the picture sketched earlier. The central aspect is called *Conceptual Necessity*: language design should include only those features which the system is designed for, namely, to correlate sound with meaning. We already saw that the bar-levels of X-bar violate the constraint; bar-levels are motivated only by theory, not by conceptual necessity. To enforce the constraint, Chomsky proposed the *Inclusiveness Condition*: no new objects are added during computation apart from rearrangement of lexical properties which are conceptually necessary.[4] That is, the computational part itself does not add any information not already stored in the lexicon; again X-bar illustrates the violation since bar-levels are introduced in the computational part. Similar remarks apply to intermediate levels of derivation, d-structure and s-structure, in the earlier frameworks (Mukherji 2010, Chapter 5).

So, how are phrase structures generated in the system if X-bar isn't there? In fact, what does phrase structure mean in the MP framework? To address this question, let me step back a little and look at two basic tasks for linguistic theory. First, a linguistic theory describes mechanisms for generating complex structures with lexical units, as noted. Phrase structures, including clause structures, are the result of such operations. Thus, roughly, in the X-bar template for a clause, the items *read* and *the book* are inserted at the lowest head and complement positions, respectively, the tense of *read* is inserted at the specifier position of the resulting verb phrase, and the item *the girl* is inserted at the subject position to generate the structure *the girl read the book*. With X-bar gone, how does MP generate structures?

Second, linguistic theory also explains how a structure so generated transforms into another structure: the *displacement problem*. I have not discussed this issue so far, except for mentioning some phenomena like active–passive transformations, *wh-* fronting and the like. Consider the somewhat deviant question: *the girl read which book*? This is the 'logical' structure since *which book*, which is the object/complement of the verbal head *read*, is placed next to the verb. Yet, it is deviant because in English the *wh-* item occurs at the front of the structure: *which book did the girl read*? So, how are *wh-* items moved or displaced to the front while retaining the logical relationship between *read* and *which book*?

For the first few decades since the advent of linguistic theory, displacement was captured with a system of transformational rules that mapped one structure into another. Beginning with language-specific and construction-specific rules – such as *wh-* fronting, passive transformation and the like – in the earlier frameworks, a vast generalization was reached in the P–P framework when all grammatical transformations were covered by a single rule Move-α, where α is any syntactic category; I am setting details aside, see Mukherji 2010 and references. We will soon see that the computational system postulated by MP contains the operation *Merge* that combines two syntactic objects α and β *both* for generating phrase structure and for executing displacement.

Since movement is computationally 'costly', we assume, again following the spirit of conceptual necessity, that movement happens with *least effort*. It is a notion of economy that endows an optimal character to a system: the preference is for the most economical movement (Marantz 1995). Finally, we ensure, following conceptual necessity, that optimal computation generates only those syntactic objects that are least costly for the external SM and CI systems to read. In other words, representations at the interfaces also must meet conditions of economy; we will see some of them as we proceed. We thus reach the *Strong Minimalist Thesis* (SMT): 'language is an optimal solution to interface conditions that FL must satisfy.' If SMT held fully, 'UG would be restricted to properties imposed by interface conditions' (Chomsky 2008).

It is crucial to note that SMT is formulated in terms of the interface conditions at SM and CI; these are the conditions that the faculty of language must satisfy. As we saw, the information for these interface conditions can be traced back exclusively to the lexicon of human language; the computational system itself does not contribute to the information encoded at the interfaces.

To be even more specific, Merge as the sole computational operation of the system is independent of the interface conditions that must be met by the flow of information from the lexicon. The only role of Merge in the system is to combine the lexical information successively under the no-tampering condition to generate 'long trains of thought'. I will appeal to these aspects of SMT over and over again as we examine whether the principles of linguistic computation meet the conditions of Principle G. With conceptual necessity and SMT in hand, we need mechanisms to address two issues: formation of phrase structures and movement of syntactic objects already in the structure. Do we need separate mechanisms for these purposes?

Since syntactic information can be picked only from the lexicon, let us think of an operation that picks two items α and β. As noted, we postulate *Merge* as an elementary operation that has the simplest possible form: Merge $(\alpha, \beta) = \{\alpha, \beta\}$, incorporating the *No Tampering Condition* (NTC) which leaves α and β intact. NTC may be viewed as a constraint on evolving structures such that once Merge generates a structure, the resulting structure cannot be modified; so $\{\alpha, \beta\}$ itself is available as a unit for further syntactic operations which can now operate at the roots of resulting structures. NTC is also an economy condition since modification of an existing structure is costlier than leaving it as is. However, once we fully appreciate that Merge is the simplest possible generative operation anyway, NTC follows as a corollary (Chomsky, pc).[5]

The effect is that Merge now projects the union of α and β simpliciter without labels, that is, without identifying the type of syntactic object constructed. As a result, the phrase structure component stands totally eliminated from the scheme, leading to the postulation of 'phases' as we will presently see. Also, Merge takes only two objects at a time, as noted, yielding 'unambiguous paths' in the form of binary branching. In effect, Merge also yields the basic X-bar format in two steps, derivationally rather than representationally. But notice that, unlike X-bar, α, β are arbitrary syntactic objects with no labels; we will see what it means in what follows.

Merge is conceptually necessary, that is, 'unbounded Merge or some equivalent is unavoidable in a system of hierarchic discrete infinity' because complex objects need to form without bound; so 'we can assume that it "comes free"' (Chomsky 2005, 2008). The present formulation of Merge is the simplest since, according to Chomsky, anything more complex, such as Merge forms the ordered pair $<\alpha, \beta>$, needs to be independently justified. The emergence of Merge signalled the 'Great Leap Forward' in evolution, according to Chomsky. Recall that, in Chapter 4, we viewed the emergence of human *language* as the great leap forward. If that event is assigned to Merge, then in effect Merge is identified with human language, contrary to our expectation that the computational principle of language is not linguistically specific. I return to the point.

To return to the design of language, unless we make the special assumption that α and β in Merge (α, β) are necessarily distinct, β could be a part of α. Since special assumptions are 'costly', we allow the latter since it comes 'free'. Call the operation that generates structures from the lexicon, *External Merge*; call the operation that works with parts of existing structures, *Internal Merge*. Now, (Internal) Merge can put parts together repeatedly as long as other things are equal. The original part will appear as copies (=traces) conjoined to other parts: *The book seems* [*the book*] *to have been stolen* [*the book*]. Here, displacement of *the book* from the original object position just means that only one of the copies, that is, the left-most one, is sounded for reasons of economy in the phonological component; others are left as covert elements to be interpreted by the CI systems. Internal Merge thus functions as Move under copy theory of movement. Thus, the simplest computational operation of combining two lexical elements yields both the effects of X-bar and movement: *External Merge* puts items together from the lexicon repeatedly, *Internal Merge* moves syntactic objects around within a structure.

Even if the phrase structure format is no longer required, something like phrase structures are still needed for the external CI and SM systems to be able to read the outputs of narrow syntax. Beyond mentioning that SM systems need something like a 'phonological phrase' (Nespor 2001) for interpreting generated structures, I will focus on the semantic component. We assume that the CI systems need structures that could be semantically interpreted as, say, individual, event, states of affairs corresponding to nominal constructions, verbal constructions, propositions and the like. There is much controversy regarding which categorial constructions correspond to which semantic requirement.

Chomsky suggests CP, vP, perhaps DP: vP is a light verb phrase headed by a light verb such as *did* in *did visit the hospital* (arguably, the required structure is not vP but v*P, a light verb phrase with full argument structure). The core idea is that syntactic configurations carry information that is propositional in character. In MP, these configurations are called *phases* which are derived online by Merge. The fact that they look like classical phrases is not surprising since classical phrase structure theory was intuitively guided by semantic considerations. In MP, they are explicitly guided by semantic requirements at the CI interface following SMT.

So, the proposal is that External Merge picks elements from the entire workspace in the lexicon to generate increasingly complex sets to target phasal domains; as structures are formed, Internal Merge moves syntactic objects around if needed depending on lexical requirements. Once a phase with its prescribed domain is formed, it is transferred to the interface for interpretation. The operation counts as a *single cycle*; hence syntax operates single cyclically, telescoping choices from the lexicon to interpretation. Once a phase has been completed and sent to the interfaces, the internal domain of a phase is not accessible to operations at the next higher phase. Only the edge of the phase remains accessible at the next higher phase; this restriction is called *phase impenetrability condition*. It is a very natural economy condition that basically says that, once a phase has left narrow syntax, it can no longer be modified inside.

Among a variety of controversial issues on this programme currently under discussion, a fundamental problem is, how to determine the character of the phase what *kind* of phase it is. Recall that, in order to meet legibility conditions at the interfaces, a phrase was framed in the specifier-head-complement structure. In X-bar theory the format was available representationally; lexical items were inserted accordingly to determine noun phrase, verb phrase and the like. In the absence of X-bar resources, how do phases meet this requirement derivationally? In the current literature, this is known as the problem of determining *labelling algorithm* (Chomsky 2013; Narita 2014; Rizzi 2016). The problem and its suggested solution(s) is (are) too technical to be discussed here fully.

Roughly, the core idea is that minimal search tracks lexical features to determine the head H in a structure {H, X} formed by Merge; the other one X is then the complement. As Epstein et al. (2014) describe the process, suppose in a structure {X, Y} minimal search locates X as a lexical item and Y as another structure XP requiring further search since XP is not a lexical item. So X is identified as the head and XP as a complement with a further head-complement structure. If the initial structure has the form {XP, YP}, then minimal search needs to search inside XP and YP, respectively, until it locates a lexical item as head – similarly, for the rest of the structure. As Chomsky (2013) shows, the method seems to work for a large variety of cases.

5.3 Set Merge

After observing some of the key features of syntactic theory in MP, let us return to the point with which the discussion started: a fundamental separation between the lexicon and the computational system. We saw that the twin minimalist conditions of inclusiveness and SMT basically render the computational system to a blind machine that transfers lexical information to the interfaces phase by phase, in a successive-cyclic manner. Although intricate and, sometimes, elaborate computations take place in C_{HL} as information from the extremely complex lexicon of human languages enters the system, C_{HL} itself constitutes just Merge which operates freely: C_{HL} contains nothing else.

Linguistic information is essentially stored in the lexicon and, working on it, C_{HL} generates symbolic objects at the interfaces which are interpreted by the external systems in terms of linguistic categories and functions such as nominal, verbal, predicate, argument, proposition and the like. The most compelling part of the design is that all linguistically specific aspects of the syntactic objects placed at the interfaces – syntactic categories, head-complement asymmetry, argument and propositional structures and the like – are traceable to lexical features which drive the computational system.

Since, in order to run, the computational system requires lexical items to be supplied as input to the system, linguistic variations in the lexicon are reflected in the output of the computational system, that is, in the representations at the interfaces. The computational system itself does not enforce linguistic variations. In that sense, the system is a truly universal feature of human languages. The significance of this distinction needs to be stressed.

The division of linguistic labour between the lexicon and the computational system is a pretty natural feature of linguistic design. The lexicon is basically a repository of items that are learned by the child by experiencing utterances of specific languages; in that sense, the lexicon stores language-specific information – the words of English, Japanese and the like. Hence, it is an efficient design that this information is morphologically marked with largely *language*-specific features and organized in *linguistically* specific categories like noun, verb and so on. These are stored locally for search and retrieval during computation.

In contrast, the computational system is not learned at all, it is just given to the child as a genetic endowment prior to the learning of specific languages; the system is triggered once lexical insertion takes place. Hence, it is a great design that language-specific and language-independent components are separated from each other; some studies suggest that these components are located at different areas in the brain (Berwick and Chomsky 2016; Friederici et al. 2017). As we will see, the language-independent character of the computational system holds much promise for developing the concept of mind.

There is no doubt that the lexicon belongs exclusively to the domain of human language: there are no CPs and VPs in music. We also saw that, under conceptual necessity, the computational system itself consists of just Merge functioning under conditions of computational efficiency. Is Merge linguistically specific? I am raising this question because, once we reach the austere design of C_{HL} under the minimalist programme, it is difficult to dispel the intuition that the system seems to be functioning 'blindly' just to sustain efficient productivity of the information coming from below.

There is a growing sense that, as the description of the human grammatical system gets progressively simple, the terms of description of the system get progressively linguistically *non*-specific as well. Let us say that a principle/ operation P of a system S_i is non-specific if P makes no reference to S_i-specific categories. Suppose that the collection of Ps is sufficient for describing a major component of S_i for us to reach some non-trivial view of the entire system. Recall that, with respect to the language system, we have called such a principle a 'purely computational principle' (PCP) earlier. It is the 'purely computational' nature of the functioning of C_{HL} that gives rise to the intuition of (the relevant notion of) non-specificity.

Intuitively, to say that P is purely computational is to say that the character – and hence the formulation – of P is such that its application need not be tied to any specific domain S_i. In that sense, P could be involved in a domain S_j which is (interestingly) different from S_i in which P was originally found. It could turn out, of course, that only S_i has P since only it requires P even if its formulation is non-specific; that is, it could be that there is no need for P anywhere else in nature. So the idea really is that, *if* a computational system other than the language system required P, then P must be non-specific; it does not follow from this statement alone that there are other computational systems requiring P. That is an empirical issue, but it interestingly opens up only when the collection of Ps in S_i begins to look conceptually as if it is non-S_i-specific. It is surely counter-intuitive, unless explicitly explained why, P is at once non-S_i-specific in its formulation but S_i-specific in its application, where S_i is a domain.

Since the computational system is the only option for P in hand, and the computational system essentially consists of Merge, let us try to find out if Merge is linguistically non-specific. For this task, we need to examine exactly what goes into the constitution of Merge, its form and content. To recall, (set) Merge is defined as an unordered set, Merge $(\alpha, \beta) = \{\alpha, \beta\}$ and Merge incorporates the *No Tampering Condition* (NTC) which leaves α and β intact. The conception of a set is central to the idea of Merge. Therefore, the issue of whether Merge is domain specific converges with the issue of what it means for sets to be domain-specific.

Merge generates a binary set, a pair. Sets are rather peculiar objects. So just as there are sets of tables and tall mountains, there are sets of imaginary quantities like $\{\sqrt{-1}, \sqrt{-2}\}$; there are sets of impossible objects as well, like {round square cupola, circular triangle}. One can even have sets of unrelated objects such as $\{\sqrt{-1}$, circular triangle}; we will soon see that Merge may operate on a 'degenerate' lexicon of two items (x, /) to generate structures of x and /. Conditions on whether these objects may combine or not come from somewhere else, Merge itself is blind. And of course, there are set of sets, set of sets of sets and so on. These are all legitimate sets because their members are represented in legible symbols.

On this basis, I assume that sets are abstract objects which contain interpretable symbols which designate members, where *symbol* means some expression that 'stands for' something. No other property of 'something' is assumed except that it is what a symbol 'stands for' or what a symbol symbolizes. To emphasize, it is the symbols inside the brackets that enable us to view sets as sets of objects. In turn, these 'objects' determine the cardinality of sets. So far, we took sets for granted, but Merge made it explicit that sets need to be constructed. Formation of a set by Merge is a very abstract operation of the mind; it is truly a great leap forward.

With this abstract perspective on sets, it is obvious that the operation Merge has nothing to do with the physical operation of merging of roads and rivers. When two roads merge, it results in one (broader) road, thus modifying the initial roads; for that reason, the merged road is not a set. Sets are not mixtures, compounds, add-ons and the like; sets are, as they say, sets. Hence, it is not helpful to suggest physical or chemical analogies to explain how Merge works.

In this connection, consider Berwick et al. (2013, 91) who formulate Merge as a set {X, Y} with X, Y unmodified. But then they go on to suggest that 'merged structures act like chemical compounds: one property or feature of a word such as *ate* is that it requires something that is eaten, here *the apples*'. There are several problems with this dramatic claim. Chemical compounds may be informally viewed as made up of a particular set of molecules; before the compound is prepared, we may think of the separate containers of hydrogen and oxygen as forming a set, but the chemical compound as a *product* is not a set, as noted: the compound H_2O is not a set {H, O} with H, O unmodified. The great thing about a set is that, unlike chemical compounds, its members continue to remain distinct in thought. As we saw, heads like *ate* do 'seek' a matching complement such as *the apples*, but it is highly misleading to say that the notion of seeking here is analogous to chemical attraction and bonding. The symbols *ate* and *the apples* retain their identity in the merged product {*ate, the apples*} visually as it were; that is why polysynthetic languages are so interesting.

Roughly similar problems arise more generally when the working of the language system is represented in terms of abstract features of dynamical systems in physics, as suggested by Piattelli-Palmarini and Vitiello (2015). I have no space here to fully examine their elaborate technical proposals. But even a cursory look at the proposals suggests that all that the authors show is that, since the minimalist programme uses binary options (branching, headedness, selection of LIs, etc.) in much of the formalism, these could be rewritten in the binary vector notation of physics; steps of syntactic derivation could then be called vector states, and so on.

Despite the heavy notation, it is not difficult to understand that the notation merely signals the adoption of the Galilean style of explanation which attempts to keep to the simplest formalism such as binary branching, either for vector states or for syntactic paths. No wonder the notation displays 'isomorphism' between 'minimalist structure, algebraic structures, and many-body field theory'. Therefore, it is difficult to evaluate the authors' claim that the notational device is 'productive', meaning perhaps that the alleged isomorphism helps ground the physical reality of the language system. Just as the product of set Merge has no relation to chemical compounds, writing syntactic phases in 'dynamical' vector notation establishes no relation between linguistic operations and physical forces. Linguistic inquiry continues to be Cartesian in character where the basic sciences fear to tread.

Another problem with Berwick et al. (2013) is that their example to show how Merge works is too linguistically guided. As we have explained the operation Merge so far, all that Merge needs is some or other symbolized object(s); there is no mention of any specific symbolic domain, such as the lexical domain of domain, in the *formulation* of Merge. In any case, the 'requirement' that *ate* attracts *the apples* is a consequence of lexical properties when Merge acts on the human lexicon. It is misleading to explain Merge itself in these terms because the choice of the example is suggestive of the operation of Merge being restricted to the domain of language. In other products of Merge, such as {1, 2}, the merged objects need not have features that 'attract' each other.

5.4 Economy principles

Some of the literature on the computational system of human language gives rather confusing signals on how Merge operates. For example, Adger and

Svenonius (2015, 12) state that the hierarchical structures generated by Merge will not be recognized as structures of language unless these structures 'interface with the systems of sound and meaning'. To that end, the authors suggest that a domain-specific 'mapping principle' is needed to link the structures with lexical information which, in turn, is read by the interface systems.

Thus, even though the authors are not directly claiming that the operation Merge is domain-specific, they are claiming that some of the computational principles around Merge are linguistically specific. This suggestion is confusing because it amounts to saying that, even if the principal operation of the computational system is not domain-specific, the system as a whole is; so Merge works under language-specific principles. Further, according to this suggestion, there is no clear separation between the language-specific lexicon and the computational system. As it muddies the neat separation of components proposed by Chomsky, it needs careful examination.

It is totally unclear why an additional mapping principle, linguistically specific or otherwise, is needed. What they have in mind, of course, is the property of phasal cyclicity of computation. It is a computational requirement that derivation cannot proceed without some or other atoms. For the sound and meaning interfaces to get triggered, there has to be lexical information in the structures generated by Merge. The particular notion of a phasal cycle from lexicon to SM and CI interfaces is no doubt specific to the domain of language entirely by virtue of the information contained in the human linguistic lexicon. Yet, the central point is that there is nothing 'linguistic' about Merge or the computational system itself.

From a different direction, Di Scuillo (2015) also claims that certain aspects of the computational system are specific to human language. Her claim arises as follows. There is a substantial literature in syntax theory that syntax is asymmetric (see Bošković 2019 for review), or even anti-symmetric (Kayne 1994; Moro 2000). Following this idea, Di Scuillo had argued in her earlier work (Di Scuillo 2005) that morphological order in human languages is also typically asymmetric. I am setting morphological order aside because even if there is asymmetry, it could just be a reflex of SM requirement, not a property of narrow syntax as we have envisaged it here.

In any case, in Di Scuillo (2015), the author is concerned with asymmetry in the computational system of human language itself. Before I study the parts of her paper that relate to my interest in domain-specificity, it is prudent to set aside the asymmetry hypothesis for syntax. This is because there is much controversy in the literature if human languages require the additional postulation of asymmetry or whether they can be more simply explained in terms of hierarchies that Merge generates by virtue of being the simplest generative operation, as we saw. Chomsky steadfastly maintains the latter: there is no asymmetry in syntax, only hierarchy. For economy of exposition, I will assume Chomsky's simpler view.

Di Scuillo's more specific claim is that two principles of computational efficiency proposed by her, Minimize Symmetrical Relations (MSR) and Minimize Externalization (ME), work only in the domain of language. According to the author, in some languages a functional element F is inserted by Merge to break the symmetry of a structure like $\{X, X\}$, thus, $\{X, \{F, X\}\}$; the author calls it 'indirect recursion'. According to Di Scuillo, the insertion of F is forced by MSR, and the element F is not pronounced at SM due to ME. 'Indirect recursion', Di Scuillo suggests, arises for complex numerals depending on the language, thus differentiating, for example, Russian from Arabic.

Before I discuss Di Scuillo's proposals about computational efficiency for generating complex numerals, let me note that there is another straightforward reason for setting aside the issue of asymmetry in this case. Di Scuillo links the issue of symmetry with the specific need for 'indirect recursion' for generating complex numerals. However, it is well known that 'direct recursion' of the form $\{X, \{X\}\}$ is rare for human languages anyway. In an interesting examination of the topic, Arsenijević and Hinzen (2012) suggest that, even when we think of X as a syntactic type, direct recursion is rare in human languages. No doubt, there are some examples of direct recursion such as

$[_{CP}$ I saw the woman $[_{CP}$ that saw the woman $[_{CP}$ that saw the woman . . .

It is not difficult to see that these cases must be rare. In the more familiar examples of CP-embedding such as

$[_{CP}$ Allegedly, $[_{TP}$ John will $[_{vP}$ deny $[_{DP}$ the very possibility $[_{CP}$ that $[_{TP} . . .]]]]]]$,

The two occurrences of CPs are invariably mediated by a phrase of another syntactic type; also notice that the D in DP, and T in TP, are functional categories in Di Scuillo's sense. In fact, as Arsenijević and Hinzen proceed to show (425), even for what appear to be a straightforward X-over-X direct recursion of nominals such as

$[_{N}[_{N}[_{N}[_{N}$ war$_{N}$ film$_{N}]$ studio$_{N}]$ committee$_{N}]$ session$_{N}]$,

a series of counter-cyclic operations are involved to place the individual nominals in the proper hierarchy for semantic interpretation as a whole. In that sense *indirect recursion* may be the typical case for human language, beyond the specific case of complex numerals. Arsenijević and Hinzen give interesting reasons as to why this is so. According to them, 'the architecture of single-phase derivation makes the rarity of the X-within-X configuration expected, given a specific semantic conception of what phases are' (424). In other words, single cyclic derivation of syntactic phases appears to require that derived phases are transferred to the CI interface with proper semantic goals in the given workspace. Arsenijević and Hinzen's analysis of why indirect recursion proliferates in human languages does not seem to require engagement with the issue of asymmetry.

Turning to Di Scuillo's paper, complex numerals such as *one thousand two hundred and twenty-three* are to be distinguished from simple numerals like *one*, *seven* and so on. Now the author's point is that in the structure *one thousand two hundred **and** twenty-three*, the conjunction *and* is working as a symmetry breaker. In some cases, symmetry-breaking 'functional' elements like ADD or MULT could be silent. For example, in the noted structure, arguably there are many silent elements: [*one* [MULT *thousand* [ADD *two* [MULT *hundred* [*and twenty-three*]]]]], which means one multiplied by thousand is added by two multiplied by hundred and added by twenty-three. The phenomenon clearly varies across languages; in Hindi, for example, the overt conjunction *and* of the English construction *one thousand two hundred and twenty-three* is not there: *ek* (one) *hazar* (thousand) *do* (two) *sow* (hundred) *teis* (twenty-three). According to Di Scuillo, the first three 'functional' elements are inserted by MSR to break symmetry, but are not pronounced due to ME. Is this form of explanation, with linguistically specific computational principles, needed?

Since we have set the issue of symmetry aside, let us suppose these functional elements are needed by CI systems for semantic interpretation, but are barred from entering the SM interface due to the general condition of economy which Chomsky (2013) calls *Pronounce Least*. As we saw, many phases contain chains of copies, empty elements and the like that are needed only for the CI interface, not the SM interface. Languages, therefore, vary in when a structure is to be transferred to SM vis-à-vis the transfer to CI (Hinzen 2006, 208). Even assuming the validity of Di Scuillo's data, with insertion of silent functional elements, there does not seem to be any need to introduce fresh language-specific and linguistically specific machinery exclusively for complex numerals. A general computational constraint suffices.

I am discussing Di Scuillo (2015) in conjunction with Adger and Svenonius (2015) because my general response to both is exactly the same. Fortunately, neither paper questions the domain-independence of Merge itself, and both target principles of computational efficiency that allegedly constrain operations of Merge in the domain of language. For Adger and Svenonius (2015), their mapping principle is explicitly linked to aspects of the lexicon. As far as I can see, Di Scuillo does the same. The author says, 'Minimize Symmetrical Relations ensures that the bundles of features of the selected elements be in a proper inclusion relation' (29); it appears that, for Di Scuillo, MSR operates on a numeration *before* it enters the main computational workspace. In other words, MSR is a restriction on the operation Select that picks elements from a (lexical) numeration to transfer them to the interfaces via the computational system. Given the separation of the lexicon and the computational system, the operation Select is conceptually necessary anyway.

My basic methodological point is that the principles of computational efficiency play a crucial conceptually necessary role in the austere programme contained in MP. As suggested in Mukherji (2010, Chapter 7), the Galilean idea of least effort may be viewed as a methodological guideline which is specifically implemented in distinct realms. In the realm of physical forces, Newton's laws, such as the inertial law, implement least effort effects. Similarly, *computational* principles of economy are likely to apply to all the domains in the realm of computable systems of organisms where principles like Minimal Search, Inclusiveness Condition, NTC and the like apply. Within this realm, special principles may apply to specific domains like language where we have Full Interpretation, Phase impenetrability condition, Pronounce Least and the like which may not apply to other domains which are not subject to SMT. As with the hierarchy of parameters for individual and groups of languages in the earlier framework (Baker 2001), hopefully further research will show that computational principles also branch out across individual and groups of computational systems in a systematic 'parametric' fashion.

In this climate of proposals on proliferating linguistically specific and even language-specific computational principles, I must mention Chomsky's heroic attempt to restrict explanation of computational efficiency to a very small set of general principles of economy such as minimal search (Chomsky 2001, 2005, 2008, 2013). The simple reason for this parsimony is that the more computational principles one postulates, the more the load on genetic endowment or on the desired simplicity of natural principles. Such a general economy principle is likely to be present for the entire realm of computational systems, but not for specific domains such as language. Merge, in any case, remains domain-independent.

Indeed, the issue of whether Merge is domain-specific appears to arise even for other parts of the broad notion of language itself! So far, we have understood the domain-independent operation of Merge in terms of the linguistic specificity of the lexicon whose lexical features trigger successive operations of Merge. However, following the work of Fabb and Halle (2006) on the distribution of syllabic stress in a metrical structure, Berwick (2011) suggests that Merge may operate in the SM part of language even without lexical features of language: to generate a metrical structure like / x / x / x / x, Merge operates on a 'degenerate lexicon' of two elements /, x. The suggestion is that, just as in syntax proper, Merge can operate successively – with projection and selection of heads – to generate 'natural metrical patterns'. Berwick calls this *pure syntax*: it is a syntax 'with no lexical features and no associated semantics; without features, there is no possibility of internal merge and the movement that we see in ordinary syntax' (464).[6]

Berwick's analysis of metrical stress could be misinterpreted. Berwick cannot be saying that x and / *represent* metrical stress because we do not express metrical stress with x and /; these are Berwick's artificial representations of the natural units of metrical stress. Nonetheless, two significant points come out of Berwick's example. First, a metrical line is divided into discrete units requiring the operation Merge to put them together; one way of doing so is to compute on higher and lower stresses; second, these discrete units have no inflectional parts showing that the lexicon of metrical stress is featureless. But then, is the proposed Merge-based computation a *symbolic* operation? This question arises because, once we remove x and / invented by Berwick from the natural scene, it is unclear which symbol represents what in the metrical scheme. We return to the issue in connection with music in Chapter 7.

So the tentative picture is, if there are lexical features of human language, Merge generates appropriate structures for both CI and SM interfaces under SMT; if there are no lexical features but a pair of weak/strong syllabic stresses, Merge generates structures for the metrical part of the SM interface. Merge itself is just a generative machine, period. Given the abstract and blind character of Merge, it is not surprising that Merge operates on a variety of human computational domains as an aspect of efficient design. The application of Merge in the metrical system raises interesting possibilities for the human music system which we discuss in Chapter 7.

As a matter of fact, Berwick indeed suggests that Merge generates the structure of birdsong. However, it is a wholly different matter to extend (metrical) operations of Merge to non-human domains such as birdsong, as Berwick proposes. I will discuss birdsong in the next chapter to argue that these so-called 'songs' are just bundles of patterned sounds, comparable perhaps to human laughter, but not to speech and music; they have no syntax at all, hence, no computation, no Merge.

No Merge for animals

Since the computational system essentially consists of Merge, we are thus beginning to understand two significant aspects of Merge. First, from the content and formulation of Merge, it appears that Merge itself is not tied to any specific operating domain; the specificities in the operations of Merge are tied to specific lexical workspaces. Second, we are beginning to find evidence that Merge operates in domains which are closely related to, but somewhat different from, the core domain of language. One of these domains is the system of metrical stress; it is different from the core language system in that it has a 'featureless' lexicon. However, it is unclear if this system is genuinely language-independent; metrical stress, arguably, is a part of the broader system of language itself, as noted.

Thus, for now, the evidence is insufficient that Merge applies to genuine non-linguistic domains; it is also not evident that Merge *fails* to apply to non-human domains. So far, the generality of the computational system just means that the system is independent of lexical variations between specific languages such as English, Hindi, Japanese and so on. It does not yet follow that identical computational principles could be involved in domains other than language. It could be that, even though these principles do not mention linguistic categories, their application is restricted to language, as the FLN hypothesis demands.

No doubt, the laws and principles postulated by a theory need to be understood in their theoretical context. The notions of action and reaction as they occur in Newton's force pair law ('every action has an equal and opposite reaction') have application only in the context of physical forces even if the law does not mention any specific domain. We cannot extend its application to, say, psychological or social settings such as two persons shaking hands. Nonetheless, as subsequent theoretical and empirical research established, we can certainly extend the application of the force pair law to all physical processes from the original projectile case to viscosity, surface tension, jet propulsion and much else (Mukherji 2010, 186 for more). It is sometimes said that Newton's three laws of motion characterize 'everything there is'. More modestly, we could say that these laws constitute our conception of the *physical* as long as these laws are not replaced by even more general laws.

In this work, we are reflecting on what could plausibly constitute our conception of the *mental*. Could we say that the principles governing the computational system of human language constitute the mental? We could reach the Newtonian conception of the physical because centuries of research showed how these laws applied to phenomena far beyond the original projectile case. Similar arguments and evidence are needed to show that the operations of the computational system need not be restricted to human language. In other words, although the system is not *language*-specific, it has to be shown that it is not *linguistically* specific as well.

To develop that argument, we need to show that the computational principles that operate in linguistic explanation also apply to other non-linguistic domains. The restriction, of course, is that, although we hope that the principles of C_{HL} apply to mental systems beyond language, their application *does not* extend beyond human systems. Thus, the C_{HL} is restricted to all and only human systems. Just to remind us, the focused study is needed to extract a Cartesian species-specific conception of the mind. To that end, I will soon review some empirical studies on different cognitive systems across organisms.

Before we venture into empirical investigation, let us be clear about what theoretical tools we have in hand. Thus we need to see how the computational principle of Merge relates to the prospects for a species-specific theory of the mind, as envisaged in this work. In the previous chapters, I expressed the hope that perhaps the notions of computation and the mind can be so narrowly construed that the conception of mind falls exclusively under the computational theory of mind. Mimicking John McDowell's famous quip on meaning – meaning is what a theory of meaning is a theory of – we could say that the mind is what the computational theory of the mind is a theory of. Is it the case that, for such a theory to emerge, all we need is Merge?

6.1 The mind and computation

We saw that Merge is a generative principle that operates in the domain of human language. In contrast, the notion of computation in the computational-representational theory of the mind is a general formal idea that is supposed to apply to a variety of domains of mental representation. So for Merge to satisfy the computational notion of the mind, we need to carefully examine the relation between the conceptions of Merge and computation.

As a preliminary step in that direction, we saw that the computational system of human languages maybe described entirely in terms of what we have called *purely computational principles* (PCPs). The brief history of biolinguistics suggested that linguistic theory may be profitably viewed as progressing from *language*-specific computational rules to *linguistically* specific computational constraints to *purely* computational principles that are devoid of any linguistic content at all. Following the extensive discussion of this issue in the last chapter, I assume that this picture has been conclusively established in the latest minimalist phase of linguistic theory. The computational principles of language – that is, the sole operation Merge and the associated principles of efficiency – are totally devoid of any linguistic content; as a consequence, all claims of domain-specificity of the computational system collapse. Given the purely computational character of Merge, can we make the further and stronger claim that the concepts of Merge and computation, in fact, coincide in the interesting cases?

At a number of places, Chomsky thinks of a computational system in terms of the availability of Merge. Thus, Chomsky (2015, 16) writes: 'The *simplest* computational operation, embedded in some manner in *every relevant* computational procedure, takes objects X, Y already constructed and forms a new object Z. Call it Merge.' (emphasis added)[1] Notice that there is no mention of the linguistic system here; Chomsky is not talking of SMT or even of sound–meaning correlation in language. He is talking just about Merge as a generative operation. Elsewhere, Chomsky views Merge as the *minimal* computational operation (Chomsky 2020). Indeed, it is difficult to think of an operation 'below' Merge if two (symbolic) objects have to be combined at all. Since a computational system is at least a generative system, it is difficult to conceive of a computational system without Merge. However, a conception of such a notion of computation without Merge is not inconceivable as we will see; there could be weaker notions of computation that are 'flatter' in character.

This issue is different from the incredible demand that Merge itself be viewed as composed of simpler non-Merge components for preferred 'evolutionary explanation' in which Merge gradually falls in place.[2] As we noted in Chapter 4, every theory of language origin – 'Darwinian' or non-Darwinian – requires at least one saltational step; Merge is that step. So it is rather surprising for Martin and Boeckx (2019) to suggest that External Merge (EM) and Internal Merge (IM) first evolved separately for generating nested and overlapping dependencies, respectively; Merge *simpliciter*, they suggest, somehow evolved from these 'simpler' operations.

As Berwick and Chomsky (2019) immediately point out, each step of this speculation is objectionable. For instance, EM and IM are individually costlier than Merge *simpliciter* since not only do they need Merge for their basic set-forming operation, but they need additional conditions as well: EM requires the condition that the entire workspace be searched, while IM requires searching within the constructed domain. In that sense, EM and IM are special applications of the operation Merge already in hand. Due to the suggested division of Merge-labour between EM and IM, it is simply false that EM and IM evolved separately for generating different dependencies. As Berwick and Chomsky point out, for the sequence *where are you going*, the associated structure is {*where* {*are* {*you* {*are* {*going where*}}}}}. Once EM forms the nested dependencies in the structure {*you* {*are* {*going where*}}} in three steps, IM forms further nested dependencies from the attained workspace by merging *where* and *are* at the edges in two more steps. It follows that Merge is the simplest general operation which creates conditions for dependencies depending on the workspace.[3]

Returning to Chomsky's remark on Merge and computation, and setting the qualifier *relevant* aside for the moment, it follows that Merge is a conceptually necessary property of a computational system; if there is no Merge, there is no computation. Let us recall also the crucial feature that Merge is a *symbolic* operation; if there are no symbols, there is no Merge and hence no computation. Therefore, in order to evaluate whether a cognitive system of an organism belongs to the mind, all we need to examine is whether the concept of symbol manipulation may be plausibly ascribed to the system. If the answer is in the negative, we may conclude that the system is non-computational. While explaining the Gaia hypothesis, the evolutionary biologist Lynn Margulis once remarked that you don't need to go to a planet to find out if there is life, just use a good telescope on the Earth to determine the atmospheric gas composition of the planet.

Recall that Chomsky views Merge as a Great Leap forward that happened recently in hominid evolution, perhaps as recently as 100 KY, according to him. To recall from Chapter 4, we assigned Principle G to Proto much earlier than the onset of language; we also saw that there is probably interesting archaeological support for the suggestion (Tattersall 2019). Pending the issue of timing, then, and assuming that Merge satisfies all the conditions of Principle G, it follows that Merge was available only in very recent phases of human evolution, and so did Merge-based computational procedures.

In effect, a computational theory of mind covers exactly the human species, as Alan Turing anticipated in my view (see Chapter 2, also Mukherji 2010). I am assuming, of course, that (the later) Proto with her saltational endowment of Merge/Principle G forms the new species *homo sapiens* at once. Notice that this narrow sapiens-based origin of Principle G follows Chomsky's view of the origin of Merge. In Chapter 4, we saw that it is more plausible to assign Principle G to later Proto who might have belonged to an earlier hominid species. I will return to the issue in Chapter 8.

For now, it is of much concern that Chomsky also maintains that 'some other organism might, in principle, have the same I-language (=brain state) as Peter, but embedded in performance systems that use it for locomotion' (Chomsky 2000, 27). Peter's 'I-language' no doubt implements a computational procedure with Merge. Chomsky seems to be suggesting, or at least not denying the possibility, that (such) computational procedures may be found in non-human species. I suppose the issue arises even if we view Chomsky's suggestion as a 'thought experiment' to exhibit the generality of Merge since a thought experiment needs to be empirically coherent. We are asking whether the notion of computation coheres with our conception of non-human cognitive systems. Chomsky's thought experiment appears to be incoherent since it requires both that Merge signalled a great leap forward at about 100 KY and that, say, insects use it for locomotion.

Chomsky's thought experiment was also suggested by Hauser et al. (2002, 1578) in their famous paper: 'comparative studies might look for evidence of such computations outside of the domain of communication (e.g., number, navigation, social relations).' Elaborating, the authors observe that 'elegant studies of insects, birds and primates reveal that individuals often search for food using an optimal strategy, one involving minimal distances, recall of locations searched and kinds of objects retrieved.'[4] Given that the very idea of a computational procedure is human-specific, what does it mean for some *other* organism to implement computational procedures while it searches for food?

As we will soon see, given the tight framework of symbols, Merge and computation, claims that the operation External Merge may be involved in various non-human activities are incoherent. As we know, External Merge is just Merge; therefore, insofar as the notion of computation involves Merge, there cannot be computation in non-human species. As far as I can see, if we do insist on computational abilities outside humans, the only option is to make sense of some notion of computation which continues to be computation without involving Merge. Recall that Chomsky thought of Merge as involved in any *relevant* notion of computation; so the alternative notion under speculation here can only be *irrelevant* for language-like human computation, but it could be relevant for insect computation, if at all.

For a conceptual feel of what may be involved here, consider some interesting suggestions by Watumull et al. (2014) on insect navigation. A species of desert ants displays the remarkable phenomenon of 'dead reckoning'; these ants appear to find a direct path to their nest after a fairly random foraging for food. Earlier, some authors, especially Charles Gallistel (1998, 2010, etc.) viewed the phenomenon in terms of the standard symbolic computation. I will discuss the phenomenon in some detail in what follows to inquire if it requires a computational explanation at all. For now, I wish to focus on an alternative explanation suggested by Watumull et al. (2014). To refresh, the 'irrelevant' explanation in this domain needs to be such that it qualifies as a genuine computational explanation without involving Merge.

After working through the complex history of ideas in the mathematical theory of computation due to Emile Post, Kurt Gödel, Alan Turing, Alonzo Church and others, the authors reach a certain notion of computation involving recursive functions; recursive functions are computable functions that take the previous output as an input, thereby forming hierarchies. After explaining the standard notion of computation in terms of recursive functions and mathematical induction, the authors show that linguistic recursion – basically, Merge – satisfies the condition of mathematical induction. Hence, Merge captures the classical notion of computation, as we saw.[5]

Now, Watumull et al. (2014) suggest that some computational systems may fail to achieve the rich notion of computation involved in linguistic recursion. For example, according to them, the dead reckoning of desert ants does not amount to linguistic recursion since such recursion 'would need its outputs to be not only returned as inputs but also represented hierarchically', as we saw with Merge. According to the authors, dead reckoning involves at best a much weaker notion of computation as in 'tail recursion' which is more of an iterative operation than a genuinely recursive one. The point is, even if tail recursion is viewed as a notion of computation, it is at best an irrelevant notion for deciding the human specificity of Merge-based computation. It follows that Merge may be realistically identified with the notion of relevant computation.

In a strong sense, the discussion of Merge and computation may be viewed as bringing to a close the main argument of this work. The argument is that Merge is an independent part of human language that puts different linguistic parts together to give human language its generative power. Apart from the conceptual independence of Merge, the analysis of metrical stress (Berwick 2011) suggests that the operation of Merge is independent of the lexicon of human language. When the lexicon varies, the output of the computing system also varies, yet Merge remains what it is. As Thomas Wasow (1985) once pointed out, knowing a language basically means knowing the words of a language; the generative part of language comes for free by human design. Merge establishes the point. Notice we are not yet concluding that Merge is domain-general.

Once we appreciate this distinctive character of Merge, it is a short step to view Merge as the human mind. Putting existing 'atomic' resources together to generate novel and unbounded expressions for associated behaviour can be justly viewed as the basic property of the thinking mind. So, even if we assume, for the sake of argument, that the mentioned generative power is restricted to the domain of language, the mind is eminently visible in the working of human language itself. Language is the mirror of the mind.

It will, then, be a proof in favour of a more substantive concept of mind if we are able to show that an identical generative capacity is available in a class of related domains such as arithmetic, music, art, tool-making, kinship and the like. For then, the proposal for an independent mind will attain further salience from the fact of its spread beyond language. Finally, the basic Cartesian intuition will be clinched if we can show that the capacity is species-specific; it does not obtain beyond humans. Needless to say, these are vast topics requiring detailed empirical research in the ongoing project. In what follows, I will study a small sample of the cross-domain research to get a feel for the direction this research is taking.

To that end, beyond conceptual considerations, we need two more essentially empirical directions, roughly paralleling the eliminative and enumerative steps suggested by Francis Bacon. First, we will study relevant aspects of cognitive behaviour of non-human systems to see if we can explain such behaviour without postulating computational systems in the sense in which computation is implicated in human domains. Second, we need to find out (other) language-like systems in the human mind which require similar computational procedures for processing *their* (domain-specific) information. Once these two steps are successfully taken, it will be reasonable to reach the hypothesis that Merge operates in all and only language-like mental systems. To emphasize, once we reach that point, we would have formed some firm idea about the scope of the computational theory of mind, and hence, on the concept of mind itself.

Before we proceed to examine assignment of computational systems to non-human species, it is instructive to be clear about what such assignment means. In my view, there is widespread confusion in scientific and philosophical circles on this issue; I have discussed the topic extensively elsewhere (Mukherji 2010, 235–42). No doubt, sophisticated mathematical tools are routinely used in physics to describe the world, such as a system of colliding particles (Flake 1998). Since computational models are also mathematical tools, they may be used to describe aspects of the world from the shape of snowflakes to the structure of continental shelves (Stewart 1995, 2001; Carroll 2005). It is no wonder that computational physics is a roaring discipline in recent times. Call it *N-computation*, 'N' for natural: investigation of various formal properties of the natural order with computational tools. However, it is always possible – indeed *necessary*, in my view – to hold an 'instrumentalist' view of the effort such that we do not make the further suggestion that the colliding particles are solving computable functions, or that snowflakes have 'internalized' fractal geometry. The genius of physics is not shareable outside the species.

For cognitive theories, the burden is more. Particles do not 'internalize' symbolic/mathematical systems, (natural) minds do. So we need to say that human infants internalize the rules of language while chimpanzees don't. To distinguish it from N-computation, call it *I-computation*, 'I' for internalized: the organism uses various computational tools to form structured expressions from lexical data. It follows that we genuinely ascribe I-computational rules only to those systems to which we can intelligibly ascribe the ability to store and process symbolic representations. To emphasize, mental systems are not only describable in N-computational terms by expert humans such as neuroscientists (Churchland and Sejnowsky 1992); they also *are* I-computational systems largely unknown to the organisms. Needless to say, only organisms endowed with I-computation are capable of coming up with explanations in terms of N-computation. In this work, I am concerned only with the endowment of I-computations. And the only way to tell whether a system is I-computational is to see whether we can view the system as a genuine symbol manipulator. Nothing less will count, nothing more is needed.

As we saw, Hauser et al. (2002, 1578) reported that 'elegant studies of insects, birds and primates reveal that individuals often search for food using an optimal strategy, one involving minimal distances, recall of locations searched and kinds of objects retrieved'. The specific mention of *optimal strategy* and *minimal search* suggests the presence of computing systems unless the authors are merely pointing out the general Galilean idea that everything in nature works under optimal strategies. I am setting aside the objection that the Galilean form of inquiry generally does not apply beyond very simple systems (see Introduction);

since biological systems are complex and messy, we cannot expect the Galilean form of inquiry to be available there (Mukherji 2017, Chapter 1). Yet, since we have entertained the Galilean form for biolinguistic inquiry, there is no immediate conceptual reason why it cannot apply elsewhere in relevant homologous biological forms.

So the reason for denying computational ability to non-human systems under consideration cannot be that these are biological systems. We can even assign some rich notion of N-computation to these systems via human ingenuity of explanation if they show some significant structural complexity that cannot be otherwise explained. But to claim that these non-human systems exhibit properties of I-computation just because they are amenable to N-computation is to take advantage of theft over honest toil, as Bertrand Russell put it in a different context.

There are three prominent areas to look at, according to Hauser and colleagues: insects, birds and primates. I will look at each of these organisms in turn to see if mental abilities may be ascribed to them, but I will not be guided by Hauser's list of domains suggesting optimal strategies. First, some species of insects exhibit pretty remarkable locomotion behaviour that appears to involve spatial and numerical computation. Second, some animals display complex vocalization. The most interesting examples are some species of birds that 'sing' impressively complicated songs to suggest that something like syntactic processing is going on. Third, some of the primates show interesting gesture patterns and call sequences which suggest at least primitive or rudimentary 'language-like' behaviour. In each case, we need to decide if the notion of a computational system applies at all.

6.2 Insect navigation

Cataglyphis fortis is a species of desert ants about 1 centimetre in length with a brain size of about 0.1 milligram. This tiny insect sets out for food such as dead arthropods from its nest (P0) in what appears to be a barren desert landscape. It can travel for over a kilometre, which is an astounding distance for its size, in a markedly wiggly path through, say, points P1 through P4 to reach food at P5, as shown in Figure 6.1.

The most remarkable feature of its foraging is that, once its feeding is done, it sets out for its nest in a straight path, called *dead reckoning*, as shown (Wehner and Srinivasan 1981; Muller and Wehner 1988). If the insect is displaced from

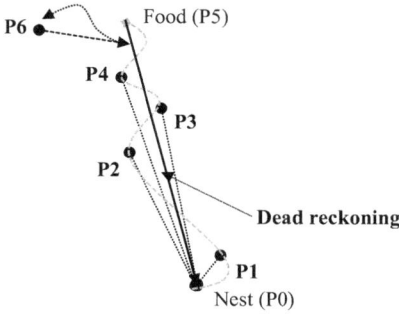

Figure 6.1 Dead reckoning of *C. fortis* © N. Mukherji

this path and released at point P6, it eventually gets back to the straight path before returning home. The basic phenomenon for this interesting ability is known as *path integration*. As Muller and Wehner (1988) explain in their classic paper, 'path integration means that the animal is able to continuously compute its present location from its past trajectory and, as a consequence, to return to the starting point by choosing the direct route rather than retracing its outbound trajectory.' Notice the informal use of *compute*. Since the authors don't explain what they mean by 'computation', for the purposes of this work I assume the authors have in mind something like N-computation.

As Muller and Wehner report further, the basic phenomenon is fairly common among insects, birds and the like. In most of the cases of minimizing their return path, animals typically use some local method based on sensory systems: some use visual cues, others dig furrows, some use olfactory information such as pheromone trails and the like. In fact, the Australian desert ant *Melophorus bagoti* navigates mostly with visual cues known as 'route learning' (Narendra 2007; Cheung et al. 2012). In hostile environments, animals often develop a distinctive sensory apparatus for navigation and foraging. Thus, similar to other desert ants of the same genus such as *C. bicolor*, but unlike ants in a relatively non-hostile terrain such as the common European ant (*Aphaenogaster sp.*), *C. fortis* also has very elongated limbs, enlarged eyes and long probes. It is natural to suppose that these specialized apparatuses are duly used for navigation and so on.

There are many dramatic examples in organic evolution in which a large part of the evolving brain is devoted to a very narrow range of cognitive features, such as the development of highly specialized sensory systems. The blind mole rat (*Spalax ehrenbergi*), illustrates the point. As the species moved underground millions of years ago under desert-like conditions, their eyes atrophied and became subcutaneous (David-Gray et al. 1998). However, the brain continued to develop an auditory system suited for the perception of vibratory stimuli as large parts of the brain previously dedicated to the visual system were transferred to the auditory system (Bronchti et al. 2002).

As we will see, *fortis* also puts its elaborate apparatus to navigational use. However, one aspect of its navigation appears to require a different form of explanation. Instead of a pheromone trail which is likely to evaporate in the hot terrain and absence of significant visual cues in a flat, barren landscape, it appears to use the location of Sun – Sun's azimuth – to form its path integration. Again, this is not a unique ability since several animals use the location of Sun to guide navigation; the classic case is the so-called 'dance' of the honeybee to mark the direction for the source of food.

What is interesting about the navigation of the desert ant is the ability to calculate the velocity of its locomotion with reference to the location of Sun while it keeps shifting in search of food. As Gallistel (2010) interprets the behaviour, the 'learning organ of desert ants takes sensory signals indicating speed and sensory signals indicating direction and combines them to get signals indicating velocity, and then it adds up those velocities to get the net change in position'. According to Gallistel, this ability shows that the phenomenon of dead reckoning of desert ants is 'strong evidence that the brain of an insect is a symbol-processing organ'; in fact, Gallistel holds that the brain of these ants exhibits an 'example of isomorphism between a computational system and the spatial world' (Gallistel 2010).

According to Gallistel, 'a system that stores and retrieves the values of variables and uses those values in the elementary operations that define arithmetic and logic is a symbol-processing system' (1998, 47). Having cited arithmetic and logic as symbolic-processing systems, Gallistel goes on to declare that 'the brain of an insect is a symbol-processing organ'. Yet, the irony is that, almost since the beginning of psychological attention to this entomological phenomenon, Gallistel had also expressed deep scepticism about this form of explanation. 'What processes enable the nervous system', Gallistel (1998, 46) asks, 'to store the value of a variable . . . to retrieve that value when it is needed in computation?' I will pick up on this genuine worry shortly.

For now, I must mention that, in more recent work, Gallistel (2018) claims to have solved this problem. The solution is too obscure to be fully discussed in the short space I have, so I will restrict myself to a brief and hopefully accurate review. Cutting through a lot of technical jargon from computer science, genetics and the like, his basic idea seems to be the following. Mentioning Jerry Fodor's work in philosophy of mind, Gallistel claims that the computational theory of the mind applies to the functioning of the brain, including insect-brain, because, as against the associationist-connectionist models of the brain, the brain can be truly viewed as a symbol processor. This is because a neuron is a symbol which attains its meaning due to the information supplied by dendrites, that is the 'semantics' of the system; the complex connectivity of neurons then displays the 'syntax' of the brain.

Far beyond the intriguing phenomenon of dead reckoning, then, every activity of every organism becomes a computational activity when the neurons are fired. Thus, the flapping of wings by a bird, the hissing of a snake, a cramp in the stomach or plain breathing are all deemed mental activities on par with cave paintings, playing baroque music or speaking Japanese. Recall that we did not view even pre-Merge Proto – our nearest ancestor by definition – to be endowed with the computational system of mind precisely because early Proto lacked Merge. This should not prevent us from assigning to early Proto a circadian clock, the ability to locate solar azimuth, finding food, returning home and so on. In fact, as we saw, there are occasions for distinguishing between putative computational and plainly non-computational explanation for non-human organisms, including desert ants, all which have dense neuron–dendrite connections. In that sense, Gallistel's hypothesis is at best irrelevant; at worst, it is unintelligible.

Returning to Gallistel's original worry, it is interesting that Chomsky (2001) mentioned Gallistel's concerns about ascribing logic and arithmetic to the brain to illustrate the general problem of unification between biology and psychology. No doubt, postulation of computational processes for, say, human language raises exactly the same problem with respect to the nervous system: we do not know with any certainty how the nervous system implements the operations assumed in any computational/ symbolic model of the processes that mediate linguistic behaviour. This is the familiar unification problem which arises in any case. In this light, Gallistel's (original) worry appears to be trivial. If we do not know how the nervous system functions as a symbol processor in the paradigmatic cases of language, logic and arithmetic, it is no wonder that the ignorance is glaring for non-paradigmatic cases such as insect navigation.

My objections are very different from the general sceptical concerns raised by Chomsky and (early) Gallistel. Granting that a variety of human-specific systems are genuinely computational in character, I am questioning the intelligibility of the idea that insects are symbol processors in the same sense because their cognitive systems simply don't fit the paradigms of arithmetic and logic, not to mention language and music, as Gallistel himself holds; hence, I do not need to argue the point. So what exactly is the phenomenon, and what are the options for interpreting it?

Insofar as 'vector summation' of the shifting distances covered by the ant, and for which Gallistel claimed elaborate computational explanation, later research conclusively showed that at the most ants use something like a step counter. As Wittlinger et al. (2006) showed, ants have a robust memory of the steps they need to take to reach home by the shortest path. They use their elaborate limbs to perform the task. When the limbs are trimmed (stunts) or further elongated (stilts) they miss the target significantly. For this part of the navigation, they just keep a measure as in a step counter; as the authors remark, although 'desert ants use a pedometer for distance measurement, the ants most probably do not literally count'. As we saw, Watumull et al. (2014) explain that this step counter involves at best a much weaker notion of computation as in 'tail recursion' which is more of an iterative operation than a genuinely recursive one.

As far as I can follow the complex literature on desert ants, the explanation of the initial part of path integration, in terms of vector calculation of speed and distance from the location of Sun's azimuth, remains largely unchallenged. I suppose such 'egocentric' measurements are largely hard-wired properties of brains displayed in many organisms such as locusts, migratory birds, insects and the like. Perhaps they are best understood in terms of N-computation of animal brains on par with formation of stripes on zebras. In any case, egocentric measurements are highly error-prone over large distances. To rectify possible errors, subsequent research has shown that desert ants use various sensory devices to overcome these errors:

(a) Ants do not require the global sky compass for negotiating inclined paths; their specially designed pedometric equipment is sufficient (Grah et al. 2007; Seidl and Wehner 2008; Heß et al. 2009; Wintergirst and Ronacher 2012, etc.). The point is, inclined paths force some modification in path integration to accommodate upward and downward climbs. But research shows that desert ants use pedometric devices to make the adjustment without using the sky compass.

(b) Although the ant's terrain appears to be devoid of landmarks to the naked human eyes, the ant itself is able to detect visual and tactile cues around the nest with the use of its enlarged eyes and extraordinary stilts (Seidl and Wehner 2006). According to some estimates, visual cues of the nest are accepted even at 66 per cent of the path vector ($\approx$ 5–10 metres), and visual cues are recognized at a distance of about 10–15 centimetres; however, tactile cues are recognized only on top of the ground.

(c) Along with visual cues, olfactory cues are also detected from at least 35–50 centimetres from the nest (Steck et al. 2011). As the two sensory cues begin to match, the vector path is rejected. Apart from the nest, olfactory cues were detected at the feeder (Wolf and Wehner 2000). In recent work, Huber and Knaden (2018) showed that these ants have a robust memory of olfaction of their nest entrance and can learn up to ten different odours of the feeder. It is obvious that olfactory information guides much of the navigation both from the nest to the feeder and back.

It is still not fully known how much of the total path is actually covered with such stimulus-dependent forms of information. It seems plausible that the more we know about such local dependence, the less there will be the need to explain the ant's behaviour with the obscure global sky compass. For example, following Huber and Knaden (2018), it seems plausible that much of the navigation of *fortis* throughout the journey depends on the strength and gradient of olfactory spread. Supposing that the olfaction of the feeder is somewhat weak, *fortis* wanders a bit to find the feeder; as the olfaction of the nest is strong, the return path is more direct. Given this general spread of olfactory information, other visual and tactile resources simply fine-tune the direction. The global sky compass may not be needed at all.

Therefore, as current research stands, egocentric path integration is only a part of the story, if at all; as we saw, this is probably the result of hard-wired properties of the brain shared with many organisms. Much of the ant's foraging movements are based on essentially non-computational specialized sensory systems – proprioceptors with stilts, visual cues with enlarged eyes, long-distance olfaction with elongated probes – without which its foraging in the hostile desert environment is not possible. The navigation of desert ants need not be explained in I-computational terms at all; hence, Gallistel's worry about symbols and their semantics appears to be unwarranted.

6.3 Birdsong

In the specific context of theories of language and mind, birdsong is discussed from two different directions in contemporary literature. The first concerns the allegedly computational properties of birdsong; the second concerns the interesting topic of vocal learning. The two are viewed as related in the following sense: the phenomenon of vocal learning shows that some birds are endowed with some mechanism for learning and vocalizing complex sound patterns, while the first shows how birdsong as complex patterns is computationally generated. Thus, an impression is created as if the two need to be held together. Yet, it is not at all evident why, while we admire the skill of vocal learning, the concerned sound pattern needs to be *computationally* generated in the sense of I-computation under discussion here. Hence, I will discuss the two directions separately.

Regarding the alleged computational abilities of songbirds, I have already discussed elsewhere the case of some European Starlings (*Sturnus vulgaris*) reported in Gentner et al. (2006) who claimed that these starlings could compute functions of the form A^nB^n (Mukherji 2010, Chapter 7). Setting details aside, there I held on to Peter Marler's opinion that these are at best examples of *phonocoding*: 'recombinations of sound components in different sequences where the components themselves are not meaningful' (Marler 2000, 36). In his review of Gentner et al. (2006), Marc Hauser made a similar complaint: the mere presence of recursion in songbirds does not imply that songbirds can acquire human languages; this is because human languages crucially involve meanings (Hauser 2006).

More interestingly, in a recent paper, Hauser et al. (2014) make a similar remark on birdsong. The long list of authors includes Noam Chomsky, Richard Lewontin, Robert Berwick, Ian Tattersall, Charles Yang and others. For this reason, I wish to cite their remark at length. Regarding recent work on the alleged computational complexity of sounds made by songbirds, these authors suggest that these observations 'do not guide understanding of language acquisition in humans' because, 'unlike human language, (i) (bird)song is a highly specialized and finite system linked to one sensory channel (acoustic)', and '(ii) when song syllables are combined to create longer structures, new creations have no impact on the function or "meaning" of the song'. As a result, 'students of child language acquisition rarely turn to work on songbirds for insights, except to make the very general point that there are analogous learning processes in early development.'

I find these remarks problematic because each of the cited authors seems convinced that birdsong involves 'generative' operations – even recursive ones – all right, but these sequences lack 'meaning' and thus they do not measure up to the attested richness of human languages. I do not know what enduring interest there is whether birdsong may be viewed as 'like' or 'unlike' human language; it appears that in some respects it is, in other respects it is not, period. What is of interest, insofar as this work is concerned, is whether birdsongs may be genuinely explained in terms of I-computation based on Merge. On that issue, the cited literature does not throw much light.

For example, Berwick et al. (2012) state that 'human language syntax, but not birdsong, is organized into "chunks" – phrases – that are labelled by features of the elements from which the chunks are constructed'. As we saw in Chapter 5, we could move beyond language to metrical stress in the human case seamlessly, and assign Merge-based I-computation even though metrical stresses contain a 'featureless' input system; for this reason, a sequence of metrical stress is not divisible into syntactic phases of the linguistic kind. Music is a more powerful computational system in the same non-linguistic genre, as we will see.

So, the question for this work is not whether birdsong simulates human language syntax, but whether we can assign Merge-based computation to whatever structures birds display. On this issue, we can set aside Gentner-type examples because, as Chomsky pointed out, Gentner's starlings were not computing at all in the sense of embedding AB's into AB's in terms of the function A^nB^n. They were simply storing sequences of A's and B's; the experiment was insufficiently structured to decide between the two alternatives. In any case, there is some consensus that the suggested form of computational ability remains unconfirmed (Beckers et al. 2012).

In the biolinguistic literature, the issue was brought to the front from a different direction in some papers by Shigeru Miyagawa and his colleagues (Miyagawa et al. 2013, 2014). The authors claimed an evolutionary explanation of where human language came from. According to these authors, human language consists of an 'adventitious combination' of two pre-existing functions from outside the hominid line. The first consists of 'expressive' functions found in birdsong, and the second in 'lexical' functions found in some primates. Since their theory proposes a combination of two functions, they call it the *Integration Hypothesis* (Miyagawa et al. 2014). I will not be discussing the hypothesis itself since its credibility depends on the credibility of its parts. Here, I will be focusing on the part concerning the expressive function of birdsong; in the next section I will discuss the lexical part.

It is not difficult to see the coveted intuition behind this proposal. Some birdsong does consist of rather complicated structures, it is another issue why it is called *song* rather than *talk*, or even *speech*. And some primate calls, importantly *not* those of chimpanzees, do point out discernible objects such as a snake or a tiger. So if you can somehow combine the complexity of birdsong with the apparently 'referential' character of primate calls, you do get something like human language. That seems to be the guiding intuition for the Integration hypothesis.

In a way the authors are unpacking what Merge does for human language which the pre-existing functions individually are unable to do. No doubt Merge occasionally combines meaningful words into complex strings without bound: 'occasionally' because Merge also generates a combination of meaningless expressions like *round square copula*, not to mention combining x and /, as we saw. But that is Merge working in specific domains; it is not intrinsic to Merge, as we saw at length, to generate wordy structures. That happens when Merge generates structures for human language. So a convenient intuition would be to assign Merge to songbirds without assigning words to them; it will then generate long sequences of whatever the birds are placing at the service of Merge; that would certainly be one way of explaining the complexity of songbird expressions. Therefore, it is surprising that Miyagawa et al. are not doing so.

I do not know why Miyagawa et al. do not assign Merge to generate the complexity of birdsong: perhaps they wish to bring out the uniqueness of Merge in taking over for humans where birds and primates fall short, perhaps they believe in Hauser et al.'s FLN hypothesis to the effect that Merge-like operations are uniquely human *and* linguistic. Be that as it may, what Miyagawa et al. do is exactly right. There is no evidence at all that the structures found in birdsong need the power of Merge-like operations. As we saw, Berwick et al. think of birdsong as a product of a finite automata; as such, even if we grant that birds, like desert ants, do compute in some sense to generate some complexity, we could announce that the notion of computation involved in this case is irrelevant for our purposes. It would have been enough for us, then, to set birdsong aside from the discussion of the range of Merge-based operations.

However, from the evidence offered by Miyagawa et al., it is unclear if birds engage in I-computation at all, relevant or irrelevant. Birds no doubt exhibit complex sound patterns which are occasionally rather pleasing and startling for humans, perhaps for birds as well, especially for the youngsters. It is reported that sometimes song-duets go on for hours; sometimes the patterns are too intricate and fine-structured for humans to mimic them easily. But none of these necessarily show that birds are using computational operations for generating them.

In my view, the correct way of interpreting birdsong is to adopt what the poet Rabindranath Tagore said about them over a hundred years ago:[6] 'You gave a song to the bird, it sings that song/ To me you gave notes, I make songs.' I have explained these lines elsewhere (Mukherji 2012). In that piece I explained in detail that Tagore's poem is misinterpreted if it is taken to mean that only humans have notes (*swara*). The poem's real meaning is that songs, as wholes, are not given to humans, they are given only to birds; humans are only given notes for them to make songs. Whether birds are (also) endowed with individual units for composition is irrelevant for Tagore.

The correct reading enables us to sidestep the intriguing issue of what counts as a note that represents a musical sound given the impressive variety of human song making. For example, classical traditions of music such as Carnatic music in India and tonal music in the West appear to share the same set of notes (Vijaykrishnan 2007), but it is unclear if similar notes are shared with Tibetan throat music and Indonesian Gamelan music. All we know of human music is that there are notes and there is a computational system. We turn to human music in the next chapter.

For birdsong, Tagore's basic point is that the birds are genetically endowed with a sound pattern which is elicited when the occasion demands. In extremely rare cases, they are endowed with more than one song. According to Kipper et al. (2006), a single nightingale's repertoire may contain several hundred 'different' songs. From their presentation of data, it is unclear though how these songs are counted. Do they have different patterns/ motifs made up of roughly the same small set of 'notes' and 'syllables'? Or, do they employ different units for forming different motifs? Most importantly, how many of them are different from one another due to performance factors causing variations within a single motif?

Whatever be the distribution of units and motifs, for Tagore each of them is simply 'given' to the bird. There is no interesting sense in which the birds 'construct' these motifs from notes and syllables. A clear evidence, in support of this sceptical conclusion is that, as Tagore emphasized, a species of birds is simply endowed with a (handful of) specific sound pattern(s) that is fixed for the species. In contrast, human music, exactly like human language (Mukherji 2021), has almost endless variety that is formed out of a small set of notes.

To say this is not to say that birdsong does not have units of notes and syllables that humans can detect, just as humans detect computable units in continental shelves and sunflowers. Miyagawa et al. (2013) reproduce some examples from the zebra finch's auditory spectrum to show what these units are; they also produce figures on how these songs sometimes loop back to an earlier point in the case of Bengalese finch. I am sure some detectable 'units' will be found in my sister's rather elaborate laughter, and my awful coughing when the monsoon begins, not to mention the distinctive 'laughter' of the hyena. After all, these are not continuous sounds, they come in fits and starts, and most individuals have their characteristic laughter and coughing. These differences are possibly due to difference in the design of the throat accompanied by external factors such as gender, state of health, age, season, time of day and the like.

It is also well known that, as with songbird babies, human children pay close attention to how their parents laugh and cough, and practice the sounds accordingly; so, often, there are similarities in the sub-laughs and sub-coughs between parents and children. However, despite these factors of complex sound patterns, imitation or vocal learning and variations due to distribution of units, no one – with the exception of Gallistel (2018) – is going to suggest that human laughter and coughing are computational systems. It is difficult to see why the case of birdsong should be treated differently.[7] If someone wishes to think of N-computations for birds, Tagore may agree with the idea, provided they are extended to human laughter as well. But the evidence offered by Miyagawa et al. (2013) and Miyagawa et al. (2014), and birdsong research in general, do not suggest that songbirds engage in I-computation.

This is simply because birds, even songbirds, need these sound patterns only for wholistic functions: guarding territory, attracting mates, drawing attention to sources of food and the like. As Kipper et al. (2006) observe, the richness of song repertoire varies with the quality of male nightingales looking for a mate; longer songs and a rich repertoire are typically displayed by healthy males who are able to attract more females. These functions do not require that individual notes be combined differently to show differences in meaning. In that sense, these units, even if they are identified by expert humans armed with technical knowledge and equipment, are not symbols in any interesting sense such that new meanings emerge when these units are differently combined. These facts about birdsong have been known for a long time. Yet, researchers are tempted to grant some notion of 'pure syntax', 'phonocoding', 'finite computation' and the like just because birds display complex sound patterns.[8] As Tagore pointed out, this fact alone does not require endowing birds with a generative device, even of the irrelevant kind.

Nevertheless, to deny I-computation to birds does not amount to denying the selective ability of vocal learning to them. As we saw, both human and songbird babies listen attentively to the sounds emitted by their parents. In some cases, they try to imitate these sounds within their restricted childish means. It is no wonder that, in both the human and non-human cases, sometimes these infantile renditions sound differently from the fully developed matured adult sound pattern. Speaking anecdotally, there was a child in the family who could not utter the sound /chandana/ in the Bangla ballad *chottopakhi chandana*; for

/chandana/, the child used to utter /nannana/. When an adult imitated him and sang *chottopakhi nannana*, the child corrected the adult by saying, 'not / nannana/, /nannana/'. The phenomenon is pretty familiar and is largely due to performance factors.

As noted, vocal learning is a pretty selective ability; importantly, except for the baboons, the great apes do not appear to have this ability. Let us also grant that humans and a small class of birds have some evolutionary convergence on this matter; perhaps they have a 'deep convergence' involving a few hundred genes (Berwick and Chomsky 2016). It is also clear that this ability is independent of the computational ability involving Merge. Even when humans are endowed with the ability to generate a complex thought, they need to come up with the complex sound pattern to externalize this thought.

For the latter ability, humans like songbirds require the ability to form complex sound patterns. The presence of these genes in the human system for the purposes of externalization does not mean that, therefore, the sounds of human language are ancillary for the linguistic system. These genes are also needed for the complexity of sound patterns in the human musical system, yet sounds are certainly not ancillary in human music. Therefore, the presence of these genes only means that these are required in any case independently of the sound-is-ancillary hypothesis. So we may grant some non-human species including songbirds the selective ability of forming complex patterns of sound while continuing to deny that songbirds have the resources to execute I-computation.

6.4 Primate cognition

The primates, especially the great apes among them, are something of a test case for the conception of the generative mind which suggests a sharp division between human and non-human animals. The primates are our closest ancestors in terms of evolutionary lineage (see Figure 3.1); they also have a much larger brain size compared to the animals we have discussed so far. While birds on an average have a brain size of less than 10 grams, chimpanzee brains measure nearly 400 grams. Although, as noted in Chapter 4, the correlation between brain size and higher cognitive functions may be questioned, among animals, chimpanzees are most likely to be comparable to humans in smartness (De Wall 2016).

Nevertheless, insofar as the verbal ability of animals is concerned, René Descartes held that 'all animals easily communicate to us, by voice or bodily movement, their natural impulses of anger, fear, hunger, and so on'. These abilities are clearly stimulus-dependent and are present in humans also, but we do not ascribe any verbal ability to organisms for shrieking in anger. Descartes thus made a careful distinction between real speech and natural impulse, and denied that animals have the former: 'no animal has attained the perfection of using real speech, that is to say, of indicating by *word or sign* something relating to thought alone and not to natural impulse.' We will review Descartes' view as we proceed. We will see that contemporary research has more or less vindicated Descartes' position on this issue.

However, it could be argued that Descartes' view is unfair to animals because Descartes seemed to expect that either animals speak or gesture like humans with words/signs or they are dumb creatures. It could be that Descartes was using too high and too selective criteria for judging the expressive abilities of animals. On the basis of studies on animal communication systems (alternatively, call systems), many authors argue not only that animals can think and express their thoughts, but also that some of the elements of animal communication systems, in fact, enter into the human linguistic system. From this perspective, some of the call systems may be viewed as preparatory steps for human language. Since we have already adopted the saltational emergence of Merge in the late hominid line as a necessary condition for human language, I am setting aside the old issue of animal protolanguage as earlier non-human stages of evolution of human language.

However, claims can still be made for some aspects of animal communication systems as a resource for human language. As we saw, Miyagawa et al. (2013) and Miyagawa et al. (2014) hold that human language arose from the 'adventitious combination of two pre-existing, simpler systems that had been evolved for other functional tasks'. I have already discussed the first of these systems, called *expressive* systems that are apparently found in birdsong; in the last section, I argued in some detail against the claim that the alleged expressive power of birdsong satisfies the computational view of the mind. I will now discuss the second of these systems, called *lexical* systems that are apparently found in some non-human primate calls, among others. The claim here is that some animals display features of lexical units that resemble those in humans.

Summarizing and simplifying over much empirical research, the situation is as follows. Some species such as bees and dolphins use a signal system which has the property of *continuous infinity*: a sonar system in the case of dolphins, a pattern of wing-vibration – called *dances* – in the case of bees. It means that the frequency of the sound (or the vibration of the wings) varies continuously over a given spectrum. There are no discrete units in the system. Since these systems are primarily used for locating objects, including other members of the species, food and the like, and since distance is a continuous function, the systems serve the purpose they are designed for.

Miyagawa et al. suggest that other species, particularly the higher primates, can use fairly complex gesture systems which have the property of *finite discreteness*. This means that the system has discrete units (first unit of the call, second unit of the call, etc.) but the units are finite in number and they combine in limited ways. After years of training with very friendly and enthusiastic human trainers, apes such as chimpanzees and gorillas could not come up with more than a few hundred gesture-equivalents of words (Premack 1986). Moreover, Premack's chimpanzees could combine words only as in 'telegraphic speech' and not more than a few at a time. Also, the 'words'/signals/calls so far studied are directly related to environmental cues.

Following the work of Kaminsky et al. (2004), Andrews (2015, 1) reports that Rico, a border collie, has acquired 200 'labels'; we will soon see whether these labels are really word-like units or merely sound–object 'associations'. Confirming earlier findings that animal vocabulary and their ability to combine them are severely limited, Miyagawa and Clarke (2019) report that old world monkeys can combine only two word-like units: 'There is no three, there is no four, there is no five. Two and infinity. And that is the break between a nonhuman primate and human primates.' Both the aspects of absence of a generative capacity and dependence on environmental cues were sharply brought out in two recent studies.

It was believed widely that animals, especially primates and higher apes, do have a variety of concepts and thoughts that are displayed in actions, but these animals fail to vocalize these thoughts because they lack the appropriate vocal machinery. William Tecumseh Fitch et al. conducted a novel experiment on a living macaque vocal tract to 'demonstrate that the macaque vocal tract could easily produce an adequate range of speech sounds to support spoken language' (Fitch et al. 2016). In fact, the scientists actually produced simulated audio suggesting that the monkeys have the vocal resources to utter *will you marry me*. Yet, the macaque produced only some low-level grunts, coos and 'threat-calls'. The authors suggest that 'the evolution of human speech capabilities required neural changes rather than modifications of vocal anatomy. Macaques have a speech-ready vocal tract but lack a speech-ready brain to control it.' I don't know whether the striking findings about the macaque brain can be generalized for other non-human species such as chimpanzees.

As we saw in Chapter 4, according to Timothy Crow (2010), the evolution of human language required a rather recent reconfiguration of the brain to implement the four quadrants of the brain needed for human language. According to Crow and his colleagues, this drastic change in the configuration of the brain happened only about 150 KY ago, many millions of years after the hominid line broke away from the primate line. The recentness of the reordering of the brain explains why these quadrants are absent in chimpanzee brains (Li et al. 2017). Therefore, there is another neural evidence why primate brains may not be viewed as language-ready. I do not know whether these two pieces of neural evidence converge.

As for the lexical aspect of non-human communication systems mentioned by Miyagawa et al. (2013), it appears that the so-called 'word-like' units of primate cognition have little to do with the corresponding aspects of human language for us to conclude that human language arose from some restructuring of pre-existing lexical systems. Laura-Ann Petitto, one of the leading researchers of primate communication and early language acquisition, observes that a chimpanzee uses the prescribed label for apple to refer to the action of eating apples, the location where apples are kept, events and locations of objects other than apples that happened to be stored with an apple (the knife used to cut it), and so on and so forth – all simultaneously, and without apparent recognition of the relevant differences or the advantages of being able to distinguish among them (Petitto 2005, 86).[9] It appears to follow that the lexicon of the chimpanzee does not contain some chimpanzee-variant of *apple*. In fact, although it is possibly a stronger claim, it is difficult to see that the chimpanzee has the concept of apple at all. In contrast, we saw that even blind children effortlessly pick up visual concepts.

Thus, Petitto's results seem to support Chomsky's view (pc) that 'there seem to be sharp differences between human concepts and anything in the animal world'. The components of animal systems seem to have a one–one association with identifiable external events (Chomsky 2020). It seems that all that happens in the animal case is that 'rustling of the leaves elicits a "warning cry", hormonal changes elicit some vocal noise' (Chomsky, pc). In this sense, the units, if any, in the animal cognitive systems are strictly stimulus-dependent. Hence, Chomsky is possibly right in suggesting that 'human concepts seem to have evolved independently of animal concepts' (Chomsky, pc). This discontinuity between human and non-human animals raises serious problems for an evolutionary explanation of human language (Berwick et al. 2013): where did human concepts come from to enter into the lexical system?

If Crow-type explanations in terms of a recent reconfiguration of the brain are valid, it might simply mean that the chimpanzee brains are not yet ready either for forming conceptual units or for combining them into complex thoughts; it is hard to detect any evolutionary pressure for either. In effect, chimpanzees do not have the resources for forming sets. As recounted by the archaeological evidence, the ability to form sets of symbols, and thus the operation Merge, is a late event in the hominid evolution. The recentness of sets, together with their abstract and symbolic character, raises doubts on regular claims of (external) Merge in animals.

Citing a range of literature, Di Sculio (2015, 40–1) writes: 'Several works seem to indicate that External Merge is not human specific: McGonigle et al. (2003) claim capuchin monkeys ordering objects; Seyfarth et al. (2005) suggest baboons' knowledge of their companions; Schino et al. (2006) argue for classification by rank and kinship in Japanese Macaques, etc.' Without going into the question of how the reported cases are to be understood, it is incredible that Di Sculio invokes Merge to explain them given the recentness of Merge. Mere ordering of some physical objects in the visual field, or collection of stones and nuts into a pile, or keeping sticks together, does not show that the agents of these activities have formed sets in their minds. As we will see in the next chapter, although animals may be ascribed some sense of numerosity, there is no evidence of arithmetical ability. Hence, it is implausible that they form sets with cardinality.

To form a set, objects have to be identified as falling under (abstract) categories that are identified in terms of a symbolic form, including 'impoverished' forms like x and /. The grouping of these *symbolic forms* counts as a set; that's how signs indicate the presence of hidden thoughts, as Descartes taught us. Before claiming that these animals can form sets in their heads, researchers have to show that these animals have symbolic ability. To take a specific case, consider the proposal by Koji Fujita (2014) that some of the uses of stone tools by chimpanzees can be described in terms of the human linguistic operation Merge {HAMMER, {NUT, ANVIL}} and so on.

The trouble is that Fujita assumes without providing evidence that chimpanzees are, in fact, endowed with concepts of HAMMER, ANVIL and the like in order for these things to qualify as symbols in the chimpanzee mind. As we saw, it is seriously doubtful if chimpanzees have such concepts at all. However, the ascription is perfectly legitimate if Fujita is describing his own mind while observing a mindless chimpanzee. As we saw in Chapter 1, it is a different matter altogether to ascribe what *we* have in mind to animals.

Merge is (perhaps) all we need

The goal of finding out if Merge, the current instance of Principle G, applies to all and only mental systems faces an uneasy methodological problem. The 'all' part of the goal requires that Merge applies to various generative systems beyond language since Merge is already seen to be working for language. In that sense, we expect Merge to define the class of generative systems. To that end, we saw some promise as Merge turned about to be a purely computational principle devoid of specifically linguistic features. Yet, since Merge first became theoretically visible with its application in the language system, the available theoretical character of Merge could well be tied to the domain-specific properties of language itself such that it may block any conception of Merge applying to non-linguistic systems.

7.1 The language bias

We have already witnessed a glimpse of the problem with some of the literature that investigates the possibility of assigning generative systems to animals. While examining alleged computational properties of dead reckoning by desert ants, Watumull et al. (2014) made the observation that navigation by ants is not up to the mark for genuine computation since it fails to meet the standards displayed in linguistic recursion. Similarly, Hauser et al. (2014) observed that birdsong doesn't qualify as a system of genuine symbolic computation because it does not satisfy the conditions of symbolic computation in human language. Beyond mentioning the point, I did not pursue the topic at that stage because neither dead reckoning nor birdsong is a computational procedure at all in my view. So, whether they meet the standards of linguistic computation is largely irrelevant from that perspective. However, the topic needs to be addressed now that we are about to explore some cases of human non-linguistic computation systems. The topic is conceptually crucial for this 'all' part.

What we saw in the case of animal studies may be called the *language bias*: either the system under study reflects the basic properties of language or it is not a generative system at all. The language bias in the literature appears to lead to the following uncomfortable consequence. If some non-linguistic systems turn out to be computational by satisfying the conditions of linguistic computation, then they do not really satisfy the crucial condition of displaying computational properties beyond language. If, however, what otherwise look like computation in some non-linguistic systems differ from linguistic computation on some measure, then, on that count alone, the language bias is reluctant to consider them as genuine cases of computation; hence, they fall outside the scope of the computational theory of mind.

Two theoretical ideas discussed so far seem to generate the bias. The first, as we saw, is that the very notion of relevant computation is tied to the idea of Merge since Merge is viewed as the simplest and, therefore, the necessary condition for computation. The second idea is that the structuring principles of language are specific to the domain of language under the FLN hypothesis; so, Merge is covered by FLN. When the two ideas combine, it follows that the linguistic system is the only relevant computational system. Other mental systems, then, if any, can be derivatively viewed as computational only if they are 'language-like'.

This consequence is uncomfortable because it becomes virtually impossible to inquire if a certain organization of sounds, actions or marks on paper is a computational system unless it is very much like a linguistic system; that is, it is difficult to ask if there are generative systems other than language. As Raffman (1993, 40–1) also points out, the very idea of symbols is portrayed so linguistically, as we saw with birdsong, that we cannot meaningfully ask if there are symbol systems other than language. There are several examples in the literature where such language bias is directly indicated. I will pick two recent cases.

Citing Chomsky (2000c), Hinzen (2014a) points out that something like theta theory is a property of any language-like system, whereas Case-checking theory is specific to human language. Setting Case theory aside, Chomsky's idea is that any 'language-like' system, apart from human language itself, contains something like theta theory. As Hinzen points out, theta theory is that part of the overall grammatical theory which assigns thematic roles such as agent, goal and the like to arguments (Mukherji 2010, 47–51). Thematic roles are arguments that fill the relevant argument places in the matrix of, say, a verb viewed as a predicate.

In the expression, *Bill hit John*, *Bill* is the agent, *hit* is the role-assigning predicate and *John* is the patient. Basically then, assignment of theta roles requires a predicate-argument structure; specifically, these predicates and their arguments are *linguistically specific* objects such as verbs and nouns. Furthermore, we know that thematic roles relate to the semantic component of languages, where the semantic component is currently viewed as a part of the external CI system. So all this organization has to be in place before we consider any system to be language-like. When such conditions are imposed, it is difficult to see how a genuinely non-linguistic system can be 'language-like'.

For another case, Hauser (2016) does grant that there could be genuine non-linguistic systems which may be classified as 'language-like'; he calls them 'Logic of Thought'. For Hauser, the idea of 'Logic of Thought' is much broader than that of language; as he puts it, the 'Logic of Thought' consists of 'computations and representations of thought, with linguistic thought being one flavour'. According to Hauser, the 'Logic of Thought' is uniquely human, and 'underpins not only language, but many other domains as well'. However, these systems must satisfy something like SMT to qualify because a 'Logic of Thought' includes all four ingredients: Merge, CI, SM and the interfaces.

Each component of SMT needs to be 'articulated in different domains' to display how the 'Logic of Thought' works only for humans across the board. Unfortunately, apart from some vague comments on abstract, a-modal concepts and some obscure queries on how Merge might look like neurologically in different domains, Hauser (2016) fails to cite a single human but significantly non-linguistic domain to illustrate the range of 'Logic of Thought'.[1] In any case, it is difficult to see how a system could be genuinely non-linguistic while satisfying the very restricted bounds set by SMT.

In my view, the language bias has severely impacted research on human generative devices outside language. As the examples suggest, the general attitude seems to be that to count as a computational-representational system, a cognitive system must contain most of the prominent features of the linguistic system. As noted, the language bias consists of two ideas. The first idea that the notions of Merge and computation converge is most salient in my view because the convergence marks a precise boundary between computational and non-computational systems. In turn, the distinction not only suggests a substantive cognitive difference between humans and animals but also posits an attractive computational theory of the mind.

Hence, the language bias may be set aside by rejecting the FLN hypothesis; the move will allow applications of Merge in other non-linguistic mental systems to anchor the generative mind. In effect, it means that we are able to show that Merge may apply in a mental system that is devoid of most of the significant linguistically specific features that identify the domain of language. Theoretically, the project seems attractive since we already know that the operation Merge itself does not contain any linguistically specific feature; it is a purely computational principle. I will illustrate these points with brief reviews of the computational properties of arithmetic in this section and music in the next.

7.1.1 Arithmetic

Consider Chomsky's remark that arithmetic is an 'offshoot' of human language; at some other places, Chomsky suggests that arithmetic is a 'concomitant of elements that enter into language' (Chomsky et al. 1982). Which elements? Chomsky had made these remarks often. To be fair to Chomsky, he has always made it clear that only the *knowledge* of arithmetic, that is, the study of how the number system is organized, is an offshoot of language; he is not claiming that the number system itself is an offshoot of language. I will argue that even the modest claim is unwarranted. To see what he means, let us examine the system of numbers under issue.

By now, it is very well understood that non-human animals have at least two forms of number sense: subitizing and quantitative estimation (Hauser et al. 1996; Gelman and Cordes 2001; Dehaene 2011). Animals have both an exact sense of small sets and a rough estimate of large quantities; these endowments vary for different species and the age of different members within a species. As we saw for desert ants, even they have something like a step counter although researchers warn us that the ants do not literally count. However, if 'counting' amounts to mastering the number system – the system of *ordinals* – then even chimpanzees do not have it.

Although it has been argued that chimpanzees have been trained to recognize individual numerals up to 9, it is unclear if these numerals correspond to the conventional notion of numbers in the cognition of chimpanzees. Thus, Spelke (2011) has argued, most animals have some 'core knowledge' of colour, geometry, numerosity and the like. Yet, according to Spelke, these are not the 'abstract concepts' available to humans. It appears to follow that chimpanzees may not possess even the *cardinal* numbers up to 9; the question of possessing *ordinal* numbers does not arise. Spelke holds that language plays a pivotal role in the development of abstract numerical and geometric concepts. So, what notion of language is involved here?

Chomsky is very specific on this point. According to him, 'we might think of the human number faculty as essentially an "abstraction" from human language, preserving the mechanism of discrete infinity and eliminating the other special features of language' (1988, 169). I am setting aside the issue of how abstract mathematical concepts are reached by just adding the mechanism of discrete infinity to the available system of core knowledge. In my view, the problem is exactly on a par with the development of the concept of apple from what we inherited from the chimpanzees (Berwick et al. 2013, see Chapter Six). In this perspective, we cannot take whatever chimpanzee number sense offers, add the procedure for generating discrete infinity to it and get ordinal numbers.

In any case, we saw in some detail that the mechanism of discrete infinity for human languages is exactly the mechanism of Merge. Furthermore, Merge is just a blind generator of discrete infinity independently of other special features of language such as the language-specific human lexicon. To emphasize, since Merge itself is not linguistically specific and Merge is the only stuff added to the existing system of numerosity, it is misleading to think of arithmetic as an offshoot of language. We can now see where this misleading idea is coming from: it is coming from the wrong conception that Merge is specific to human language, the FLN hypothesis (Hauser et al. 2002).

The non-linguistic character of arithmetic is further illustrated by Chomsky's recent suggestion that if we take Merge and we reduce the rest of the lexical system to the absolute minimum, that is, a lexicon which contains one element, we get the successor function (Chomsky 2008). According to Chomsky (2007), Merge operates on a single lexicon 0, and the result is the successor function: 0, {0}, {{0}}, {{{0}}} and so on. It is important to understand that that's all that Merge does; Merge generates an abstract representation of the ordinal series in the mind, which maybe dubbed *knowledge of arithmetic*.

In a further mapping operation, we may call {0} as 1, {{0}} as 2, and so on, to enumerate the familiar series of digits in the 'language' of arithmetic for those who have access to the digital notation. The lexical mapping may as well be done in more language-specific, say, English, terms to form the sequence of numerals *one, two, three* and so on to say *one plus one equals two*.[2] In that derivative sense, the digital sequence 1, 2, 3, . . . or the numeral sequence *one, two, three* represents the structure generated by Merge. Let us suppose arithmetical operations such as summation (+) and equality (=) are also products of Merge via the successor function. In that way, repeated operations of Merge ultimately generate the arithmetical expression 1 + 1 = 2. The point of great interest is that, Merge-generated digital expressions, unlike metrical stress, obviously carry truth values and, therefore, have a propositional semantics.

In this connection, it is interesting that Ken Hiraiwa (2017) argues that 'linguistic representations of number, grammatical number, and numerals do not incorporate anything like the successor function'. Setting aside the issue of grammatical number, it is not clear what more Hiraiwa wants to establish that the successor function is 'incorporated'. His argument appears to be that the number system is independently formed by the system of numerals in language: he says, 'numeral systems reflect both of the core systems of number and Merge'. Thus, Hiraiwa obviously thinks of Merge as a linguistic operation while the successor function is a non-linguistic arithmetical operation; so, according to him, the discrete infinity reflected in the system of numerals is a linguistic contribution due to Merge.

According to this view, language owners re-create the arithmetical system specifically in their preferred linguistic terms in their minds. As we have presented the matter, the numeral sequence *one, two, three* and so on, is formed out of mapping on to the abstract arithmetical sequence which is already a product of Merge implementing the successor function; so, there is no further need of the successor function specifically in language. All language-specific numeral systems simply label the abstract arithmetic system in the mind; the digital notation is a convenient marking of this 'hidden' system.

There is interesting evidence that arithmetical functions remain in place despite severe language impairment (Varley et al. 2005). The study was conducted on three patients who suffered from some difficulty in processing phonological and orthographic properties of number words; that is, the concerned patients had problems in accessing the lexical numerals of a language. The authors report that, otherwise, all three patients solved mathematical problems involving recursiveness and structure-dependent operations (for example, solving bracketing problems) when arithmetical problems were posed in digits. This result indicates that the computational procedures of arithmetic, when conducted in digits, remain unaffected despite linguistic impairment affecting number words. More recent studies from a variety of angles seem to confirm that linguistic processing occurs in brain areas distinct from those that support arithmetical processing (Fedorenko and Varley 2016). Hence, insofar as Merge operates in arithmetic to generate digits as we saw, the operation of Merge remains unaffected by language impairment.

However, some authors appear to think just the opposite. Thus, Arsenijević and Hinzen (2012) argue that the recursion displayed in arithmetic is not Merge because Merge, for them, does not strictly follow the standard x-over-x recursion. As we saw, the recursive generation of ordinal numbers strictly obeys the x-over-x principle, as in Chomsky's scheme. In contrast, we saw in Chapter 5 that generative structures of language typically require incorporation of different syntactic categories in order to complete the phase (see Section 5.4). Arsenijević and Hinzen's argument is a clear demonstration of language bias in their understanding of Merge. Merge in the language case is taken to be the real Merge such that if any computational operation differs from the language case, it is no longer Merge.

Once we delink the idea of Merge from its domain-specific operations in language, the basic operation could be viewed as more abstract than any of its specific local applications. Of course, we need to show carefully how the products of Merge vary in structure in terms of the demands of the lexicon in respective domains, but that is a separate issue (but see Chapter 8). Here my only concern is to point out the language bias in the decision to characterize Merge in terms of the specificity of its operations in the domain of language, rather than in arithmetic.

In this connection, it is interesting to note how non-linguistic arithmetic really is. For example, there is nothing like thematic roles in arithmetic which Chomsky thinks is a property of any language-like system. Furthermore, even if arguably the discourse of arithmetic satisfies Hauser's criteria of 'Logic of Thought' in terms of Merge and the two interfaces, the sound–meaning correlation for arithmetic is likely to be direct. This is because the lexicon of arithmetic does not contain the required features for driving Internal Merge, as we saw with metrical stresses (Berwick 2011, but see Chapter Eight). Arithmetic, then, is best viewed as a kindred system of language rather than as a 'language-like' system in Chomsky's narrow sense; it is certainly not an offshoot of language.

The comparison of arithmetic with the kindred system of metrical stress suggests another way of looking at their differences from the language system. Despite all its differences, arithmetic, as noted, may still be viewed as akin to language because the discourse of arithmetic admits of the standard Tarski-type satisfaction conditions, but not in the categorial terms of language: for example, '5 > 3'. In contrast, the system of metrical stress with its 'impoverished lexicon' of x and / (see Chapter 5), does not seem to have such affiliations with the language system. It is meaningless to think of a sequence of metrical stresses as a proposition with some truth value attached. In that sense, the system of metrical stress is further away from language than arithmetic. All we can say is that human languages, arithmetic and the system of metrical stress belong to a kindred class exactly because they are all Merge-based systems.

7.2 Music

The domain of music, another discretely infinite system, seems to be a more interesting candidate for the suggested class of kindred systems precisely because it is phenomenally almost totally distinct from the domain of language. Locating the same computational system in two phenomenally distinct domains promises significant theoretical unification towards the concept of mind. In what follows in this section on music, I will be mostly focusing on the phenomenal differences between language and music to insist that the only thing they have in common is the computational system. In fact, as we will see, the organization of music is, indeed, like birdsong in appearance with the exact difference that human music is a genuinely generative system of I-computation.

Although I have written about these differences between language and music earlier at length (Mukherji 2000, 2010), I wish to emphasize some of the crucial points because, unlike the focus on differences here, earlier I was also anxious to stress the stark similarities between the two systems to suggest something like a musilanguage hypothesis, even a strong musilanguage hypothesis. At that point, it seemed to me that showing Merge-like computational operations to explain the generativity of music was the only convincing way of demonstrating the domain-independence of Merge within a class of language-like systems. Now that we have Principle G in hand and a strong sense of separation between the lexicon and the computational system, we no longer have the preceding anxiety about the domain-independence of Merge: Merge *is* domain-independent whether it applies to music or not. Therefore, there is no need for a specific musilanguage thesis. The application of Merge in the domain of music simply expands the scope of Merge.

The generative character of human music is pretty obvious and was recognized for ages. Every musical system consists of a small set of notes and syllables as units that enter into computation. These units are compiled over and over again to generate progressively complex objects such as chords, scales, modes, phrases, passages, movements and so on; as we will see, some of these are viewed as forming the lexicon of music. The generation of non-lexical complex objects is unbounded, hierarchical and countable (Brown 2000, 273; Merker 2002; Fitch 2006). Even then authors continue to think that 'there are no unambiguous demonstrations of recursion in other human cognitive domains, with the only clear exceptions (mathematical formulas, computer programming) being clearly dependent upon language' (Fitch et al. 2005). I return to the remark in what follows.

7.2.1 Merge in music

Several attempts have been made in recent years to align some aspects of the linguistic framework to music (Pesetsky 2007; Katz and Pesetsky 2011; Rohrmeier 2011). I will keep to the work by Pesetsky and Katz since they directly use Merge to characterize musical syntax. As to the recursive character of progression in music, following Pesetsky (2007), Mukherji (2010, 221) reports that musical progression can be displayed as structures with binary branching and headed phrases. They are thus characterizable as products of Merge. For example, the progression of the opening part of Mozart's piano sonata K. 331 can be represented in the form of a tree structure generated by the repeated operation of Merge. Pesetsky's basic idea is to treat 'I' and 'V' as heads of phrases, where 'I' is the tonic chord and 'V' the dominant chord.[3] Many more diagrams for a variety of tonal music were offered in Katz and Pesetsky (2011) and (Mukherji 2013). Similar structures were displayed for Indian classical music in the set notation (Mukherji 2010).

Before we proceed, I wish to point out a general problem with musical notation as with Berwick's notation for metrical stress in Berwick (2011). As we saw there, the symbols x and / cannot be the symbols on which Merge operates; these are Berwick's inventions for making a theoretical point – similarly, for Pesetsky's notational scheme. Even if 'I' and 'V' are taken to be theoretical notations like N and V as in the language case, the stave notation for notes are not the symbols on which Merge operates. In the language case, in contrast, the syntactic structure '{*saw* {*the man*}' contains words of English, which are not artificial notations. These words are symbols as they are the articulated forms of mental representations; thus, Merge can operate on these symbols. The artificial notation in music at best suggests that certain mental representations are involved, but the notation does not specify what these mental representations are. Hence we do not yet have a clear idea of the mental representations or symbols in music on which Merge operates. Near the end of this section, I engage in some speculation on what these mental representations are likely to be. Needless to say, for the purposes of this project, I am only concerned about the application of Merge in musical contexts; hence, I am not concerned about the study of music cognition in general.[4]

Returning to other aspects of Pesetsky's proposals, when a sequence is generated by Merge, as we saw with metrical stress, it is natural to assign some selections even from the 'impoverished' lexicon as heads with projections to show the growth of the structure. My claim is that, beyond this structural convergence due to Merge, there is nothing linguistic about music. Which input items are selected as heads and how the projections are to be interpreted depends entirely on the concerned domain. Hence, I am not at all convinced about what Katz and Pesetsky call the 'Identity' between language and music. Again, the system of metrical stress can be used as a point of departure.

For the system of metrical stress, Berwick remarked that it was an example of syntax 'with no lexical features and no associated semantics; without features, there is no possibility of internal merge and the movement that we see in ordinary syntax'; he calls it 'pure syntax' (464). It is unclear why the system of metrical stress should be called *syntax* at all when it has no other language-like features, especially with no associated semantics. If, however, by 'syntax' Berwick means just the presence of the generative operation Merge, then, of course, there is no substantive problem – similarly, for music.

In my view, the very fact that Pesetsky was able to describe musical progression with Merge, then other things being equal, it refutes the language bias of Fitch et al. (2005) that 'there are no unambiguous demonstrations of recursion in other human cognitive domains'. More significantly, a demonstration of convergence between language and music in this very specific generative respect finally answered the long-standing problem of explaining unbounded, hierarchical, countable generativity in music. To my knowledge, no other form of work in music theory has a satisfactory answer to this problem; for example, the otherwise classic work of Lerdahl and Jackendoff (1983) suffers from this defect (Mukherji 2010).[5] On that count, if we wish to call Pesetsky's Merge-based account of musical progression 'musical syntax', there is no problem. We can still uphold the view that core language and music share nothing else.

However, to motivate the 'identity thesis' between language and music, Katz and Pesetsky claim more. According to them, 'All formal differences between language and music are a consequence of differences in their fundamental building blocks. In all other respects, language and music are identical.' As the authors clarify, the 'building blocks' of language consist of lexical items which are arbitrary sound–meaning pairings, while music consists of pitch classes (roughly, notes) and combinations of pitch classes such as chords, scales, ragas, motifs and so on. Later in the section, I discuss what these things mean in mental terms so that Merge can operate on them; the discussion will thereby indicate how musical thought looks like.

As we know, the arbitrary pairing between sound and meaning in the language case ultimately receives interpretation of complex sequences at two independent interfaces of SM and CI. So we have two representations, say, PHON and SEM and the pairing between them, <PHON, SEM>. The syntax of human language is such that it generates the pair. In the musical case, however, there is no such arbitrariness and independence between pitch classes and complex objects, say, chords since pitch classes (notes) constitute the chords. In that way, what constitutes the lexicon of music is more like units of phonology and morphology which constitute PHON. This raises the question if music has semantics at all in any interesting sense.[6] Since Katz and Pesetsky do not discuss the question, I will discuss it later. Setting semantics aside for now, what remains in music syntax, beyond Merge, that enables the authors to claim the formal identity thesis?

As far as I can see, the only other aspect of syntax pointed out by Katz and Pesetsky concerns movement or displacement of syntactic objects by Internal Merge. As we saw, Internal Merge is just Merge and it comes for free.[7] Yet, the availability of some feature does not mean that it is actually availed of. Recall that movement in the language case is triggered by some morphological feature of the lexical head; also, movement consists of copies. So there are morphological properties that force placement of copies at vacant places such that some syntactic requirement, such as agreement, may be met.

The operations of Internal Merge produce the phenomenon of displacement: a syntactic object is heard at one place while it is interpreted somewhere else. Hence, sound and meaning are mostly indirectly related in the language case. It is doubtful whether these aspects of movement are simulated in the music case. Berwick (2011) denied movement in metrical stress precisely because the heads in metrical stress were featureless. However, it is possible that Berwick reached that conclusion due to his language bias: nothing moves unless it moves in the way syntactic objects move in language.

Katz and Pesetsky (2011) argue for a different form of movement in music. They suggest that cadences in compositions of music may be viewed as products of Internal Merge.[8] Western classical tonal music typically imposes an adjacency condition: some chords of certain types must be adjacent to meet the phrase closure requirement; the adjacent chords form a cadence (Mukherji 2013). According to Katz and Pesetsky, syntactic objects in music sometimes move to meet the adjacency constraint on phrases and, in so moving, they form cadences. Several problems with this explanation of movement in music have been pointed out.

For example, cadences for phrasal closure are typically found in Western classical tonal tradition – they are not found in rock music; hence such cadences are not universal features of music, probably they are imposed by idioms. A more formal objection is that it is not evident that in the suggested cases some syntactic movement is actually taking place (Mukherji 2013). Be that as it may, since there are no cadences in human languages, the suggested case of Internal Merge in music, even if it is valid, is not an evidence in support of the identity thesis. It is clear where the Katz-Pesetsky identity thesis is coming from: it is coming from a language bias that Merge is a linguistic operation and hence any evidence of Internal Merge is further evidence that language and music are identical. The assumption that Merge is dedicated to language is essentially false, as we saw.

The point that language and music are formally entirely different can be advanced further if we consider the notion of musical interpretation vis-à-vis linguistic interpretation. Although Katz and Pesetsky do sketch how the generative structure of music looks like, they do not say anything about how the interfaces, where these structures are interpreted, look like. Assuming that musical organization also contains interfaces with 'external' systems in some sense, they cannot be the external systems of language because interpretation of music centrally involves the tonal organization of music, not the phonetic and semantic representations of language.[9]

In any case, as with arithmetic, there is much evidence by now of neural dissociation between language-specific and music-specific abilities; hence, there is no marked correlation between either healthy or impaired individuals for performance in structural processing in the concerned domains (Patel 2003; Peretz et al. 2015; Fedorenko and Varley 2016; Faroqi-Shah et al. 2019). In fact, musical structural processing was not affected even in the case of severe agrammatic aphasia. In view of the marked differences between language and music in their domain-specific properties, the domain-general operation Merge may be viewed as forming just the generative structure of linguistic and musical expressions (Mukherji 2010).

7.2.2 Significance in music

In fact, any form of identity thesis between language and music is suspect because of the predominance of the sound component in music. As we saw, if we wish to pursue the analogy of language design, we can at best say, if at all, that music consists only of a PHON-like component. In the absence of an overt SEM component, music is starkly different from language. Indeed, the recent proposal that the sound part of language is ancillary (Berwick and Chomsky 2016) could mean that language is essentially geared to meet the conditions at the CI interface. There is no such thing as a CI interface for music; musical objects do not express any 'external' concepts or refer to any item in the world. In that sense, musical sequences do not *say* anything which could be expressed in words.

Sometimes this phenomenon is misleadingly characterized as an 'ineffability problem' (Raffman 1993). Ludwig Wittgenstein clarified why it is misleading to view the alleged property of music as a problem: 'it is a strange illusion that possesses us when we say "This tune says *something*", and it is as though I have to find *what* it says' (1958, 178). The solution to the ineffability problem, as Wittgenstein characteristically suggested, is to whistle the tune. Since I have written extensively on this topic (Mukherji 2010), I will not pursue it any further here. Nevertheless, I will mention one specific issue briefly to draw the analogy with birdsong.

The language bias, pointed out by Wittgenstein to address the so-called ineffability problem, explains why authors devote so much effort to locate some 'external' system in the music case as well. Since it is well understood by now (Fitch 2006; Boghossian 2007) that we cannot associate a musical sound with either a concept or something in the world, many authors insist that music is best understood as expressing emotions. Authors such as Jackendoff and Lerdahl (2006) often come up with elaborate lists of these emotions: gentle, forceful, awkward, abrupt, static, earnest, reverent, tender, ecstatic, sentimental, longing, striving, resolute, depressive, playful, witty, ironic, tense, unsettled, heroic and the like (see Mukherji 2010 for more).

The basic problem, among many, is that even if we are able to ascribe specific emotions to given pieces of music, emotions can only be global properties of music. Typically, emotions are assigned to an entire piece of music; for example, according to Roger Scruton, the last movement of the *Jupiter Symphony* is 'morose and life-negating' (cited in Raffman 1993, 42). But music is a complex organization of notes which we hear on a note-by-note basis, forming larger and larger groups as we proceed. It is hard to see how the global (emotional) property of the piece is computationally reached from its smaller parts; emotions just don't compute in the desired sense (Mukherji 2010). But this is not to deny that expression of emotions is a significant aspect of music.

The point of interest here is that expression of emotions as global properties of large chunks of music is exactly how birdsong is associated with some global significance for the species, as we saw. In fact, songbirds sometimes display songs out of pleasure. If pleasure falls under emotions, then birdsong is also associated with emotions as global factors. Now we can see why it is misleading to complain, both for birdsong and human music, that 'when song syllables are combined to create longer structures, new creations have no impact on the function or "meaning" of the song' (Hauser et al. 2014).

It follows that these global associations are not to be viewed in terms of the local features of computation at all; in that sense, their task *is* to serve a global function. The intimate association between music and emotions holds without tracing the association to the internal structure of music. As songs – that is music with lyrics – attest, outputs of both language and music certainly access emotions. It is a common experience that most complex human activities are globally associated with emotions: watching soccer or cooking 'Mama's pasta', for example. To my knowledge, it is not very clear why such associations take place at all.

For the music case, one speculation is that music accesses emotions more directly and definitively because music is fundamentally an 'internal' system; music has nothing else to access (Mukherji 2010). For another explanation, Dan Sperber (1994) suggests that the human music 'module' could have been a cultural adaptation of 'acoustic properties of early human vocal communications'. According to Sperber, 'sounds that the module analyzes thereby causing pleasure to the organism . . . are not often found in nature (with the obvious exception of bird songs)'. The mention of birdsong in this rather exclusive context suggests that we can view human music as an adaptation of some pre-existing vocal system that we shared with songbirds.

In any case, the critical difference between the two is that human music is generative in character, birdsong is just patterns of complex sound. Under the simplest assumption that some version of Merge instantiates Principle G, it is not surprising that musical form is the result of successive applications of Merge, as Katz and Pesetsky showed. But Merge is a computational device that needs some lexical workspace constituting symbols. In the absence of conceptual, referential and emotional properties in musical meaning, what could be the symbols in the music case?

No doubt, the most prominent part of interpretation in music concerns internal relations between musical elements themselves without any computational connection with external factors such as concepts and emotions. As Diana Raffman (1993, 59) explains the phenomenon, musicians are typically concerned with *structural* issues such as whether a given phrase ends at E-natural. Three possibilities arise: the phrase ends before the E-natural, the phrase ends at the E-natural, and the phrase extends beyond the E-natural. As anyone familiar with music knows, these structural variations make substantial differences in the interpretation of music. Depending on the group of notes at issue, and the location of the group in a passage, some of the structural decisions may even lead to bad music. This is because these decisions often make a difference to how a given sequence of notes is to be resolved. Any moderately experienced listener of music can tell the differences phenomenologically, though its explicit explanation requires technical knowledge of music (such as modulation to the dominant).

In my view, this aspect of musical interpretation is on a par with much of grammatical interpretation in language since, at the level of grammar, linguistic interpretations are restricted to structural issues such as scope distinction, distribution of arguments, agreement between syntactic objects and the like (Mukherji 2010). Arguably, no mention is made at this level of the conceptual, referential and other 'external' features of lexical items.[10] But it would be facile to draw any deep connection between language and music on this count. It could be just a reflex of Merge-like operations that lexical items, and groups of them, form various structural relations at different hierarchies. Which of these structural relations are salient and which violate conditions on interpretation depends on the concerned domain. For example, in the language case, grammatical computation has to satisfy conditions at the semantic interface. It does not follow that music also needs to have something like semantic representation in its overall grammatical organization, as suggested in Mukherji (2010).

In any case, the query about individual symbols in music persists because, after all, most lexical items of language receive progressively wider interpretation in the vast CI system, as the so-called semantic features associated with lexical items display. In the absence of a CI system in the music case, the notion of a musical symbol thus poses a bit of a problem if we suffer from language bias with respect to the notion of a symbol. In the absence of a language-like CI interface for music, some authors, indeed, suggest that music is not a symbol system at all. As noted, the trouble is that Merge can operate only in a symbolic domain.

Setting aside the history of language bias in this area, one way to approach the problem is to ask the following: what are the constituents of musical thought? What is the composer 'looking up' when he is writing a piece of music? What does a competent user of music hold in the mind when there is no sound in a context? No doubt, a composer occasionally hits some keys on the nearest piano to elicit the sound he wants. But suppose there is no sound of the piano and no associated humming, as we are told happened with Beethoven in his later years.[11]

To explain the content of musical thought in such noise-free contexts, suppose we assume that the musician, as well as the experienced music listener, have some abstract images of the basic sounds stored. These images are 'abstract' in the sense that the image remains invariant while the stimulus, the actual sound, changes, say, as octaves change. I am assuming for the sake of some informal description that these prior images in the memory explain the responses of assent or dissent from an experienced listener regarding a particular sound elicited from the keyboard.[12]

My guess is that even lay listeners have some loose images of musical sound as they track intonation and sameness of notes across a vast range of common music. They may not have stable images for individual notes, and fail to appreciate idiom-specific structural nuances especially in classical music, but they can recognize whether the intended note has been reached or the same group of notes have been transposed to a different octave, perhaps even in the transposition to a different key.[13] I am assuming roughly the same mechanism for the production of sound when other physical conditions are fulfilled.

My contention is that these mental representations of musical sound, in the form of abstract images, are the symbols on which Merge in music operates; these imagistic symbols stand for musical sounds, pitch classes, in thought. However, how these images turn into symbols to enter into Merge-like computation is not entirely clear. Part of the symbolization must have to do with the somewhat abstract character of these images which qualifies them to be viewed as stimulus-independent representations; but the real explanatory challenge of how these images acquire the abstract character continues to fall under dark matter, to my knowledge.[14]

In some cultures, especially those with written notation, these symbols are associated with phonetic or orthographic forms such as A, B, C, D, E, F, G or do-re-mi-fa-so-la-ti or sa-re-ga-ma-pa-dha-ni; sometimes they are indicated in more technical notations such as the stave notation, Pesetsky's chord notation and the like. But these are not concept-bearing names, these are artificial markers of (stored) images of sound, on a par with Berwick's invention of x and / to mark metrical stress (Berwick 2011). These notational devices play a role in the analysis of music, but they are not needed in the music itself. They do not constitute musical thought. People completely ignorant of these notations can hum a tune.

To say this is not to deny that the vast range of musical concepts such as tonic, dominant, chord, melody, rondo, allegro and the like can enter into discussion of music in the language of music theory. Human languages are used to talk about almost anything, including human musical experiences. For those who are versed in the vocabulary of music theory, these concepts indicate what a sequence of notes 'says'. I am not denying that they also enter into (advanced) musical thinking as an assistance to, say, composition or recall of music, for those who are competent with these notational schemes.[15] But they do not enter the composition itself. Indeed, classical musicians in India sometimes use the notion of 'saying' by showing how a musical piece sounds like, that is what the piece 'says'. As Wittgenstein pointed out, all you need to do to display the symbolic form of musical thought is whistle.

In my view, it is plausible to assume, then, that symbols of music incorporate imagistic information by accessing the relevant perceptual system. But the non-conceptual, imagistic nature of information in music does not prevent music from attaining its generative power. The generative power of music comes from the operations of Merge; for Merge, it does not matter if it operates on images or concepts as long as some information is packaged in a symbolic form. Except for Merge, the musical system is fundamentally different from the language system.

From the discussion on the nature of Merge so far, we may identify three conjectures: (a) Merge is essential for any relevant notion of I-computation; (b) Merge is possibly available in an array of human domains beyond language proper; (c) Merge is probably not available outside human domains. If these results become established, then the FLN hypothesis – that the computational system of language is unique to the faculty of language (see 5.1) – will collapse due to (b). Moreover, on the basis of these results, it will not be unreasonable to form the expectation that the availability of Merge suggests the (exact) scope of the computational theory of mind.

7.3 Questionable domains: Concepts, morality

The perspective on FLN suggests the presence of the generative mind in other mental domains beyond language. At the current stage of inquiry, though, in view of the underlying historical influence of the FLN hypothesis, it is likely that the application of Merge will be confined to domains that are viewed as adjacent to language since current conceptions of generativity, as we saw for music and arithmetic, emanate from the generative features of language. Although the domains of melodic stress, arithmetic and music turned out to be genuinely non-linguistic after analysis, it is still possible that the domains where Merge is seen to apply could be too close to language to be viewed as genuinely non-linguistic; the application of Merge in such proximal domains, then, may not expand the scope of the generative mind.

With the suggested uncertainty in mind, we will briefly explore some apparently non-linguistic mental domains such as the conceptual system, morality, kinship and the arts. The generative character of these systems does indicate some version of Principle G in operation. Nonetheless, it appears that where the operation Merge or something very similar is said to be operating, it is unclear if the domain is genuinely distinct from language; in contrast, when a domain is genuinely non-linguistic, it is unclear if Merge is applying. A further consolidation of the conception of the generative mind therefore depends on theoretical progress on two issues. First, we need a more careful understanding of how mental systems and their distribution are to be identified so that they may be viewed as falling under the proposed conception of the mind. Second, there is a need for closer investigation into the relation between Principle G as the putative sole generative operation of the mind, and the formulation of Merge initially found in the language system, so that Merge may be viewed both as a real version of Principle G and as operating in individual systems to generate structured thoughts in them.

7.3.1 The conceptual system

In Chapter 3, following Chomsky's distinction between the computational and the conceptual systems of language, we adopted a narrow core conception of language for which the concept of meaning is restricted to the internal significance of the structure generated at the CI interface. Except for readability conditions imposed by the CI systems, no external system or condition influenced the notion of meaning for determining the sound–meaning correlations in the core language. In that sense, as noted, the language system did not appeal to traditional semantic notions such as truth, denotation, conceptual structure and the like. The conceptual system, in particular, was viewed as a 'dark matter' that is separate from but linked to the core language system in unknown ways.

To my knowledge, the conceptual system continues to be a dark matter for which we do not really know which elements constitute the system in what structural arrangement; so it may be premature to ask whether the conceptual system, if any, is a generative one. Perhaps there is a genus–species structure governing the system, as evidenced by some inferential uses of words, but it is unclear how to identify the 'lexical' elements of the system in a coherent organization (Mukherji 2010, Chapter Four). Therefore, I am myself not assuming that there is an independent conceptual system that requires a generative account. In fact, I am not ruling out the possibility, as sketched in

Chapter 3, that the conceptual system could well be a product of the language system in a certain generative sense in interaction with the perceptual systems, especially the visual system.[16]

However, we do express thoughts such as *brown bread,* *happy old man,* *the present King of France* and so on that seem to suggest a combination of concepts, perhaps due to links between the conceptual and the language systems. For authors, who are apparently not content with the narrow notion of language with internal significance, these facts suggest that a broader theory of meaning for natural languages may be developed by harnessing such combinatorial properties of concepts. This can be done from two opposite directions, either by semanticizing the theory of language or by syntactification of the conceptual system. I look at them in turn. Since we have already adopted a core view of language and have located the generative part of the design, I will be concerned only with the generative aspects of the suggested incorporation of the conceptual system into a broader language system; in particular, I will restrict my attention to whether Merge is working, and how. I will not be concerned with the viability of these projects as theories of meaning for human languages.

For the first, more directly semantic, approach, consider Thornton (2016). Assuming some common idea and organization of concepts, Thornton suggests that the linguistic operation Merge may be viewed as combining these concepts; for example, Thornton holds that Merge combines the concepts of lawn and flower-bed to generate the more complex concept of garden, so we can think of garden as the 'root' of a structure with lawn and flower-bed as elements. Following this direction, the idea of a meal of steak and salad with dressing yields the semantic phrase marker: [**meal** steak [**salad** lettuce cucumber [**dressing** oil vinegar salt]]]. It is totally unclear to me what this structure is a representation of. To me, the suggested structure looks like a menu for the table written in English; but whether it qualifies as a structure description of the external conceptual system as it interfaces with language is a wholly different matter which I set aside for reasons already stated.

Continuing with such constructions for more and more complex expressions, and adopting familiar semantic markers for various parts of an event, Thornton proposes the structure [**seeing.action** [**subject** John] [**object** [**definite.thi ng** book]]] as an output when Merge operates in the conceptual system. The structured thought apparently is thus already formed by repeated operations of Merge. In due course, this structure is to be transferred to the SM systems to yield the articulated expression *John sees the book* for English users; in Hindi, it yields *dekha John-ne kitab-ko.* Details aside, it appears that all the thought-generating formal apparatus of the core language is now available semantically within the conceptual system itself, so the conceptual system itself works as a phrase generator. In effect, Merge is conceptualized as operating in the conceptually organized language system itself. The conceptual system can no longer be viewed as an independent non-linguistic domain. As a result, the scheme fails to show that there are two independent domains, language and conceptual system, and Merge operates in both.

Paul Pietroski (2005, 2010, 2020) in contrast assumes the basic architecture of the core language with narrow syntax and interfaces, with the conceptual system linked as an external system. Once a structure reaches the CI interface, Pietroski asks which notion of meaning now applies to this structure. Pietroski's answer has two parts: rhetorical and substantive. In the rhetorical part, Pietroski engages critically with much contemporary debate on whether linguistic meaning consists of 'externalist' notions like reference, truth conditions and the like (Mukherji 2010, Chapter Three, Chomsky 2000a; Chomsky and Collins 2021). Pietroski's main claim is that an intermediate theory of meaning for natural languages can be developed which lies between narrow syntax with internal significance and very broad semantics with truth conditions (Pietroski 2005, 2010); the appeal to the conceptual system is made for the intermediate system of meaning.

Pietroski's basic idea is that 'humans use available concepts to *introduce* formally new concepts that can be fetched via lexical items and combined via certain operations that are invoked by the human faculty of language' to generate more complex phrasal meanings (2010). Thus, according to Pietroski (2020), the meaning of *green bottle* is a 'tripartite instruction': access a concept via *bottle*, access a concept via *green*, and conjoin the results. So there are concepts like BOTTLE, GREEN stored somewhere which are 'accessed' by an English user with the help of lexical items *bottle, green* and so on. These concepts are first accessed via the lexical items to generate some 'special kind' of concepts, *then* these special kinds of concepts are conjoined. It follows that there is no combinatorial operation in the conceptual store itself; the conjunctions happen in the language system. To that extent, Pietroski's scheme does not extend the scope of the generative mind.

We saw in Chapter 5 that, in acquiring the word *read* (in English), the child is, in fact, acquiring a transitive predicate of the form x(read)y. Pietroski exploits this structural fact to claim that the child has 'fetched' the available concept READ (X, Y) to introduce the monadic concept E for the 'event' (of reading). The idea aligns Pietroski's project with the formal structure of neo-Davidsonian event semantics; all we need to do now is 'fetch' saturable concepts for X and Y, and then conjoin them in a structure by using the formal machinery of first-order logic. Thus, the meaning of the English predicate *kicked a brown cow* is given in the structure, $\exists(X)\bullet[\text{PATIENT}(E, X), \bullet[\text{BROWN}(X), \text{COW}(X)]]$, representing someone kicking a brown cow. As noted, my only concern is with the conjoining operations.

As we set up Pietroski's project, the conjoined structure for meaning appears at the CI interface linked to the conceptual system. For this to happen, Merge must have already operated to get the syntactic structure to the interface. This arrangement seems plausible since the concerned lexical items need to be already in place to start 'fetching' regular concepts and introducing special concepts. These special concepts are then placed in the neo-Davidsonian event structure by certain operations that are invoked by the human faculty of language. But this operation cannot be Merge because Merge can only operate on lexical elements at the base; in any case, the conjoined structure contains first-order resources that are not in the base and Merge cannot introduce them online.[17]

In any case, both Thornton and Pietroski assume that there is an independent progenitive system of concepts from which conceptual information is somehow drawn to reach some enriched notion of meaning. I have already argued against progenitive concepts in Chapter 3. Therefore, the arguments against an independent generative conceptual component of meaning sketched here apply to all 'meaning-first' views of linguistic architecture, such as Sauerland and Alexiadou (2020).[18] As emphasized throughout, the generative conception of human language is entirely restricted to structured thoughts formed from words. In some sense, words do contain conceptual information drawn from the CI systems. Yet the understanding of the conceptual system itself, if any and as separate from language, is currently a dark matter. The core language with internal semantics is all we have. I return to the issue in the next chapter.

7.3.2 Morality

Another domain of thought and action that is increasingly cited as a language-like computational system is the domain of morality. For example, John Mikhail (2007) claims that there is a universal moral grammar on par with the universal grammar of language. Hauser and Watumull (2017) view morality as falling under a more general 'Logic of Thought'. Is the domain of morality a non-linguistic generative domain enlarging the conception of the generative mind?

As we have construed the idea of a generative domain so far, it satisfies the following criteria. A generative domain contains the unique human-specific generative operation Principle G; the current hypothesis is that Merge is that operation. Thus a generative domain constitutes of Merge and the domain-specific 'lexicon' with which the domain is identified (Hauser and Watumull 2017): the domain of language is identified with its lexicon, words; music is identified by the system of notes standing for sound-images; and so on. Thus a domain is identified only when its lexicon is identified. The domain is non-linguistic if its 'lexicon' is different from language.

A domain is generative in that it generates structured thoughts when the generative principle works on its lexicon. The lexicon is thus viewed as consisting of unstructured units of thought with a symbolic form. Hence, even when generativity is noticed in human actions, such as knitting, the generative factor must be traceable to the thoughts that guide these actions. As we saw, this condition raises problems for a salient generative conception of the conceptual system. In sum, it follows that, in order to count as a non-linguistic generative system, a generative system contains units of non-linguistic thought. I will argue that it is implausible that the domain of morality is a non-linguistic generative system in the sense outlined.

The problems begin with some unclarity about what counts as a moral domain. Abstracting over a long history of philosophical discussion on this topic, we may broadly think of morality in three ways. At one extreme, there is something like instinctive morality that we largely share with animals. These include moral actions such as display of courage for the care of offspring, helping conspecifics in distress, sometimes even sharing food and other resources with offspring and conspecifics and the like. By definition, instinctive morality is not a mental system at all because it is shared with animals who are not endowed with the generative mind. At the other extreme, there are abstract ethical principles such as detachment from self-interest, sacrifices for others, ensuring peace and justice at all costs and so on; some like Gandhi will say that that is the real domain of morality. I am also setting these ethical principles aside because they are practised by very few individuals and are, thus, not part of our daily lives.

Between these extremes, there is the vast area of regular practice in human societies which we may view as judicial morality. As social creatures, humans need to devise various complex forms of cooperative living, formulate and maintain rights of individuals and recognized groups, implement some sense of distributive justice, responsibility, punishment and the rule of law and so on. Much of this is explicitly codified in the form of statutes, rules, injunctions, obligations and the like. So the use of language is a necessary condition for this moral domain; by now, much of these have been written down as codes in literal cultures. The problem is, it is hard to conceptualize this area of human thinking without the aid of language.

In this area of human thought, moral concepts appear to be intrinsically connected with moral terms in a language. As Mikhail shows from a study of moral terms in languages, most cultures use a familiar set of moral concepts which are classified in three broad categories of obligatory, forbidden and permissible moral actions (Mikhail 2007). His study also shows remarkable similarity in judicial procedures and constitutions with respect to these categories across a wide variety of cultures (Mikhail 2009). Hence, it is reasonable to view this range of moral thinking and action as universal features of human societies as they evolved and developed various forms of sustainable social living. The study of the universal bases of morality suggests that relativistic and culture-specific views of morality are largely mistaken for this area of moral practice; they may be more relevant for the third area of ethical principles (Williams 1985).

However, the evidence for universal bases of morality by itself does not enlarge the scope of the generative mind. As we saw, much of the moral thinking in this area is codified in human language with a specific range of vocabulary dedicated to guiding human actions; the generative properties of language suffice to characterize the structure of moral thought. Therefore, no additional aspect of the generative mind is needed to capture the generative properties of, say, the Indian Penal Code. There is no doubt that there are various specialized vocabularies within the assorted lexicon of languages. Human languages are used to talk about almost everything. For example, there is a specialized geographical vocabulary in English that articulates concepts such as equator, latitude, continental divide, rain forest and so on. However, there is no additional generative device for producing structured thoughts in geography that employ such concepts. Moral and geographical thoughts are simply components of linguistic thought.

In some cases, the specialized vocabulary does indicate interactions with independent generative systems. The linguistic lexicon of music contains words for articulation of musical concepts such as chords, rondo, arpeggio, allegro and the like; the vocabulary for cooking contains labels for various ingredients, utensils and steps of cooking. Yet, the domains of music and cooking are independent precisely because they are non-linguistic, for which we have distinguishing evidence. So the structured thoughts generated in these specialized lexical areas of language will interact with independent domains of music and cooking, as we saw for music. Hence, the claim of an independent moral module will be valid when we have evidence that morality is non-linguistic in character; just specialized vocabulary is not enough. The required evidence seems to be unavailable in the moral case because moral thought is necessarily codified in human language. In that sense, moral thoughts do not expand the scope of the generative mind beyond language.

The distinction between the domains of religion and creek-crossing further illustrates the crucial issue of identification of non-linguistic mental systems. There is much controversy on the universality of religious concepts. Some authors believe that religiosity is culture-specific (Banerjee and Bloom 2013), others hold that the emergence of religion is a universal phenomenon (Johnson and Bering 2006). In view of the widespread use of religious concepts like God, divinity, sin, hell, heaven, afterlife and so on in most human cultures, let us suppose that a non-trivial set of religious concepts are universal. Even then it is implausible that religious ideas may be entertained by a non-linguistic mind. This is because religious concepts, involving imaginary scenarios and hypothetical causes, are not connected with direct perceptual conditions; as discussed in Sections 1.3.2 and 3.1 such abstract concepts need the scaffolding of language.

In contrast, people often place suitable bricks and stones in the shallow parts of a creek to form a bridge to cross the creek. One can codify this elaborate generative activity in language in the form of instructions, say for children or for travellers unfamiliar with the area. The practice is unlikely to vary in form between Africa and Canada; therefore, it is plausible to view the activity as universal. Also, it is likely to be restricted to humans because of the generative factor.[19] Yet, since the practice is entirely based on locally and perceptually available material, there is a clear intuition that the practice must have been available to hominids with Principle G much before the advent of language, as the widespread migration of early hominids suggests. Thus, we have two other generative systems, one of which falls under language and the other has possibly non-linguistic origins.

Mikhail's work on morality does include elaborate charts and tree diagrams to show the 'causal structure' of moral actions, such as particular responses to the trolley problem, in terms of categories like Agent, Patient, Cause and the like (Mikhail 2007). In view of the linguistic character of moral thoughts, these trees for moral actions can be viewed only as something like 'event semantics' or 'theory of meaning' for moral discourse, on a par with theories of meaning discussed previously. In other words, these charts and diagrams can be interpreted only in terms of accompanying instructions phrased in language, unlike the creek-crossing case.

As with Thornton and Pietroski, Mikhail gives no indication that the conceptual conditions of moral actions may be entertained independently of language. Therefore, the suggestion by Hauser and Watumull (2017) that graphical representations of moral action – as characterized, say, by Mikhail's diagrams and flow charts – may be constructed by Merge is not striking at all; the demonstration simply shows that moral action is guided by the moral component of linguistic thought. Therefore, Mikhail's contention that morality constitutes an independent 'grammar' in the mind is questionable.

In my view, in thinking of morality as an independent mental domain, both Mikhail and Hauser-Watumull project a wrong conception of the human mind. According to Mikhail, morality forms a class with such disparate domains as language, vision, musical cognition and face recognition (2007, 144). As discussed in Chapter 2, this class is incoherent even without morality because it includes vision and face recognition where the structuring principles are widely different from the others like language; Nelson Goodman (1951) would have called it a class of 'imperfect community' where the members do not cohere despite some resemblance. In any case, inclusion of morality in this class is pointless because morality falls under language which is already included. Similarly, Hauser and Watumull are mistaken in including morality as a domain distinct from language in what they consider to be the class of domains falling under the 'Logic of Thought'. According to them, the members of 'Logic of Thought' share the operation Merge, but differ in their lexicon; however, the lexicon of morality just forms a component in the broad and open-ended lexicon of language.

7.4 Promising domains: Kinship, arts

The domain of kinship relations throws interesting light on the issue of demarcating genuinely non-linguistic domains. *Prima facie*, the alleged domain shows a similarity with the area of morality in that, to my knowledge, most researchers on kinship relations focus on how kinship relations are expressed in language; hence, kinship thoughts appear to be linguistic thoughts. Thus the apparent generativity of the system is just the generativity of language.

Consider the pioneering work by Kenneth Hale in this area. In his classic work, Hale (1966) showed that the pronominal system of indigenous languages in Australia reflects various kinship properties of those societies. For example, the kinship system of Lardil speakers consists of two very interesting categories that Hale calls *harmonic* and *agnatic*. Keeping to the category of harmonic, the kinship system forms two sets based on alternate lineage. This distinction is reflected in the use of non-singular pronouns. So, when Lardil speakers use the equivalent of *you* in the sense of dual, they pick pronouns depending on whether the two persons addressed belong to a harmonic or a disharmonic set. In fact, as Hale shows, there are syntactic rules for reducing compounds like *my father and I* based on the harmonic information. Although Hale mentions that such kinship information is used elsewhere, such as in performing rituals, the tight fit between kinship relations and language suggests that the generative processes are linguistic in character.

The close connection between the generative properties of kinship relations and grammar seems to be a settled matter with more recent and extensive data. Thus, according to Jones (2010), kinship terms display hierarchical properties 'homologous with conceptual structure in other domains'. In fact, Jones holds that there is no dedicated acquisition device for kinship terms, meaning that kinship terms are learned in a similar fashion with terms from other domains.[20] As for the grammar of kinship, it has all the components such as semantics, syntax and phonology that are traditionally associated with grammars. Without going into the details, it looks like kinship terms are simply a component of the lexicon of language, much like the cases of morality, religiosity and geography. Therefore, the design features of language apply to kinship thoughts.

Nonetheless, there seems to be a strong intuition that, unlike morality and geography and more like music, the kinship system is what it is, independently of whether it may be captured in language. In other words, even if the organization of kinship terms appears to be an 'offshoot' of language, kinship organization itself, which possibly predates human language, seems to reflect generative properties. The sustained survival and rapid growth of human populations are often ascribed to the development of complex social networks (Stringer 2011). For example, there was the 'grandmother phenomenon' in which older women lived long enough to take care of the children while the parents left for hunting, collecting material for cooking, organizing agriculture and so on. The arrangement has obvious survival value for the species.

Supposing such complex social joints to have developed before the onset of language, it is plausible that early humans formed some conception of kinship organization in non-linguistic observational terms. Such information could have included biological information about lineage, gender, ageing and some way of numerically arranging a cluster of conspecifics in some genealogical order. The structural information so obtained could have helped form something like a mental map of kinship hierarchy.

Following the research programme of Optimality Theory, Jones (2010) lists a range of 'constraints' under which the organization of kinship terms works. Setting Optimality Theory aside, some of these constraints seem relatively independent of language. For example, all kinship terms require a distinction of gender for determining lineage. Perhaps the most important constraint for our purposes is the distinction of distance such that one is able to form some conception of Younger Brother, Father's Daughter, Mother's Sister and the like. Then there is the constraint of distinction of grade with which one determines if a relation is fully or partially reciprocal. My point is, it is not obvious why a conception of these things necessarily requires language. Needless to say, we are assuming that, although language is yet to emerge, some generative device, Principle G, is already available.

No doubt, when these hierarchies are marked with kinship terms, one can form more complex hierarchies such as Older Mother's Mother's Brother's Son's Son, once the initial hierarchies such as Son's Son and Brother's Son are available independently of language. If these speculations have some merit, kinship organization itself could be viewed as a generative system of the mind that was further enhanced by language via the use of kinship terms. Interestingly, Jones suggests that the grammar of kinship (in language) may be understood 'as an offshoot of a uniquely human capacity for playing coordination games', meaning perhaps that the notion of grammar may be viewed more abstractly as a generative mechanism. We explore the speculation in the next chapter.

The application of Merge to incorporate imagistic information contained in the flow of music suggests that Merge may also be working in other imagistic domains such as the arts, especially painting and sculpture which represent visual images. However, I am not aware of any work that attempts to understand the human-specific generativity of the arts in terms of Merge-like procedures available in language, arithmetic and music. For example, in a sweeping review of the substantial archaeological literature on cave paintings, Miyagawa et al. (2018) report that literally hundreds of thousands of cave paintings have now been located in prehistoric human habitations across the world. Some of them in Indonesia and Australia have been uranium dated to between 40 and 50 KY (Aubert et al. 2014; Marchant 2016).

In fact, it is well known by now that pigment ochre, the basic ingredient for these paintings, was extracted and used in the making of adhesives through various chemical processes much before the journey out of Africa started, perhaps dating as far back as the Middle Stone Age, about 200 KY (Stringer 2011, 138). Assuming that much of the earlier paintings have been lost or remain undiscovered, it is very plausible that painting originated in the hominid line at least at the same time as language, if not earlier; furthermore, the evidence seems to be that cave painting appeared only in the later stage of the hominid line, far away from any early hominids.

It stands to reason that visual images, like auditory images of music, are more naturally and thus directly available to the concerned organisms than the conventional correlations between sound and meaning needed for the basic units of the language faculty. Thus, it will not be surprising at all if it turns out that paintings and other art objects are found independently or even earlier than language. In line with the basic thesis of this work that the human mind in the form of Principle G was available independently of the emergence of language, it is most interesting to find out if the unbounded structural – perhaps even hierarchical – character of artistic creativity can also be explained in terms of Merge, in line with proposals for music.

Unfortunately, I have not been able to locate any direct literature on the topic. Despite its tantalizing title 'Prehistoric Cave Paintings, Symbolic Thinking, and the Emergence of Language', the cited paper by Miyagawa et al. (2018) does not examine the relationship between the formal properties of language and cave painting at all. All it does is record scattered instances of what they call 'symbolic objects', and darkly suggest that the sound of hoofs deep inside ancient caves may have something to do with the 'articulatory' character of these objects. In particular, Miyagawa et al. throw no light on what could have been the lexicon of cave paintings and how they gave rise to the symbolic objects. Perhaps one problem is that there is no clear idea of how the basic elements of arts, such as line and colour, contribute to the growth of an art object in a discrete manner such that we are able to examine whether Merge may operate in the given workspace.[21]

Douglas Hofstadter's classic work (1980) did examine some intriguing art objects, such as Escher's paintings of 'impossible objects', to study their formal unity vis-à-vis mathematical and musical representations. However, except for suggesting that familiar computational terms such as recursion, loop, self-reference and the like may be used to describe some of the peculiar properties of these representations, Hofstadter appears to be too engaged with classical artificial intelligence to study the natural generative processes of art.

Nonetheless, Hofstadter's study appears to suggest broadly that artworks contain discernible 'chunks' in the form of visual images in the artist's mind that are used to generate even 'impossible objects'. For example, in Escher's drawing of *Waterfall*, images of pillars are inserted at the second level to break the spatial continuity of the flow of water; so we know that visual images of these pillars are stored in the mind as 'chunks'. The painting then can be viewed in terms of chunk-by-chunk computation at different levels. But Hofstadter never explains what goes into the chunks themselves; so we don't know what kind of computation is involved.

Implications

The discussion of arithmetic and music in the last chapter conclusively showed, in my view, that the reigning FLN hypothesis is fundamentally wrong. As we saw, not only is there nothing linguistically specific in the formulation of Merge, but the operation of Merge is also implicated in the non-linguistic systems of arithmetic and music. With the growing intuition about the domain-general character of Merge in hand, we could engage in some speculation on the possibility that a similar operation created primitive art and some conception of kinship relations independently of language; perhaps these generative systems were formed before the advent of language in human history.

Hence, there is a real possibility that Principal G, or one of its manifestations such as Merge, may well have applied to distant non-linguistic domains, perhaps even to non-human hominids in the later stages of hominid evolution, as suggested in Chapter 4. Pending deeper empirical and theoretical inquiry on the generative origin of various mental systems, it seems that the model of the origin of the human mind sketched in Chapter 4 is conceptually plausible.

8.1 Stone tools and early mind

In fact, recent archaeological literature seems to indicate some preliminary evidence which may be viewed as promising for developing the conception of the hominid but non-human generative mind (Stout 2011; Joordens et al. 2015). By studying fossils of freshwater shells collected in Trinil, Indonesia, Joordens et al. suggest that 'engraving abstract patterns was in the realm of Asian Homo erectus cognition and neuromotor control'; their study was based on tools made of shells and geometric engravings on them. The discovery is pretty remarkable because these fossils have been dated to over half a million years ago and are linked to the later stages of *Homo erectus*; therefore, such abstract engravings were done much before the advent of *Homo sapiens*.

A more direct evidence of language-like generative ability was reported on the basis of the study of stone tools. For example, archaeologists sometimes explain the making of stone tools and weapons by earlier hominids in terms of hierarchical structures imposed by the early hominid mind. Dietrich Stout (2011) identifies four phases in the production of prehistoric stone tools during the palaeolithic era. Interestingly, even the last of these phases, Late Acheulean, dates back to at least about 300 KY, if not earlier; the earliest, Oldowan, dates between 2.6 and 1.4 MY. The emergence of this ability during the later stages of non-human hominid evolution raises interesting issues about the relation between language and stone tool-making.[1]

Stout's general methodological observation is that the process of making of these tools is better described in terms of 'hierarchical organization that has received much attention in the study of language' under the heading of 'discrete infinity', than in terms of a 'flat' behavioural chain. Following this suggestion, Stout presents a series of diagrams, similar to syntactic trees, covering each of the phases to show how the steps of tool-making might have been organized. For the Late Acheulean shaping of stone tools, Stout identifies at least six levels of hierarchical operations such as hammerstone selection, platform preparation, percussion, target selection, complex flake detachment and suchlike.

I wish to point out that Stout's description of these steps as 'actions' may be misleading. As his comparative example of coffee-making suggests, instructions such as *add sugar* and *grasp spoon* are better understood as thoughts directing actions, rather than as actions themselves, even if these were not designed as thoughts with language-like conceptual content. Of course, these thoughts are such that they are deemed to be followed by suitable actions, yet it is not difficult to see that these actions might fail to ensue despite the thoughts; so these are distinct things. On analogy with the music and art cases, it is plausible to suppose that these thoughts were constituted of action-guiding images, perhaps in the form of abstract visual images. In due course, these thoughts could have been recast in language when the visual images were marked with words.

The difficulty, of course, is that it is hardly feasible to view these thoughts as linguistic in character at such an early date; this could be the reason why Stout is not yet ready to reject the behaviourist framework of action and motor control, even if he replaces flat chains of behaviour with hierarchies. However, a methodologically and conceptually safer alternative is to view these thoughts as composed of icons in some form of visual imagery as suggested, perhaps involving some schematic and graphical symbolism of the sort we use when we give instructions for road direction or cooking, either with gestures or in diagrams.

So the suggestion is that symbol manipulation of visual images is likely to be based on its own 'vocabulary'. An organization of some form of symbolic thought in at least six hierarchical planes, with similar instructions replicated at different levels, suggests computational ordering involving hierarchical operation. In that sense, something language-like seems to have been there, but we do not know how it relates to language primarily because we do not know how to specify the lexicon of the rule system that generated the order.

Interestingly, Tattersall (2019) mentions a debate between two schools of thought in this connection. From the measurements of flow of blood in the brain, archaeologists Uomini and Meyer (2013) conclude that the 'neural processes underpinning language' are the same as those 'underlying Acheulean stone-working techniques'. As we saw from Stout's work, these stone-working techniques date back to 300 KY, much before the estimated origin of human language. Yet, the authors are clearly suggesting that the same, or very similar, structural principles underlie language and Acheulean stone-working.

I am setting a range of intriguing theoretical issues aside, such as the actual formal operations of stone-working that suggest convergence with language, the evidence of neural processes for such operations and the like. So I am not making the empirical claim that Principle G is already operating in Acheulean stone-shaping. In any case, formal research in such obscure domains has not even reached infancy. For conceptual purposes, then, let us adopt the functional idea that similar formal processes were involved in Acheulean stone-shaping, and structuring of thought in human languages, for generating 'longer sequences and sub-sequences' to execute 'complex, goal-directed action', as Uomini and Meyer interpret the processes of stone-working.[2] Whether this functional idea is actually corroborated, as the authors suggest, by measures on flow of blood in the brain is a very different issue.

In contrast to Uomini and Meyer, Tattersall (2019) argues, following Derek Bickerton (1995), that language with its syntax emerged in a catastrophic event, occurring much later in hominid evolution within the first generation of *Homo sapiens*. Therefore, according to Tattersall, Uomini and Meyer have a wrong diagnosis of their findings because such language-like operations could not have been available so early in hominid evolution in the absence of language. Nevertheless, from what we have seen so far, Tattersall could be simply wrong about the origin of language-like operations such as Principle G. This is because, given the untenability of FLN, the saltational emergence of the generative mind could have happened much earlier than what Tattersall believes. The untenability of FLN suggests that the alleged debate could be pointless because it is now credible to suggest that Principle G in the form of a generative operation appeared in the late hominid line much earlier than the emergence of human language to operate on other more 'primitive' mental systems.

The system of graphical representation that is likely to be involved in tool-making thoughts would have been 'primitive' because it is simpler and more easily available than the system of words. Since graphical representations/symbols are directly linked to visual images, much like the auditory images of musical sounds, they are likely to be available to hominids with advanced mental powers, much ahead of words, as Darwin thought (cf. Chapter 4). If these reflections are credible, then we can explain the striking computational features of Acheulean stone tool-making without involving human language.

The conceptual point is that, in his objection to Uomini and Meyer, Tattersall assumes that the required generative device emerged only with the emergence of language. This assumption is in accord with the Chomsky–Hauser FLN hypothesis. Since, according to FLN, the structuring principles of language are restricted to the domain of language, they can only emerge in association with language. In fact, Tattersall almost paraphrases the Chomskyan programme in linguistic theory in evolutionary terms to suggest that language is 'underpinned by an algorithmically simple interface between sensorimotor and conceptual-intentional systems that were co-opted from pre-existing functions or potentials' at some definable point in the human past. Thus, following Chomsky, Tattersall appears to hold that the origins of language and the generative device are coterminous, with the CI and SM systems already in place.

Chomsky, in fact, *identifies* the language faculty with the generative device. As we saw in Chapter 4, Chomsky imagined that 'there were primates with pretty much our sensorimotor (SM) and conceptual-intentional (CI) systems, but no language faculty, and some natural event took place that brought about a mutation that installed a language faculty' (Chomsky 2012, 14–15). Clearly, Chomsky thinks of Merge itself as the language faculty. Since Merge is by definition the language faculty in this view, it is no wonder that Chomsky (1988, 169) thinks of arithmetic as 'essentially an "abstraction" from human language, preserving the mechanism of discrete infinity and eliminating the other special features of language'. So, the aspect of discrete infinity in arithmetic, implemented by Merge, is viewed as borrowed from the language faculty, even though the lexicon of human language does not contain numbers and the successor function (Hiraiwa 2017).

The alleged identification of language with Merge perhaps explains why Katz and Pesetsky (2011) mooted the otherwise puzzling identity thesis between music and language, even though the 'lexicon' of music has nothing to do with the lexicon of language. In this FLN-based perspective, mental domains are identified principally in terms of their structuring principles, notwithstanding differences in their lexicon (Hauser and Watumull 2017); therefore, each domain that contains Merge is thought of as identical with language. Such has been the effect of the FLN hypothesis in this area of cognitive research.

Be that as it may, the rejection of FLN suggests a very different organization of mental systems. Clearly, what Chomsky thinks of narrowly as the language faculty may now be viewed more broadly as the generative mind as it covers a vast range of human-specific thoughts and actions. As to the organization of human language, the alternative perspective suggests that human languages formed when several things fell in one place from pre-existing sources, including, importantly, the structuring principle. We discuss some consequences of this picture for different aspects of linguistic theory in the next three sections.

In the alternative picture, the mental system of language is not identified by its structuring principles at all; in that sense, there is no language faculty, just as there are no music or arithmetic faculties. Instead, there are mental systems that are distinguished in terms of the ways in which pre-existing resources fell in one place. In the case of language, the system formed when Principle G started operating in the domain of words to generate structured expressions at the interfaces with pre-existing systems of CI and SM. The system of music formed when Principle G started operating in the domain of tones. Perhaps the system of numbers formed when, with advanced brains and resources as indicated earlier, hominids developed the conception of individual objects (Strawson 1959), rather than clusters of them; Principle G could have then been applied to help form hierarchies of numbers in a limitless way. This has obvious implications for the origin of the kinship system and the number feature in syntax.

As recounted with suggestive cases of kinship relations, creek-crossing ability, stone tool-making, graphical representations, painting and other generative activities, it is not difficult to appreciate how the presence of Principle G might have helped in the rapid development and expansion of the species. Each of these systems is based on pre-existing resources available to late hominids in the usual course of evolution as Darwin suggested. Hence, except for the saltational emergence of Principle G, no evolutionarily significant notion of emergence or saltation applies to the systems themselves. The generative mind is viewed as constituted of these mental systems with Principle G at the core.

For now, we are investigating whether the erstwhile linguistic principle Merge may be viewed as Principle G. As we saw, the conception of the generative mind was arrived at essentially by incorporating what Chomsky thinks is the faculty of language, namely Merge. In Chomsky's picture, the language-specific principle Merge is viewed as forming linguistic structures by working on the lexicon. In the alternative picture, the domain-general principle adapts to the specific domain of language for generating linguistic structures. As we will soon see, the shift in perspective will not alter the synchronic view of language, provided other things are equal. Nevertheless, the incorporation significantly alters the evolutionary pictures for language and the mind.

Independently of the alternative picture, it is well known that the task of fitting the generative device to the lexicon is stupendous for the language system since there are thousands of languages with their own lexicon that are typically marked by wide differences in sound (Mukherji 2021). Each of these lexical systems is a finite but very large and open-ended store of words as sound–meaning correlations; these finite systems are capable of generating virtually infinite expressions for the interfaces. After decades of exciting work across a wide variety of languages, it has been a marvellous achievement of linguistic theory under the evolving minimalist framework to fit these extremely complex systems of languages to a simple computational principle for optimal generation of structured expressions (Chomsky 2020). Thus, generative grammar was anyway occupied with fitting complex lexical systems to simple structuring principles to solve the tension between descriptive and explanatory adequacies (Chomsky 1965, 1995). Now we can look at the entire effort as fitting the resources of the generative mind to the domain of language.

In the process of solving the internal problem of complexity in linguistic theory, the minimalist framework prepared some basis for explaining the evolution of language: 'the less attributed to genetic information (in our case, the topic of UG) for determining the development of an organism, the more feasible the study of its evolution' (Chomsky 2007). As we saw, the minimalist programme introduced Merge as the relevant component of UG which may be viewed as the simplest computational operation. The search for simplicity in the language system thus led to a more general and biologically viable conception of computational systems. With the incorporation of Merge as a domain-general operation of the generative mind, nothing is therefore left in the domain-specific UG (provided other things are equal); there is no language faculty.

We can now see that the incorporation of Merge enabled the convergence of two biological conditions on mind design. As noted, Principle G was designed to reduce the load of saltation in mental explanation to just one event. Merge was designed to reduce genetic load in linguistic explanation to just one simple combinatorial operation. With the rejection of FLN, the genetic condition on Merge is now available to the generative mind. In effect, the generative mind emerged when a simple combinatorial operation was inserted in the human design in a single saltational event. This is the theoretical interest in finding out if some version of Merge satisfies Principle G.

8.2 Mind and core language

This work is meant to propose and develop a general concept of mind covering all mental systems. Hence, the study of any specific mental system in detail is not part of the agenda. However, since the generative conception of mind is developed in intimate connection with the generative theory of language, some programmatic remarks on the implications of the suggested conception of mind for linguistic inquiry may be appropriate. This is because the rejection of the FLN hypothesis, and the consequent change in perspective on the notion of the language faculty, lead to some alternative conception of how the language system works within the overall framework of the generative mind. The discussion will be restricted basically to sketching a range of unresolved issues that need to be addressed more fully to develop the conception of the generative mind.

As noted, the distinguishing feature of the language system in the emerging picture is the human lexicon, which supplies linguistic information to the interfaces via the Inclusiveness Condition; the distinguishing feature is no longer the structuring principle that puts lexical items together. Suppose we view the lexicon informally as consisting of words which are themselves units of sound–meaning correlation in that each word carries a specific meaning and a specific sound (Mukherji 2021). In that sense, as Thomas Wasow (1985) once pointed out, knowing a language basically means knowing the words of a language; the generative part of language, Principle G, comes for free by human mental design. Near the end, I will make some brief remarks on the unresolved issue of how words might have been formed for the language system to fall in place.

In the new perspective on the language system, the basic difference with earlier conceptions of the language faculty concerns the domain-general character of Principle G; in fact, it is eminently plausible that the principle was available to the human cognitive architecture prior to the evolution of human language. However, once words formed and Principle G started working in the domain of words, the earlier picture of core language continues to obtain. More specifically, since SMT is independent of the timing of language evolution, SMT continues to be available as a synchronic description of the language system as various components of the core language fell in place.

Arguably, the conception of core language via SMT is even more firmly established in this picture because the sole task of Principle G in the language system, as with other mental systems, is to generate structured outputs consisting of domain-specific information so that these structures may be put to use in external contexts; in the language case, the structured outputs display lexical information that are put to use to generate further thoughts in the human mind and action in the world. In other words, Principle G works on the lexicon for constructing resources for other systems to use; that was essentially the conception of core language via SMT. To emphasize, how linguistic structures, that are formed via SMT, are put to use is no part of the description of core language. Earlier, Chomsky used to say that the grammar by itself is 'useless' (Chomsky 1991; Mukherji 2000); in his view, it is an abstract system which needs to be embedded in 'performance systems' to come to life. The core language is useless in the same sense.

The use of linguistic structures may involve interaction with other non-linguistic mental systems such as arithmetic, metrical stress, music and, let us assume, the conceptual system for producing further thought and action of various sorts; for example, the system of metrical stress just adds a metrical contour to the structured thought during articulation. Similarly, the output of core language interacts with conceptual systems to add something like a conceptual order to the thoughts expressed, beginning, say, with the requirements of the theta system. Yet, the point of saying that SM and CI systems are *external* systems is just that they add a variety of information to the expressions of core language so that they may be used in the world for planning, imagination, articulation and dialogue. None of these things are part of the core language at all. It is important to stress this point because it is often missed. For example, Chomsky (2020) and elsewhere stresses strongly that every form of articulation, even in inner speech, is external to the core language. But it is unclear if Chomsky also thinks the same way of the CI systems. I will return to the point briefly.

Apart from non-linguistic mental systems, the language system, of course, interacts with other cognitive systems such as perceptual and emotional systems which are mostly shared with animals; understanding the information content of the linguistic structure, *shadows are lengthening*, certainly requires interaction with the visual system, among others. However, the basic point is that the description of the core language *does not* include either the descriptions of other mental and non-mental systems that interact with language, or the products of such interactions. The core language is all there is to languagehood. This thesis was defended in some detail in Mukherji (2010), in terms of the primacy of grammar. In my view, the strong sense of autonomy of the core language system forestalls any wider conception of language, especially on the meaning-side, in terms of semantic theories, theories of meaning and the like.

However, there is an interesting recent angle on this topic which holds that the language system is *structurally* designed for thought. This novel view does not require that an independent theory of thought be *attached* to the core language system. According to this perspective, the structures generated by the core language are themselves structures of thought or, at least, they strongly determine the essential format of thought. In that sense, this thesis may be viewed as a very strong 'language as thought' hypothesis. It has been forcefully advocated by Wolfram Hinzen in a number of important publications. A detailed review of this work falls outside the scope of this work. However, some general remarks are warranted because the 'language as thought' hypothesis is threatened by the idea that Merge is domain-general.

As Chomsky (2007) reports, Hinzen (2006) suggests that 'syntax carved the path interpretation must blindly follow'. Thus, Berwick and Chomsky (2016, 71) hold that the central components of thought basically follow from the 'optimally constructed generative procedure'. Going a step further, Tattersall (2019) agrees with Hinzen (2012) that thought is inherently grammatical; in fact, Tattersall suggests that language and thought are not two independent domains of inquiry. As Hinzen (2014b) puts it, it is a natural suggestion that the cognitive mechanisms generating human-specific thought and those generating language should be the same.

In the light of the emerging picture of the generative mind, the idea that language was specifically designed for human thought needs clarification. The suggested perspective is trivial if the view is that the operation Merge is designed to generate human thought. As we saw, pending further empirical confirmation, it is plausible to view Merge, as an instance of Principle G, as generating thoughts across all forms of human generative domains: linguistic, non-linguistic, imagistic, graphical, iconic and the like. In this emerging picture, Merge is no doubt sapiens-specific such that it is restricted to all and only human domains for implementing the generative procedure.

However, Hinzen (2014b) clarifies that he is concerned only with thoughts generated in the domain of language. In this narrower perspective, then, the claim is that the design of the language faculty is uniquely suited to determine the structure of linguistic thought. In that sense, the perspective leans on FLN to ground the idea of optimal design in terms of the domain-specificity of the structural principles of language.[3] Since FLN is invalid, the perspective does not obtain in terms of the structuring principle; there are no dedicated structuring principles in any mental domain; there is no UG in language or its equivalent in other systems. Principle G is all we have and this principle is designed to determine the structuring of thought in all mental domains, not just in a specific domain.

A shallower version of the language as thought perspective may still obtain, not in terms of the structuring principles, but vide the domain-specific lexicon in a domain. Thus, suppose, as Merge operates in a specific domain D, it attains a form Merge (D) suitable for that domain. Chomsky (2007) seems to be saying something very similar: 'The conclusion that Merge falls within UG holds whether such recursive generation is unique to FL or is appropriated from other systems. If the latter, there still must be a genetic instruction to use Merge to form structured linguistic expressions satisfying the interface conditions.' So the 'sameness' between grammar and linguistic thought can still be framed in terms of Merge (L), a possible component of UG. Similarly, the structure of musical thought can also be viewed as a product of dedicated principles obtained from the domain-specific lexicon by Merge (M).

To pursue the shallower view for language, one may incorporate, as an informal intuitive guide, notions like object, event, proposition and the like from the familiar uses of language to form semantically loaded computational units such as DP, v*P, CP and so on; in each case, the chosen phases are aligned to specific features of the lexicon, as we saw. For example, Hinzen claims that the phase structure CP, typically triggered by complementizers, is meant to carve out propositional interpretation.[4] Both the empirical and theoretical aspects of this claim of thought–syntax congruence may be questioned. It is theoretically questionable because no theory-internal reasons are given as to why the computational system must generate these structures and not others.[5] Informally, of course, the intuitive answer is that these structures are readable at the CI interface because we happen to use them. But that suggestion assumes knowledge of how semantic information is organized in the CI system and put to use. Until that knowledge is available, DP, CP and the like are suggestive 'Fregean' tools to see whether intuitive semantic ideas may be built into structural configuration.

Empirically, it is deeply controversial which phases actually and uniformly obtain in different languages. Even for something as classical as CP, it is unclear whether all human languages do have CP in a similar form, and even when they do, whether they carry the same semantic interpretation; it is even doubtful if CP is a phase in all languages. These doubts about even the shallower thesis linger because, as Berwick and Chomsky (2016, 7) remark, there is no substantive evidence on how the language-independent thought systems are organized. Until our knowledge improves, core language is all we have.

8.3 MERGE and Principle G

Although the core language obeying SMT is in place, the rejection of FLN places some constraints on how the structuring principles in a domain may be formulated. As the computational device can no longer be viewed as dedicated to language, the language system needs to solve the problem of how a domain-general operation responds to the specific properties of the human lexicon in different domains, just as the general laws of motion operate in the specific environment of viscosity or jet propulsion. For mental domains, the computational system uses the general 'law of generativity' to construct structures in accordance with the properties of domain-specific lexicon. Giving an optimal account of these structures is thus the principal task for linguistic theory, music theory and so on.

We have already had some idea of how the general operation Merge adapts to different lexical domains. Let us review. In arithmetic, Merge operates on a single lexicon, 0, hence Merge adopts the 'pure' form X-in-X to repeatedly generate sets, set of sets and so on. In the case of metrical stress, Merge operates on a pair of 'impoverished lexicon', x and / (with the qualification noted); it is unclear if the pure form X-in-X applies for metrical stress with two items in the lexicon. In the case of music, computation becomes more complex due to a much larger lexicon of over a dozen items. As a result perhaps, computation proceeds in phrases, melodies and motifs. For language, as Arsenijević and Hinzen (2012) insist, there is nothing like 'pure' Merge since linguistic computation proceeds in cyclic phases in a vast lexicon; whether these cycles are semantically motivated, as the authors believe, is a different issue, as noted. It looks like the operation of Merge in a domain is at least partially dependent on the available lexical resources and the constructions thereof.

Drawing on recent controversies on the character of Merge, Chomsky (2020) makes a range of novel suggestions, some of which throw interesting light on how to understand the relation between the generative mind and the specific domain of language falling under it. For example, earlier we saw that Berwick (2011) links Internal Merge (IM) to specific lexical features of language, especially 'edge features' like *wh-* that are associated with nouns. Now, Chomsky (2020) suggests that the construction of the number series in arithmetic is entirely based on IM since there is one lexicon, despite the absence of triggering features. Let us suppose it means that IM applies throughout because the lexical resource is too small for EM to apply. Thus, since 0 is the only term available, IM constructs {0}, {0, {0}} and so on, the successor function. As we will see later, computations on the lexicon for arithmetic automatically guarantees the least set of integers.

For linguistic computation, Chomsky introduces the notion of a workspace (WS) to denote the resources available during computation. Chomsky points out that this aspect of the functioning of Merge was left unspecified in the original formulation, so Merge was viewed as operating without restrictions. Chomsky raises a variety of problems with the unrestricted conception of Merge in the domain of language. Since I am not directly concerned with technical problems in linguistic theory, I will just state two of the major problems and proceed to the conception of restricted Merge, called MERGE.

First, if the WS in Merge is not strictly specified, Merge may freely generate structures that violate well-known linguistic conditions, such as Island Constraint. An island is a closed structure such that extraction of elements from the structure is barred. We can topicalize *Phyllis* in the context *Phyllis, I don't believe that Harold likes___*, but not in **Phyllis, I don't believe the claim that Harold likes___*, because *the claim that Harold likes Phyllis* is an island (Soames and Perlmutter 1979, 284). There are innumerable cases like this. Thus, somehow we need to specify that certain elements are no longer available in WS for merging.

Second, Chomsky argues that unrestricted Merge allows various additional formulations of Merge such as Parallel Merge, Late Merge, Sideward Merge and the like that proliferate in the literature and clutter the theory of universal grammar with unprincipled descriptive devices. Chomsky shows that they are all really consequences of unrestricted Merge; hence they can be eliminated with suitable restrictions on Merge. This leads to impressive simplification and unification of the theory of Merge. Following empirical exposition, Chomsky proposes the following reformulation of Merge in terms of workspaces: MERGE WS [a, b] = WS' [{a, b}, . . .], that is, the workspace containing a and b maps onto a new workspace that contains the merged object {a, b} as before, and some other objects satisfying restrictions on resources, the details of which we set aside.

From the form, it appears that MERGE is a special case of Merge since MERGE contains Merge, in the form of {a, b}, in the new workspace; in other words MERGE is a more restricted version of Merge with WS specified as desired. In that sense, MERGE is costlier than Merge since incorporation of any special condition is always costlier. So it is a bit puzzling that Chomsky thinks of MERGE as the simplest computational principle. Let us suppose then that MERGE is not to be viewed as a special case of Merge, but as the computational operation that *replaces* Merge, since the original Merge is simply inadequate. A discussion of the empirical significance of MERGE for linguistic theory falls beyond the scope of this work.

The only issue I wish to discuss briefly is whether MERGE may be viewed as Principle G, since the original Merge is no longer available for that role. The way we developed the idea of MERGE suggests that MERGE is designed to address linguistically specific problems. Hence, MERGE could be specific to language; as Freidin (2020) puts it, 'recursion for language differs from recursion in general'. So, it looks as though MERGE can only be a linguistically special case of some general operation, if at all. But MERGE cannot be viewed as a special case of Merge, say, Merge (L) as mentioned in Section 8.2, because Merge no longer exists. As a result, Principle G apparently becomes devoid of both Merge and MERGE.

However, as with Merge before, there is nothing in the formulation of MERGE to suggest that MERGE itself is linguistically specific although it does address specific linguistic phenomena. Instead of mapping between sets of lexical objects as in Merge, MERGE simply denotes mapping between workspaces that contain lexical objects and products containing them. Every computational operation, of course, may be viewed as mapping of WSs. For example, Chomsky shows explicitly that the notion of the least set for integers in arithmetic need not be stated anymore because the WS factor in the computation of integers guarantees the least set.

Interestingly, Chomsky suggests a totally general reason for restricting workspaces for computation. In the cited paper and in more recent lectures, Chomsky mentions the work of the neuroscientist Sandi Fong to suggest that the brain is a slow computer and it throws out much of the information that comes in. Therefore, restrictions on the information in the computational workspace is a natural consequence of brain design. Fong's observation obviously applies to any brain, including animal brains. Thus, the suggested restriction on workspaces is a perfectly general idea if the restrictions on computations may be traced to the slowness of the brain.

The idea is intriguing for the Cartesian perspective adopted here because it attempts to unify the processes in the immune or visual systems of animals with computational systems of the generative mind. *Prima facie*, it is not even obvious that the observation holds for all forms of computations in the generative mind. For example, Chomsky contrasts the restricted workspace for human language with the workspace in proof theory in which all constructed items such as axioms and theorems are available all the time. One wonders how the human brain of a mathematician is able to retain the information for computation. However, following the discussion in Chapter 6, let us restrict our attention to systems of I-computation that are naturally displayed by humans as part of their organic design. Since proof theory is an artificial system that works with technological aids, it may be set aside. Therefore, as with Merge, both in its formulation and in its computational requirements the operation MERGE appears to be a general operation of the mind implementing Principle G in mental systems.[6]

Assuming so, there is the need to specify how MERGE applies in different domains, just as there was the need to specify the working of Merge in specific domains. In other words, as with any formulation of Principle G, it needs to be shown how the specific forms of MERGE – MERGE (L), MERGE (M) and the like – are to be derived from the domain-general MERGE (=Principle G) to explain domain-specific forms, if any, of the structured thoughts so generated. We have some explanation of the computational effects of MERGE in arithmetic and language, but we need to be able to extend it to other domains of the mind without enhancing computational resources in view of the saltation problem. As indicated, we need to know how the factor of workspaces, which is the only real difference between Merge and MERGE, plays out in non-linguistic domains beyond arithmetic. Otherwise, we will be stuck with two virtually indistinguishable operations in the generative mind: Merge for, say, music, kinship and a host of other systems where workspaces apparently play no role, and MERGE for language and arithmetic.[7]

8.4 Words and Pair-Merge

Chomsky (2020) officially introduces another basic operation in UG, called *Pair-Merge*: Pair-Merge (a, b) = <a, b>, where a, b, are syntactic objects, but there is no mention of workspace; Pair-Merge generates a sequence, not a set.[8] According to Chomsky, Pair-Merge explained many unresolved linguistic phenomena such as adjuncts and coordinated sequences. As Freidin (2020) shows, adjunct structures like *someone young* cannot be constructed by standard MERGE principally because the two lexical items are in an asymmetric relation. So, Pair-Merge is applied to generate the sequence <someone, young> and then MERGE the whole thing into regular phase-derivation: {met, <someone, young>}. As for structures such as *I met someone young, happy, eager to go to college, tired of wasting his time,* which contain indefinitely long sequences like 'beads on a string', each of the adjectives is predicated on *someone* by Pair-Merge in different dimensions, and then merged in the derivation (Chomsky 2020). Chomsky also extends the use of Pair-Merge to perception verbs and quasi-causatives. So there is a large unification of theory.

Setting details of language-theory aside, the basic issue for us is to form some idea of what it means to have Pair-Merge as an additional operation in the generative mind. There are two concerns: whether Pair-Merge is to be viewed as a general mental operation, and, whether Pair-Merge is needed as an additional operation. As with MERGE, Pair-Merge is introduced in the language system to address a range of specific problems. Yet, there is nothing in the formulation of Pair-Merge to indicate that its application is restricted to language; apparently, Pair-Merge just requires syntactic objects for generating sequenced pairs, wherever these objects are coming from.

As to its possible general application, we may appeal to the general problem about coordination structures that Freidin (2020) cites from Chomsky and Miller (1963): 'in the case of true coordination, by the very meaning of this term, no internal structure should be assigned at all within the sequence of coordinate items.' So Pair-Merge is invoked to address this problem of apparent lack of structure in a cluster of syntactic objects. In that wide sense, it is not difficult to think of such 'structureless' sequences as playing a significant role in many mental domains, especially because they may be inserted inside the main derivation from different planes. For example, it seems that such sequences are inserted inside regular progression in music, say, for ornamentation or highlight; the generative activity of cooking perhaps requires such structures for assembling different flavours, and the like. Suppose so. Pair-Merge thus could well be a general property of the mind.

Regarding the second concern about whether there is another operating principle in the mind apart from MERGE, we need to know where Pair-Merge is coming from. Chomsky mentions that it could be 'easier' to explain the evolution of Pair-Merge than other 'things', meaning perhaps that other options for explaining the data are more problematic in evolutionary terms; but Chomsky did not specify what that easier explanation is. So I will engage in some speculation for what it is worth.

Chomsky does say that Pair-Merge is costlier or more complex than MERGE because Pair-Merge imposes asymmetry, unlike a set. But it is not exactly clear why asymmetry is a necessary feature in general. Perhaps, it is a legibility condition at the CI interface for attaching interpretation to the complex predicate structure of coordinated sequences. If so, then it is a special condition for language, which needs to be explicitly specified in the formulation of Pair-Merge for language. That is one way of keeping the general idea of pair-formation free from the property of asymmetry. Otherwise, we face the saltation problem for Pair-Merge and its relation to the other generative operation MERGE. The point is, Chomsky's contention that it is a genuine advance in explanation to reduce the operations of the linguistic system to just two, MERGE and Pair-Merge, may still be viewed as problematic in the face of the saltation problem.

Let us suppose, then, to begin the speculation, that the special condition for language is attached to some simpler form (a, b) which is then viewed as a property of the generative mind: call it *Binary Merge*. So the idea is that Binary Merge, (a, b), somehow turns into Pair-Merge, <a, b>, in the domain of language. The issue is where Binary Merge is coming from. The most comfortable answer would be that Binary Merge is simply adopted from pre-hominid sources, much like the visual and the emotional systems, and then modified according to human needs; a simpler form is likely to be available more generally.

Recall that Miyagawa and Clarke (2019) suggested that old world monkeys can combine two word-like units, but not three or four, possibly because they don't have Merge or MERGE. Setting aside the intriguing issue of whether whatever the monkeys were combining are genuine words, perhaps we may think of the combinatorial operation in terms of something like Binary Merge. In fact, the presence of such a rudimentary combinatorial operation may help explain various complex behaviours of animals. These may include the sense of causality displayed in behaviour, the use of natural objects as artefacts and so on. If so, then there would not be any need for a saltation to insert the operation in the human mind.

However, I am setting this tempting option aside because we do not know what it means to adopt non-hominid resources for computation on symbolic forms (Miyagawa 2021). Earlier in Chapter 6, we denied the idea of *any* form of computation to animals on this ground. Methodologically then, it is safer to suppose that Binary Merge is closely related to MERGE/Merge in terms of access to symbolic forms. In fact, it would be nice if Binary Merge (a, b) is simply derived from MERGE as a special case for forming pairs, so the dreaded saltation would have been needed only for MERGE, as desired.[9] To emphasize, let us suppose there is only MERGE, with Binary Merge obtaining as a special case of MERGE for forming pairs. Assuming all this, a simple pair-forming operation in the generative mind of some early hominid could go a long way to address a lingering problem for the language system.

From his study of archaeological records, the archaeologist Ian Tattersall has reported over the years that the human species developed two novel capacities: the ability to process information symbolically to form ideas which are then used to form structured articulate language (Tattersall 2016, 2017, 2019). In more familiar terms, humans developed the abilities for word formation and word combination (Mukherji 2021). A word has a sound and a meaning; so we can think of a word as a unit of sound–meaning correlation.

The reason for thinking that words are a novelty in hominid evolution is that, as we saw, it is difficult to assign word-like units even to great apes like chimpanzees (Petitto 2005). In fact, it is unclear if individual concepts, in the human sense, may be assigned to chimpanzees at all. In any case, even if there is a rudimentary set of concepts that may be borrowed from animal resources, there is nothing like human words in the rest of the organic world. So words, in the sense of sound–meaning correlations need to be generated specifically for hominids.

Human language with its syntax emerged when the process of word formation was plugged in to some generative operation for constructing unbounded structures of word combination which Darwin viewed as 'long trains of thought'. In effect, the notion of syntax of human languages consists of two independent parts: words and Principle G. In this picture, Principle G was already available prior to word formation for words to be plugged in to an existing generative process. To emphasize, the process of human language begins with a prior stock of words which are viewed as products of some combinatorial operation that yields sound–meaning correlation. To minimize the saltation problem, it will be useful to think of Principle G, which already exists, as supplying the resources for word formation; that, in gist, is the idea of Binary Merge.

Viewing word-like units of human language itself as a combinatorial product is nothing new. For example, Collins and Kayne (2020) define a lexical item (LI) as a binary set of formal features (FF) and phonological segments (PHON): LI = {FF, PHON}. In their model, lexical items are 'paired up' pre-syntactically in the lexicon. Interestingly, Collins and Kayne use the same notation of set formation for both Merge and the operation that pairs up elements of LI, thereby suggesting that the same syntactic operation Merge obtains throughout. A discussion of this model is beyond the scope of this work.

In our picture, formation of words requires the combination of selections from a stock of concepts and a stock of sounds.[10] We assume that a rudimentary stock of 'hidden' atomic concepts are already in place; the origin of these atomic concepts continues to be a mystery (Berwick et al. 2013). As noted, the stocks of sounds are themselves formed from representations of simple sounds called *phonemes* and combined into more complex forms called *morphemes*; the concepts are then combined with morphemes to generate words. Human languages progressively developed as the stocks of words expanded.

As reflected in Chapter 4, the complex process of origin of words suggests that words appeared much later in hominid evolution than the emergence of the generative mind; the complex process probably led to a 'fallow' before language fully emerged. Also, it is plausible that the process occurred in a very restricted class of advanced hominids, perhaps just one, as most of the other hominids could have died out during the period between the emergence of Principle G and the much later origin of words. Thus, even if Principle G was available to earlier hominids, perhaps as far back as 300 KY as the Late Acheulean stone-shaping suggests, human language appeared much later when a sufficient stock of words was formed, and Principle G started working with this stock (Figure 4.2).

So the net picture is that the pair-forming operation Binary Merge, which is viewed as derived from Merge/MERGE, combines the sound /banana/ with the concept BANANA, whatever it is. In effect, a combinatorial operation (a, b) forms a pair-list (/banana/, BANANA), represented by the word *banana*. The combinatorial operation enables humans, and *only* humans, to symbolize a concept with the mark of a sound; needless to say, sound is not the only marker. In Chapter 5, we saw that Merge has the versatility of combining otherwise unrelated symbols from different domains. Hence, thinking of Binary Merge as a derivative of Merge enables us to view Binary Merge as inheriting this versatility for combining concepts and representations of sound (Mukherji 2021). In this way, the 'sign' signals the presence of 'hidden' thought, as Descartes put it. This form of symbolization could be relatively rare in hominid evolution; for example, it is unclear if musical symbolism has this form.

The unique process of word formation seems to have other interests. Once words were available as sound–meaning pairs, then assuming other human facilities such as demonstration, imitation and the like, some form of communication was also available as an ancillary capability. In this perspective, communication was a bonus, it was not a part of either the basic structure or the primary function of language. This proposal fits well with the widely attested phenomenon that human languages are not very well designed for communication.

In this connection, we recall that we never quite made sense of the idea of what it means for 'pure' concepts to be there, how they 'look' like and what it means to combine them. According to the suggested reading of Darwin's cryptic proposals, words were needed precisely to mark what Descartes called 'hidden thoughts'; the marked objects of thought both acquired perceptual identity and facilitated combinatorial operations. Perhaps, we may be able to strengthen this idea to argue that, in fact, there were no concepts before there were words; human concepts *emerged* with words. No wonder non-human animals do not have concepts like us because they do not have words (Mukherji 2019). Needless to say, more work is needed to develop the idea.

This work suggests that generative principles were operating throughout the evolution of late hominids in various guises, from prehistoric tool-making, cave painting, music, arithmetic to human language. The simplest assumption is that all these human-specific generative operations are executed by a single and the simplest computational operation, Principle G. The existence of Principle G may therefore explain both the unique origin of symbolic forms in humans and the subsequent production of structured thoughts in language that created human history and altered the character of the planet.

Notes

Introduction

1   Chomsky (2006) repeatedly cites the expression 'mirror of mind' and ascribes it to the rationalist tradition, see p. xv and p. 67; also, Chomsky (1975, 4).

Chapter 1

1   Even here, Descartes gives conflicting signals regarding what happens during sleep. In his letter to Arnauld, dated 29 July 1648, he says: 'we do not have any thoughts in sleep without being conscious of them at the moment they occur; though commonly we forget them immediately' (Cottingham et al. 1991, 357). He seems to be suggesting that while having thoughts is always accompanied by consciousness, there is a distinction between two notions of consciousness: sleeping-consciousness and waking-consciousness. In Indian philosophy, the former is often called *Sakshi Chaitanya*, witness consciousness.

2   Block (2009) holds that 'separation of consciousness and cognition has been crucial to the success of the scientific study of consciousness'. We can see that Descartes made the distinction between consciousness and cognition precisely for animals.

3   Davidson (1975) also raised a similar problem, but his formulation of the problem requires the concept of belief, which is problematic (see Mukherji 2017, Chapter 9).

4   As in note 2, Descartes introduced a different notion of consciousness to account for this.

5   By primate talk I mean something like inner symbolic representations since chimpanzees obviously do not speak.

Chapter 2

1   Here is a list of some of the most popular topics in the cognitive sciences selected from top downloads of very influential journals in recent years.
Behavioural and brain sciences: Does the chimpanzee have a theory of mind?;
The magical number 4 in short-term memory: A reconsideration of mental storage capacity; Is the P300 component a manifestation of context updating?; Sex

differences in human mate preferences: Evolutionary hypotheses tested in thirty-seven cultures; The Theory of Event Coding (TEC): A framework for perception and action planning, among others.

Trends in cognitive science: Inhibition and the right inferior frontal cortex: One decade on; Network hubs in the human brain; Human cooperation; Interoceptive inference, emotion, and the embodied self; Bridging animal and human models of exercise-induced brain plasticity; The ventral visual pathway: An expanded neural framework for the processing of object quality; Frontal theta as a mechanism for cognitive control, among others.

Cognition: Alignment as a consequence of expectation adaptation: Syntactic priming is affected by the prime's prediction error given both prior and recent experience; Using regression to measure holistic face processing reveals a strong link with face recognition ability; Rational snacking: Young children's decision-making on the marshmallow task is moderated by beliefs about environmental reliability; The essential moral self, among others.

Mind and language: Against Darwinism; Illocutionary forces and what is said; Dreaming and imagination; Natural compatibilism versus natural incompatibilism; Mirroring, simulating and mindreading; Pretence as individual and collective intentionality; Epistemic Vigilance, among others.

2   Elsewhere, Chomsky (pc) wrote: 'We have no theoretical notion of body (matter, physical) in either the traditional sense or any more modern version. That seems to me to undermine the basis for a "theory of mind" in anything like the form it has ever been conceived, other than as an informal cover term for certain aspects of the world (like a theory of optics, or chemistry).' For Chomsky, then, the mind is to be viewed in terms of the mind–body dualism, failing which, mind can only be viewed as a loose, informal term.

3   In contrast, there are seven entries on vision itself apart from three entries on colour, and individual entries on blindsight, face recognition, gestalt perception, high-level vision, imagery, illusions, lightness perception, machine vision, mid-level vision, perception of motion, eye movements and visual attention, object recognition, oculomotor control, pattern recognition, perceptual development, pictorial art and vision, retina, shape perception, spatial perception and so on. In fact, the cumulative entries for vision are exceeded only by the cumulative entries on language.

4   According to one reviewer, Turing's proposals can only be viewed as 'materialistic'. I don't agree, but the topic is too exegetical to be pursued here. In any case, we have already rejected materialism as an incoherent doctrine in Chapter 1.

5   Similar remarks apply to the recently popular notion of 'the predictive mind' (Hohwy 2014) insofar as this approach in cognitive science studies the stable and largely accurate cognitive functioning of the brain in dealing with the sensory systems. This notion of 'predictive mind' certainly applies to non-human organisms, perhaps more so because that is all they've got for survival.

6   However, I do have sociological and political issues with the use of computerism and neuroscientism as forms of inquiry into the human condition. These technological displays raise fundamental questions of funding of projects, inequities in the distribution of facilities, corporatization of science, massive waste of resources including depletion of resources of the planet and the like. But these concerns are separate from the explanatory issues under discussion.

7   More recently, the linguist Henk Reimsdijk (2007) observed: 'we don't really know how to talk about biological systems that are dealing with DNA, with biochemistry, with cell structure, and so on, and how to connect that sort of thing with the sort of notions that we work with in linguistics.'

8   Hence, despite strong objections raised by some scholars (Martin and Boeckx 2016) against my view on this topic, I see no reason to change my opinion expressed over a decade ago: 'Biolinguistics is currently suggesting that the structure of language may be "perfect" in design, not unlike the arrangement of petals in the sunflower and the double helix of the DNA. Yet these advances have been accomplished essentially independently of the natural sciences, especially biology. In that sense, biolinguistics has initiated a (basic) science in its own terms' (Mukherji, 2010, xv).

9   Or, perhaps, keeping to Fodor's basic idea of 'quick and dirty' modular systems, it is possible to suggest a divide between modular and non-modular systems by appealing to other notions of a domain without affecting the classical notion of a cognitive system. For example, Carruthers (2014) suggests a similar distinction for broad and loose *processing* domains such as learning, conditional and probabilistic reasoning, decision-making and social cognition of various sorts. Clearly, such modules cut across classical domains like language, music, arithmetic, kinship system and the like.

10 Sperber (1994) spawned a huge literature in which scholars argued for a modular distribution of even central systems. This implied that the *entire* mind is modular unlike Fodor who diligently argued for a distinction between modular and non-modular aspects of mind. Since I am sceptical about Fodor's conception of a module, I will not discuss the popular notion of 'massive modularity' of cognitive systems. This is because Sperber's conception of a module is an extension of Fodor's conception involving cognitive impenetrability and the like; thus it carries all the infirmities of Fodor's conception. Moreover, as Fodor himself has pointed out (Fodor 2000), application of Fodor's notion to (central) cognitive systems is illegitimate.

Chapter 3

1   Since we are looking for some naturalistic understanding of the human mind, I am setting aside the artificial computational model suggested by Newell and Simon.

2   In recent work by Hinzen (2007) and Pietroski (2020), among others, semantic issues of reference, predication and truth are addressed with grammatical tools.

However, it is unclear if this work really explores something like CSU or it continues to be 'pure syntax', perhaps 'analogous to phonology', as Chomsky (2020) puts it. I discuss both Pietroski and Hinzen from the perspective of the generative mind in Chapters 7 and 8, respectively.

3 The system continues to remain complex in the desired sense even if we 'take away' the SM interface as suggested in Berwick and Chomsky (2016).

4 As we saw, Descartes makes a distinction between human sensations and general animal sensations because, according to him, thought was included in human sensations. Whether thoughtful sensations arise in the human case because of interaction between language and animal sensation, or because human sensations belong to a different category, appears to be a verbal issue.

5 Another option is to argue, against appearances, that the computational properties of human vision are not shared by non-linguistic species, including early Proto.

Chapter 4

1 I am unsure if Descartes, who was one of the principal proponents of the classical view, would have agreed that sound is ancillary even if he subscribed to the primacy of thought. As repeatedly mentioned in this work, Descartes viewed 'signs' as the only sure 'mark' of 'hidden thoughts'. For most humans, sounds are those signs; however, the deaf and dumb use gestures as signs instead, as Descartes also pointed out. To think of signs as ancillary is to set aside possibly the only entry into the realm of thoughts for Descartes.

2 Adopted from Raichlen and Polk (2013) and *Encyclopaedia Britannica* article on evolution of brain size. https://www.britannica.com/science/human-evolution/Increasing-brain-size.

3 There are many dramatic examples in organic evolution in which a large part of the evolving brain was devoted to a very narrow range of cognitive features, such as the development of highly specialized sensory systems; I discuss the blind mole rat (*Spalax ehrenbergi*) in Chapter 6 to illustrate the point.

4 Elsewhere in the same book, Darwin makes some obscure and assorted unorganized remarks on evolution of language: language has its origins in the 'imitation and modification, aided by signs and gestures, of various natural sounds, the voices of other animals, and man's own instinctive cries' (1871, 56); he also links the evolution of language with sexual selection of vocal chords, and the like.

5 According to Hauser (2016), the language system itself falls under the 'Logic of Thought' which includes concepts and interfaces, among other things. If so, then the CI system was basically empty prior to the emergence of language; hence, there could not have been a wandering hominid with 'pretty much' our CI systems already in place. Berwick and Chomsky cannot have it both ways.

6   I don't know if chimpanzees can combine colour concept with material concept, material concept with place concept; as far as I know, Elizabeth Spelke's work on this topic (Spelke 2000) does not go beyond rats. But we are not talking about a chimpanzee, we are thinking of Darwin's Proto, with nearly four times the size of a chimp's brain which grew for six million years.

7   'It could turn out that there would be richer or more appropriate mathematical ideas that would capture other, maybe deeper properties of language than context-free grammars do' (Chomsky et al. 1982).

8   I have in mind something like the Chomsky Hierarchy which describes a range of finite, transfinite and infinite symbol systems (Chomsky 1956, 1963, etc.). The idea is that, while infinite systems cover finite systems, the reverse is not true. Since Principle G is viewed as an infinite generator, it could generate all the finite states also. The issue is too technical to be pursued here; see Uriagereka (2008), Hauser and Watumull (2017) for similar ideas.

9   For example, in her study of the origins of the Khoisan language group, Rini Huybregts (2017) argues that even though the internal computation of thought appears to have originated much earlier, externalization took place much later. The proposed narrative still requires that the hierarchical structured thoughts already in place be transferred somehow to the linear articulatory system later.

10 I am not suggesting that the shift from word formation to word combination with full syntactic structure is the only reason for the fallow. As Huybregts (2017) points out, the step from internal structures to externalized (articulated) structures might also have taken considerable time. However, as indicated, there are reasons to be sceptical about a prolonged period of 'silent' use of language; a language without the resources for externalization cannot be used between conspecifics.

Chapter 5

1   Setting 'fringe' expressions, such as alternative communication aids, aside (Chomsky, pc).

2   I am setting aside the more technical problem that X-bar theory wrongly assumes *endocentricity* for all constructions (Chomsky 2013, 2020).

3   I am setting aside the problematic case of polysynthetic languages where, arguably, the strict separation between lexicon and hierarchical organization of lexical elements generated by the computational system is not directly visible, as we saw. However, computational hierarchy may still be located abstractly as Julia Legate's work on Warlpiri suggests (Chomsky pc); see Legate (2003).

4   As one referee correctly pointed out, the Inclusiveness Condition was proposed earlier than Chomsky (1995b). However, as long as X-bar theory with its bar-levels

continued, the condition was not strictly implemented. In my view, it became fully operational only with Bare Phrase Structures. The issue is too exegetical for discussion here.

5   For more recent and alternative formulations of Merge, see Chapter 8 for some discussion.

6   Needless to say, the conceptual attraction of Berwick's example does not depend on whether it is a valid description of SM. We can draw a nice picture of unicorns without the existence of unicorns.

Chapter 6

1   In the cited text, Chomsky did not explain what he meant by 'relevant' computation. It could be that Chomsky had in mind the variety of computational procedures listed in the *Chomsky Hierarchy*, not all of which are equivalent to Merge, hence not relevant. See Chomsky (1956), Miller and Chomsky (1963), Uriagereka (2008), Berwick and Chomsky (2016).

2   This issue is also different from the more interesting issue of whether recursive Merge found in language could have originated from earlier human non-linguistic domains such as tool-making and music. The thought was mooted in Chapter 4; we discuss it in Chapters 7 and 8.

3   Basically, similar remarks apply to Hornstein and Pietroski (2009) in which they propose Combine (=Merge) as a complex operation consisting of Concatenation and labelling. I will not discuss their proposal fully because, as we saw, labelling is no longer viewed as a primitive operation in the system. Further, as Chomsky pointed out, Concatenation is a more complex operation than Merge. These remarks extend to Hornstein and Pietroski's proposal about minimal semantics as well.

4   To be fair, the authors do suggest these studies to be a testing case for determining the uniqueness of human grammar. However, until the case for human uniqueness is made, the suggestion does amount to ascribing minimalist computation to insects.

5   As an aside, for what it may be worth, personally I do not find much interest in the historical survey of mathematical logic for the project in hand since it seems to me that ideas of mathematical induction and recursive functions presuppose some intuitive underlying notion of Merge as a basic human endowment. In other words, only an organism endowed with Merge may form some intuition about 'infinite in finite means' and the like to be able to formulate functions with recursive clauses, as in mathematical induction. To put the intuition somewhat differently, it is unclear how to conceptualize some general notion of recursion without the notion of Merge subliminally in mind. For example, if we think of elementary arithmetical operations as recursive, we already know they are all instances of Merge in the domain of

numbers. In that sense, the concept of Merge precedes the mathematical concept of recursion.

In any case, as Berwick and Chomsky (2019) have argued recently, much of the history of mathematical linguistics, which was based on fragments of formal languages developed by logicians in terms of rewriting rules, may be viewed as irrelevant once we have the primitive operation Merge in hand (Mukherji 2010, Chapter 2).

6 পাখীরে দিয়েছ গান, গায় সেই গান
   তার বেশী করে না সে দান।
   আমারে দিয়েছ স্বর, আমি তার বেশী করি দান
   আমি গাই গান। (রবীন্দ্রনাথ ঠাকুর, *বলাকা,* ২৮)

7 It is thus rather puzzling that even expert linguists fall into the illusion that birdsong is an example of 'pure syntax' just because young birds try to imitate them.

8 From the opposite direction, analogous problems seem to clutter much of recent thinking on music. Since music obviously displays complex sound patterns, but no specific meaning in the linguistic sense can be assigned to the units of music, music is supposed to have only phonocoding, phono-syntax, and the like (Asano and Boeckx 2015). It is as if music has only half of 'real' syntax. Needless to say, linguistic syntax is taken to be the real syntax.

9 This result falls in place with Daniel Povinelli's classic work suggesting that apes cannot demonstrate individual objects (Povinelli 2000). In a sense, chimpanzees have nothing to point to.

Chapter 7

1 Similar considerations appear to lead Hauser and Watumull (2017) to suggest that there is a 'universal generative faculty' (UGF) that governs the domains of language, mathematics, morality and music. However, apart from the familiar general suggestion that the universal generative faculty is something like a Universal Turing Machine and that Merge 'may also play a role in moral judgment' and so on, the authors fail to offer any principled explanation of why the UGF covers exactly the four domains mentioned. There are a variety of other problems with the proposal.

2 Interestingly, although the digits 1, 2, 3 and so on are called 'Arabic numbers', the Arabic language has language-specific expressions for them; in Roman, they are written as *wahid, ithnan, thalathah* and so on. 'Arabic numbers' probably refer to the country of origin, not the language.

3 By drawing attention to the structural convergence, I am not claiming that Pesetsky's selection of musical heads is correct or that the piece of music has the

suggested structure description; that is for the music theorists to decide (Mukherji 2013; Lerdahl 2013, 2015).

4 So, I will not comment on the voluminous and complex literature on the overall organization of music from the multidisciplinary dimensions of acoustics, evolution, neural architecture and cognition (Peretz 2001; Fitch 2006; Patel 2008, 2019; Asano and Boeckx 2015 etc.). But I do not deny that ultimately a theoretically salient account of mental representation in music depends on these music-internal factors.

5 Although Lerdahl and Jackendoff (1983) assure readers that 'the process of subordination (or domination) can continue indefinitely' (p. 13) and describe how 'recursive elaboration' may look like in music (p. 214), there is no principled explanation of why these things happen.

6 The absence of language-like semantics in music leads some authors such as Vijaykrishnan (2007) to conclude that music has only 'phonetics'. For Carnatic music, he declares that it has neither syntax nor semantics. I have critically discussed Vijaykrishnan's optimality theory of Carnatic music in Mukherji (2009b).

7 In more recent work, Chomsky (2020) suggests that IM is, in fact, more fundamental – it is less costly as it operates on a restricted workspace. I discuss the idea briefly in Chapter 8.

8 Earlier Pesetsky (2007) argued that the transfer of a syntactic phrase to the rhythmic phrase required Internal Merge. See Mukherji (2010) for a criticism of this argument.

9 It follows that, if anything, musical structures require something like interpretive systems internal to the faculty of music (Quintana 2019). In Mukherji 2010, Chapter 7, these systems were called 'interface conditions driven by the faculty of music', FMI.

10 'Arguably' because some authors do hold that grammatical computation proceeds with an eye on referential properties to be established within a wider notion of grammar (Hinzen and Sheehan 2013). I am setting this suggestion aside because it is unclear to me if the authors work with the same conception of grammatical organization of language. I return to the issue for a brief discussion near the end.

11 Needless to say, Beethoven is mentioned just to indicate the soundless context of musical composition; the explanation of how the mind of a musical genius works is an entirely different issue, even if feasible.

12 According to some music psychologists, the understanding involved of musical sounds is made up of representation of acoustic properties such as timbre, pitch and volume, but involve some cognitive categories as well like consonance, dissonance, tonal centre, semitone and the like. (Krumhansl et al. 2000, 14).

13 Even though these images are abstract in the sense indicated, there is no mystery about them since they are fundamentally guided – but not wholly determined, as noted – by physical principles of sound such as certain parts of the Fourier series.

14 It also raises uneasy questions about the species-specificity of these images.

15 Recall the fascinating scene near the end of Foreman's film *Amadeus* where Mozart on his deathbed dictates his last music to Salieri. Mozart was portrayed as uttering things like *C Major*, *measure five* and the like. What was Mozart dictating these things *from*?

16 If valid, this consequence raises interesting prospects for addressing the problem of 'dark matter'. I will return to the possibility near the end of Chapter 8.

17 As with the literature on formal semantics, Pietroski seems to have exactly two options. First, he can start afresh with Merge on a redesigned (first-order) lexicon, somewhat like Thornton's scheme, but that will not give him the neo-Davidsonian structure he wants, apart from raising disciplinary problems. Second, he can use, as he does, the formal computational apparatus of first-order logic to attach his semantic structure to the syntactic structure already reached by Merge. But then, the effort will be a duplication of the computation of structured thought already constructed within the mental system of language.

18 Some of this work leans on Fodor's alleged idea of a separate existence of 'language of thought', see Fodor (2008). As discussed in Chapter 3, Fodor's ideas do not reveal any independent evidence for a generative conceptual structure.

19 In a Google search on 'bridges made by animals' to verify the point, fifty admirable examples were displayed on human construction of bridges for safe animal-crossing.

20 One of the other domains frequently mentioned in Jones (2010) is that of physical space that is characterized by various spatial terms denoting spatial concepts.

21 Creation of art objects with pixels and graphics in a digital computer is a very different issue.

Chapter 8

1 Interestingly, Chomsky (2020) mentions the Blombos Cave in South Africa as the only site for prehistoric symbolic objects. The engravings in the Blombos caves are dated to about 73,000 years ago; by that time, of course, both *Homo sapiens* and human language were firmly in place.

2 The authors have other things to say about 'proto-speech, proto-sign, or multimodal communication', which I am setting aside.

3 In the light of the 'language as thought' hypothesis, it is now clear why some form of FLN is needed to distinguish between recursion in arithmetic and recursion in language as in (Arsenijević and Hinzen 2012).

4 Hinzen (2016) even claims that some of the basic referential features of linguistic thought may be predicted from grammatical configurations.

5 Chomsky (2020) suggests that in a genuine explanation it should be possible to predict the structure of a phase from computational principles alone, which he calls a 'third factor'.

6 If it is not, that is, if the restriction on workspaces is not needed in some domain D, then MERGE cannot be viewed as the general operation meeting Principle G. In that case, there must be some other operation of which MERGE is a special case for language. The burden is certainly on the linguist.

7 For what it is worth, my own hunch is that it is theoretically more satisfying to keep to the original Merge and explain the restrictions in each domain in terms of domain-specific properties of workspaces. There is a strong intuition that how the workspaces get restricted is closely related to the specific lexicon in a domain, even if there is a general basis for restricting workspaces due to the restrictions of the brain.

8 Since there is no distinction between Pair-MERGE and Pair-Merge, I will keep to the latter unlike Freidin (2020) who prefers the former. Earlier, Chomsky also used List Merge, apart from MERGE and Pair-Merge (Langendoen 2003). In Chomsky (2020), List Merge is no longer used.

9 As noted in Chapter 4, it is inelegant design to have a small door and a big door in the same dog house; in contrast, a chef's knife both cuts meat and slices ginger. See note 29 regarding the Chomsky Hierarchy.

10 The informal notion of 'word' is needed as a starter in any case to form the roots of a language, which are then categorized in grammar as nouns, verbs and so on; these syntactic categories carry formal features such as number, person, tense and the like.

References

Adger, D. and P. Svenonius (2015). 'Linguistic explanation and domain specialization: A case study in bound variable anaphora'. *Frontiers in Psychology*, 6: 1421. doi:10.3389/fpsyg.2015.01421

Andrews, K. (2015). *The Animal Mind: An Introduction to the Philosophy of Animal Cognition*. London: Routledge.

Arnauld, A. and C. Lancelot (1975). *General and Rational Grammar: The Port-Royal Grammar*. J. Rieux and B. Rollin (Trans.). The Hague: Mouton.

Arsenijević, B. and W. Hinzen (2012). 'On the absence of X-within-X recursion in human grammar'. *Linguistic Inquiry*, 43 (3): 423–40.

Asano, R. and C. Boeckx (2015). 'Syntax in language and music: What is the right level of comparison?'. *Frontiers in Psychology*, 6: 942. doi:10.3389/fpsyg.2015.00942

Aubert, M., A. Brumm, M. Ramli, T. Sutikna, E. Saptomo and B. Hakim (2014). 'Pleistocene cave art from Sulawesi, Indonesia'. *Nature*, 514: 223–7. doi:10.1038/nature13422

Baker, M. (2001). *The Atoms of Language: The Mind's Hidden Rules of Grammar*. New York: Basic Books.

Banerjee, K. and P. Bloom (2013). 'Would Tarzan believe in God? Conditions for the emergence of religious belief'. *Trends in Cognitive Science*, 17 (1): 7–8.

Baron-Cohen, S., A. Leslie and U. Frith (1985). 'Does the autistic child have a "theory of mind"?' *Cognition*, 21 (1): 37–46.

Barrett, H. and R. Kurzban (2006). 'Modularity in cognition: Framing the debate'. *Psychological Review*, 113 (3): 628–47.

Beckers, G., J. Bolhuis, K. Okanoya and R. Berwick (2012). 'Birdsong neurolinguistics: Songbird context-free grammar claim is premature'. *Neuroreport*, 23: 139–45.

Behar, D., R. Villems, H. Soodyall, J. Blue-Smith, L. Pereira, E. Metspalu, R. Scozzari, H. Makkan, S. Tzur, D. Comas, J. Bertranpetit, L. Quintana-Murci, C. Tyler-Smith, R. Spencer Wells, S. Rosset and The Genographic Consortium (2008). 'The dawn of human matrilineal diversity'. *The American Journal of Human Genetics*, 82: 1130–40.

Benítez-Burraco, A. and E. Murphy (2016). 'The oscillopatic nature of language deficits in autism: From genes to language evolution'. *Frontiers in Human Neuroscience*, 10: 120. doi:10.3389/fnhum.2016.00120

Bennett, M. and P. Hacker (2003). *Philosophical Foundations of Neuroscience*. London: Blackwell Publishing.

Bermudez, J. (2003). *Thinking Without Words*. New York: Oxford University Press.

Berwick, R. (2011). 'All you need is merge'. In A. M. Di Sciullo (Ed.), *Biolinguistic Investigations*, 461–91. Oxford: Oxford University Press.

Berwick, R., G. Beckers, K. Okanoya and J. Bolhuis (2012). 'A bird's eye view of human language evolution'. *Evolutionary Neuroscience*, 4: Article 5. doi:10.3389/fnevo.2012.00005

Berwick, R. and N. Chomsky (2016). *Why Only Us: Language and Evolution*. Cambridge, MA: MIT Press.

Berwick, R. and N. Chomsky (2019). 'All or nothing: No half-merge and the evolution of syntax'. *PLOS Biology*, 27 November. doi:10.1371/journal.pbio.3000539

Berwick, R., A. Friedrici, N. Chomsky and J. Bolhuis (2013). 'Evolution, brain and the nature of language'. *Trends in Cognitive Science*, 17: 2.

Bickerton, D. (1995). *Language and Human Behaviour*. Seattle: University of Washington Press.

Block, N. (2009). 'Comparing the major theories of consciousness'. In M. Gazzaniga (Ed.), *The Cognitive Neurosciences, IV*, 1111–22. Cambridge, MA: MIT Press.

Boeckx, C. (2017). 'Not only us'. *Inference*, 3 (1, April).

Boghossian, P. (2007). 'Explaining musical experience'. In K. Stock (Ed.), *Philosophers on Music: Experience, Meaning, and Work*, 117–31. Oxford: Oxford University Press.

Bolender, J. (2007). 'Prehistoric cognition by description: A Russellian approach to the upper palaeolithic'. *Biology and Philosophy*, 22: 383–99. doi:10.1007/s10539-006-9058-2

Bolhuis, J., I. Tattersall, N. Chomsky and R. Berwick (2014). 'How could language have evolved?' *PLOS Biology*, 12: 8. Available online: www.plosbiology.org.

Boruah, B. (2007). 'Language, mind and consciousness'. *Journal of Indian Council of Philosophical Research*, 24 (4): 91–111.

Bošković, Z. (2019). 'Generalized asymmetry'. Available online: https://ling.auf.net/lingbuzz/004711

Bracken, H. (1993). 'Some reflections on our sceptical crisis'. In E. Reuland and W. Abraham (Eds), *Knowledge and Language*, Vol. I, 59–70. Dordrecht: Kluwer Academic Publishers.

Brentano, F. (1874). *Psychology from an Empirical Standpoint*. Leipzig: Duncker and Humblot. Trans. A. Rancurello, D. Rerrell and L. McAlister. London: Routledge, 1973.

Bronchti, G., P. Heil, R. Sadka, A. Hess, H. Scheich and Z. Wollberg (2002). 'Auditory activation of "visual" cortical areas in the blind mole rat (*Spalax ehrenbergi*)'. *European Journal of Neuroscience*, 16: 311–29.

Brooks, A., J. Yellen, R. Potts, A. Behrensmeyer, A. Deino, D. Leslie, S. Ambrose, J. Ferguson, F. d'Errico, A. Zipkin, S. Whittaker, J. Post, E. Veatch, K. Foecke and J. Clark (2018). 'Long-distance stone transport and pigment use in the earliest Middle Stone Age'. *Science*, 360 (6 April): 90–4.

Brooks, R. (1991). 'Intelligence without representation'. *Artificial Intelligence*, 47: 139–59.

Brown, S. (2000). 'The "musilanguage" model of music evolution'. In N. Wallin, B. Merker and S. Brown (Eds), *The Origins of Music*, 271–300. Cambridge, MA: MIT Press.

Butterfill, S. and I. Apperly (2013). 'How to construct a minimal theory of mind?', *Mind and Language*, 28 (5, November): 579–698.

Carey, S. (1985). *Conceptual Change in Childhood*. Cambridge, MA: MIT Press.

Carey, S. (2009). *The Origin of Concepts*. Oxford: Oxford University Press.

Carruthers, P. (2009). 'How we know our own minds'. *Behavioural and Brain Sciences*, 32: 121–82.

Carruthers, P. (2014). 'The fragmentation of reasoning'. In P. Quintanilla, C. Mantilla and P. Cépeda (Eds), *Cognición social y lenguaje. La intersubjetividad en la evolución de la especie y en el desarrollo del niño*, 113–23. Lima: Pontificia Universidad Católica del Perú.

Carroll, S. (2005). *Endless Forms Most Beautiful*. New York: Norton.

Cassam, Q. (2008). 'Contemporary responses to Descartes' philosophy of mind'. In J. Broughton and J. Carriero (Eds), *A Companion to Descartes*, 482–95. London: Blackwell.

Chalmers, D. (1996). *The Conscious Mind: In Search of a Fundamental Theory*. Oxford: Oxford University Press.

Cherniak, C. (2005). 'Innateness and brain-wiring optimization: Non-genomic nativism'. In A. Zilhao (Ed.), *Evolution, Rationality and Cognition*, 103–12. London: Routledge.

Cheung, A., L. Hiby and A. Narandra (2012). 'Ant navigation: Fractional use of the home vector'. *PLoS One*, 7 (11, 29 Nov). doi:10.1371/journal.pone.0050451

Chomsky, N. (1956). 'Three models for the description of language'. *IRE Transactions on Information Theory*, 2 (3): 113–24. doi:10.1109/TIT.1956.1056813

Chomsky, N. (1957). *Syntactic Structures*. The Hague: Mouton.

Chomsky, N. (1963). 'Formal properties of grammars'. In R. Luce, R. Bush and E. Galanter (Eds), *Handbook of Mathematical Psychology*, Volume II. New York; London: John Wiley and Sons, Inc., 323–418.

Chomsky, N. (1965). *Aspects of the Theory of Syntax*. Cambridge, MA: MIT Press.

Chomsky, N. (1966). *Cartesian Linguistics*. New York: Harper and Row.

Chomsky, N. (1972a). *Language and Mind*. New York: Harcourt Brace Jovanovich (expanded Edition).

Chomsky, N. (1972b). 'Remarks on nominalization'. In *Studies On Semantics In Generative Grammar*, 11–61. The Hague: Mouton.

Chomsky, N. (1975). *Reflections on Language*. New York: Pantheon Press.

Chomsky, N. (1980). *Rules and Representations*. Oxford: Basil Blackwell.

Chomsky, N. (1981). *Lectures on Government and Binding*. Dordrecht: Foris.

Chomsky, N. (1986). *Knowledge of Language*. New York: Praeger.

Chomsky, N. (1988). *Language and the Problem of Knowledge: The Managua Lectures*. Cambridge, MA: MIT Press.

Chomsky, N. (1991). 'Linguistics and cognitive science: Problems and mysteries'. In A. Kasher (Ed.) *The Chomskyan Turn*, 26–53. Oxford: Basil Blackwell.

Chomsky, N. (1993). 'A minimalist programme for linguistic theory'. *MIT Working Papers In Linguistics*, reprinted as Chapter 3 in Chomsky (1995a).

Chomsky, N. (1994a). *Language and Thought*. London: Moyer Bell.

Chomsky, N. (1994b). 'Bare phrase structure'. *MIT Working Papers In Linguistics*, reprinted in G. Webelhuth (Ed.) *Government and Binding Theory and The Minimalist program*. Oxford: Basil Blackwell.

Chomsky, N. (1994c). 'Naturalism and dualism in the study of language and mind'. *International Journal of Philosophical Studies*, 2: 181–209.

Chomsky, N. (1995a). *The Minimalist Program*. Cambridge, MA: MIT Press.

Chomsky, N. (1995b). 'Language and nature'. *Mind*, 104: 1–61.

Chomsky, N. (1997). 'Language and mind: Current thoughts on ancient problems, Parts 1 and 2'. Reprinted in L. Jenkins (Ed.), *Variation and Universals in Biolinguistics*. Amsterdam: Elsevier, 2004, 379–405.

Chomsky, N. (2000a). *The Architecture of Language*. N. Mukherji, B. N. Patnaik and R. K. Agnihotri (Eds). New Delhi: Oxford University Press.

Chomsky, N. (2000b). *New Horizons in the Study of Language and Mind*. Cambridge: Cambridge University Press.

Chomsky, N. (2000c). 'Minimalist inquiries'. In R. Martin, D. Michaels and J. Uriagereka (Eds), *Step by Step*, 89–155. Cambridge, MA: MIT Press.

Chomsky, N. (2001). 'Language and the rest of the world'. *Bose Memorial Lecture in Philosophy*, Delhi University, 4 November.

Chomsky, N. (2002). *On Nature and Language*. Cambridge: Cambridge University Press.

Chomsky, N. (2004). *The Generative Enterprise Revisited*. Berlin: Mouton de Gruyter.

Chomsky, N. (2005). 'Three factors in language design'. *Linguistic Inquiry*, 36 (1): 1–22.

Chomsky, N. (2006). *Language and Mind*. Enlarged 3rd edn. Cambridge: Cambridge University Press.

Chomsky, N. (2007). 'Approaching UG from below'. In U. Sauerland and H. Gärtner (Eds), *Interfaces + Recursion = Language? Chomsky's Minimalism and the View from Syntax-Semantics*. De Gruyter Mouton. doi:10.1515/9783110207552

Chomsky, N. (2008). 'On phases'. In R. Freidin, C. Otero and M. Zubizarreta (Eds), *Foundational Issues in Linguistic Theory. Essays in Honor of Jean-Roger Vergnaud*, 133–66. Cambridge, MA: MIT Press.

Chomsky, N. (2012). *The Science of Language: Interviews with James McGilvray*. Cambridge: Cambridge University Press.

Chomsky, N. (2013). 'Problems of projection'. *Lingua*, 130: 33–49.

Chomsky, N. (2014). 'Minimal recursion: Exploring the prospects'. In T. Roeper and M. Speas (Eds), *Recursion: Complexity in Cognition. Studies in Theoretical Psycholinguistics*, Vol. 43. Switzerland: Springer International Publishing.

Chomsky, N. (2015). *What Kind of Creatures are We?* New York: Columbia University Press.

Chomsky, N. (2018). 'Two notions of modularity'. In R. Almeida and L. Gleitman (Eds), *On Concepts, Modules, and Language: Cognitive Science at Its Core*, 25–40. New York: Oxford University Press.

Chomsky, N. (2020). *The UCLA Lectures*. Available online: https://lingbuzz.net/lingbuzz/005485

Chomsky, N. and C. Collins (2021). 'Interview on Formal Semantics'. Available online: https://www.dropbox.com/s/638rxon8tslxp00/Chomsky%20Semantics%20June%2028%202021.pdf?dl=0

Chomsky, N., A. Gallego and D. Ott (2019). 'Generative grammar and the faculty of language: Insights, questions, and challenges'. *Catalan Journal of Linguistics, Special Issue*, 229–61. doi:10.5565/rev/catjl.288

Chomsky, N., R. Huybregts and H. Riemsdijk (1982). *The Generative Enterprise*. Dordrecht: Foris.

Chomsky, N. and G. Miller (1963). 'Introduction to the formal analysis of natural languages'. In R. D. Luce, R. Bush and E. Galanter (Eds), *Handbook of Mathematical Psychology*, Vol. 2, 269–322. New York and London: John Wiley and Sons, Inc.

Church, A. (1936). 'An unsolvable problem of elementary number theory'. *American Journal of Mathematics*, 58: 345–63.

Churchland, P. (1984). 'Eliminative materialism'. In P. Churchland (Ed.), *Matter and Consciousness: A Contemporary Introduction to the Philosophy of Mind*, 43–50. Cambridge, MA: MIT Press.

Churchland, P. (1986). *Neurophilosophy*. Cambridge, MA: MIT Press.

Churchland, P. and R. Grush (1999). 'Computation and the brain'. In R. Wilson and F. Keil (Eds), *MIT Encyclopaedia of the Cognitive Sciences*, 155–8. Cambridge, MA: MIT Press.

Churchland, P. and T. Sejnowski (1992). *The Computational Brain*. Cambridge, MA: MIT Press.

Clark, B. (2013). 'Syntactic theory and the evolution of syntax'. *Biolinguistics*, 7: 169–97. Available online: http://www.biolinguistics.eu

Clarke, D. (2003). *Descartes's Theory of Mind*. Oxford: Oxford University Press.

Collins, C. and R. Kayne (2020). 'Towards a theory of morphology as syntax'. Available online: https://lingbuzz.net/lingbuzz/005693

Corballis, M. (2011). *The Recursive Mind*. Princeton: Princeton University Press.

Cottingham, J., R. Stoothoff, D. Murdoch and A. Kenny (Eds) (1991). *The Philosophical Writings of Descartes, Volume III: The Correspondence*. Cambridge: Cambridge University Press.

Crow, T. (2010). 'The nuclear symptoms of schizophrenia reveal the four quadrant structure of language and its deictic frame'. *Journal of Neurolinguistics*, 23: 1–9.

Crow, T. J. (2008). 'The "big bang" theory of the origin of psychosis and the faculty of language'. *Schizophrenia Research*, 102: 31–52.

Cudworth, R. (1731/1996). 'A treatise concerning eternal and immutable morality'. In S. Hutton (Ed.) *Cambridge Texts in the History of Philosophy*, 1–152. Cambridge: Cambridge University Press.

Curtiss, S. (2013). 'Revisiting modularity: Using language as a window to the mind'.
   In M. Piattelli-Palmerini and R. Berwick, (Eds), *Rich Languages From Poor Inputs*,
   68–96. Oxford: Oxford University Press.

Darwin, C. (1871). *The Descent of Man, and Selection in Relation to Sex*. London: John
   Murray.

David-Gray, Z., J. Janssen, W. DeGrip, E. Nevo and R. Foster (1998). 'Light detection in
   a "blind" mammal'. *Nature Neuroscience*, 1 (8): 655–6.

Davidson, D. (1970/2001). 'Mental events'. In D. Davidson (Ed.), *Essays on Actions and
   Events*, 170–86. Oxford: Clarendon Press.

Davidson, D. (1974/1984). 'On the very idea of a conceptual scheme'. Reprinted in D.
   Davidson, *Inquiries into Truth and Interpretation*. Oxford: Clarendon Press.

Davidson, D. (1975). 'Thought and talk'. In S. Guttenplan (Ed.), *Mind and Language*.
   Oxford: Clarendon Press. Reprinted in D. Davidson. *Inquiries into Truth and
   Interpretation*. Oxford: Clarendon Press, 1984.

Davidson, D. (1984). 'The method of truth in metaphysics'. Reprinted in D. Davidson.
   Inquiries into Truth and Interpretation. Oxford: Clarendon Press.

Davies, M. (1989). 'Tacit knowledge and subdoxastic states'. In A. George (Ed.),
   Reflections on Chomsky, 131–52. Oxford: Basil Blackwell.

Dediu, D. and S. Levinson (2013). 'On the antiquity of language: The reinterpretation of
   Neandertal linguistic capacities and its consequences'. *Frontiers in Psychology*, 4: 397.
   doi:10.3389/fpsyg.2013.00397

Dehaene, S. (2011). *The Number Sense: How the Mind Creates Mathematics*. Oxford:
   Oxford University Press.

DeMarco, D. (1999). 'Descartes, mathematics and music'. In B. Sweetman (Ed.), *The
   Failure of Modernism: The Cartesian Legacy and Contemporary Pluralism*, 35–44.
   Indiana: American Maritain Association.

Dennett, D. (1991).*Consciousness Explained*. Boston: Little Brown and Co.

Dennett, D. (1995). *Darwin's Dangerous Idea*. New York: Simon and Schuster.

Descartes, R. (1637/1641). *Discours de la Méthode* 1637; *Meditationes de Prima
   Philosophia* 1641. English Tr. F. E. Sutcliffe, *Discourse on Method and The
   Meditations*. Penguin Books, 1968.

Descartes, R. (1961). *Compendium of Music*. W. Robert and C. Kent (Eds). American
   Institute of Musicology.

Descartes, R. (1970). *Descartes: Philosophical Letters*. A. Kenny (Trans. and Ed.).
   Oxford: Clarendon Press.

De Wall, F. (2016). *Are We Smart Enough to Know How Smart Animals Are?* New York:
   W. W. W. Norton.

Diesing, M. (1992). *Indefinites*. Cambridge, MA: MIT Press.

Ding, N., L. Melloni, H. Zhang, X. Tian and D. Poeppel (2015). 'Cortical tracking
   of hierarchical linguistic structures in connected speech'. *Nature Neuroscience*,
   7 December. doi:10.1038/nn.4186

Di Scuillo, A. (2005). *Asymmetry in Morphology*. Cambridge, MA: MIT Press.

Di Scuillo, A. (2015). 'On the domain specificity of the human language faculty and the effects of principles of computational efficiency: Contrasting language and mathematics'. *Revista Linguística*, 11 (1): 28–56.

Elsabbagh, M. and A. Karmiloff-Smith (2004). 'Modularity of mind and language'. In K. Brown (Ed.), *Encyclopaedia of Language and Linguistics*, 2nd edn, 218–224. Pergamon Press.

Embick, D. and D. Poeppel (2015). 'Towards a computational(ist) neurobiology of language: Correlational, integrated and explanatory neurolinguistics'. *Language, Cognition and Neuroscience*, 30 (4): 357–66. doi:10.1080/23273798.2014.980750

Epstein, S., H. Kitahara and T. Seely (2014). 'Labeling by minimal search: Implications for successive-cyclic a-movement and the conception of the postulate "phase"'. *Linguistic Inquiry*, 45 (3): 463–81.

Evans, G. (1982). *Varieties of Reference*. Oxford: Oxford University Press.

Everett, D. (2005). 'Cultural constraints on grammar and cognition in Pirahã'. *Current Anthropology*, 46: 621–46.

Fabb, N. and M. Halle (2006). 'Telling the numbers: A unified account of syllabotonic English and syllabic French and Polish verse'. *Research in Language*, 4: 5–30.

Faroqi-Shah, Y., L. Slevc, S. Saxena, S. Fisher and M. Pifer (2019). 'Relationship between musical and language abilities in post-stroke aphasia'. *Aphasiology*. doi:10.1080/0268 7038.2019.1650159

Fedorenko, E. and R. Varley (2016). 'Language and thought are not the same thing: Evidence from neuroimaging and neurological patients'. *Annals of the New York Academy of Sciences*, 1369 (1): 132–53.

Fitch, W. (2006). 'The biology and evolution of music: A comparative perspective'. *Cognition*, 100: 173–215.

Fitch, W. (2010). *The Evolution of Language*. New York: Cambridge University Press.

Fitch, W., B. de Boer, N. Mathur and A. Ghazanfar (2016). 'Monkey vocal tracts are speech-ready'. *Science Advances*, 2 (9 December): e1600723.

Fitch, W., M. Hauser and N. Chomsky (2005). 'The evolution of the language faculty: Clarifications and implications'. *Cognition*, 97 (2): 179–210.

Flake, G. (1998). *The Computational Beauty of Nature: Computer Explorations of Fractals, Chaos, Complex Systems, and Adaptation*. Cambridge, MA: MIT Press.

Flanagan, O. (1998). *The Nature of Consciousness*. Cambridge, MA: MIT Press.

Fodor, J. (1975). *The Language of Thought*. Cambridge, MA: Harvard University Press.

Fodor, J. (1981). *Representations: Philosophical Essays on the Foundations of Cognitive Science*. Cambridge, MA: MIT Press.

Fodor, J. (1983). *The Modularity of Mind*. Cambridge, MA: MIT Press.

Fodor, J. (1994). *The Elm and the Expert*. Cambridge, MA: MIT Press.

Fodor, J. (1998). *Concepts: Where Cognitive Science Went Wrong*. Oxford: Clarendon Press.

Fodor, J. (2000). *The Mind Doesn't Work That Way: Scope and Limits of Computational Psychology*. Cambridge, MA: MIT Press.

Fodor, J. (2008). *Lot 2: The Language of Thought Revisited*. Oxford: Oxford University Press.

Fodor, J. and Z. Pylyshyn (1988). 'Connectionism and cognitive architecture: A critical analysis'. *Cognition*, 28: 1–2.

Fodor, J. and Z. Pylyshyn (2015). *Minds without Meanings: An Essay on the Content of Concepts*. Cambridge, MA: MIT Press.

Fridin, R. (2020). 'Introduction to Chomsky (2020)'.

Friederici, A. (2011). 'The brain basis of language processing: From structure to function'. *Physiological Reviews*, 91: 1357–92. doi:10.1152/physrev.00006.2011

Friederici, A., N. Chomsky, R. Berwick, A. Moro and J. Bolhuis (2017). 'Language, mind and brain'. *Nature Human Behaviour*, 1: 713–22.

Fujita, K. (2014). 'Recursive merge and human language evolution'. In T. Roeper and M. Speas (Eds), *Recursion: Complexity in Cognition*, 243–64. Heidelberg: Springer.

Galilei, Galileo (1632). *Dialogue Concerning the Two Chief World Systems*. Berkeley: University of California Press, 1962.

Gallistel, C. (1998). 'Symbolic processes in the brain; the case of insect navigation'. In D. Scarborough and S. Sternberg (Eds), *An Invitation to Cognitive Science: Methods, Models, and Conceptual Issues*, Vol. 4, 1–51. Cambridge, MA: MIT Press.

Gallistel, C. (2010). 'Learning organs'. In J. Bricmont and J. Franck (Eds), *Chomsky Notebook*, 193–202. New York: Columbia University Press.

Gallistel, C. (2018). 'The neurobiological bases for the computational theory of mind'. In R. Almeida and L. Gleitman (Eds), *On Concepts, Modules, and Language: Cognitive Science at Its Core*, 275–96. New York: Oxford University Press.

Gallup, G., J. Anderson and D. Shillito (2002). 'The mirror test'. In M. Bekoff, C. Allen, G. Burghardt (Eds), *The Cognitive Animal*, 325–34. Cambridge, MA: MIT Press.

Gardner, H. (1975). *The Shattered Mind*. New York: Alfred Knopf.

Gelman, R. and S. Cordes (2001). 'Counting in animals and humans'. In E. Dupoux (Ed.), *Essays in Honor of Jacques Mehler*, 279–301. Cambridge, MA: MIT Press.

Gentner, D. (1982). 'Why nouns are learned before verbs: Linguistic relativity vs. natural partitioning'. In S. Kuczaj (Ed.), *Language Development: Language, Culture, and Cognition*, 301–32. Hillsdale: Erlbaum.

Gentner, D. and S. Goldin-Meadow (2003). 'Whither Whorf'. In D. Gentner and S. Goldin-Meadow (Eds), *Language in Mind: Advances in the Study of Language and Thought*, 3–14. Cambridge, MA: MIT Press.

Gentner, T., K. Fenn, D. Margoliash and H. Nusbaum (2006). 'Recursive syntactic pattern learning by songbirds'. *Nature*, 440: 1204–7.

Gillette, J., H. Gleitman, L. Gleitman and A. Lederer (1999). 'Human simulations of vocabulary learning'. *Cognition*, 73: 135–76.

Gleitman, L. and E. Newport (1995). 'The invention of language by children: Environmental and biological influences on the acquisition of language'. In D. Osherson (Ed.), *An Invitation to Cognitive Science*, Volume 1. L. Gleitman and M. Liberman (Ed.). Cambridge, MA: MIT Press.

Gleitman, L., E. Newport and H. Gleitman (1984). 'The current status of the motherese hypothesis'. *Journal of Child Language*, 11 (1): 43–79.

Gleitman, L. and P. Bloom (1998). 'Language acquisition'. In R. Wilson and F. Keil (Eds), *MIT Encyclopedia of Cognitive Science*, 434–8. Cambridge, MA: MIT Press.

Gleitman, L. and A. Papafragou (2005). 'Language and thought'. In K. Holoyoak and R. Morrison (Eds), *The Cambridge Handbook of Thinking and Reasoning*, 633–61. New York: Cambridge University Press.

Goldin-Meadow, S. and H. Feldman (1979). 'The development of language-like communication without a language model'. *Science*, 197: 401–3.

Goodall, J. (1971). *In the Shadow of Man*. Boston: Houghton Mifflin; London: Collins.

Goodman, N. (1951). *The Structure of Appearances*. Cambridge, MA: Harvard University Press.

Grah, G., R. Wehner and B. Ronacher (2007). 'Desert ants do not acquire and use a three-dimensional global vector'. *Frontiers in Zoology*, 4: 12.

Gregory, R. (1970). 'The grammar of vision'. *The Listener*, 19 February.

Griffin, D. (2001). *Animal Minds: Beyond Cognition to Consciousness*. Chicago: University of Chicago Press.

Grodzinsky, Y. (2000). 'The neurology of syntax: Language use without Broca's area'. *Behavioral and Brain Sciences*, 23: 1–71.

Hale, K. (1966). 'Kinship reflections in syntax: Some Australian languages'. *Word*, 22: 1.

Haugeland, J. (1997). 'What is mind design?' In J. Haugeland (Ed.), *Mind Design II: Philosophy, Psychology, Artificial Intelligence*, 1–28. Cambridge, MA: MIT Press.

Hauser, M. (1996). *The Evolution of Communication*. Cambridge, MA: MIT Press.

Hauser, M. (1999). 'Primate cognition'. In R. Wilson and F. Keil (Eds), *The MIT Encyclopedia of the Cognitive Sciences*, 666–7. Cambridge, MA: MIT Press.

Hauser, M. (2001). 'What's so special about speech?' In E. Dupoux (Ed.), *Language, Brain, and Cognitive Development: Essays in Honor of Jacques Mehler*, 417–34. Cambridge, MA: MIT Press.

Hauser, M. (2006). 'Songbirds learn grammar'. *The Hindu*, 27 April.

Hauser, M. (2009). 'The illusion of biological variation'. In M. Piattelli-Palmarini, J. Uriagereka and P. Salaburu (Eds), *Of Minds and Language: A Dialogue with Noam Chomsky in the Basque Country*, 299–328. Oxford: Oxford University Press.

Hauser, M. (2016). 'Challenges to the what, when, and why?' *Biolinguistics*, 10: 1–5.

Hauser, M., N. Chomsky and W. Fitch (2002). 'The faculty of language: What is it, who has it, and how did it evolve?' *Science*, 298: 1569–79.

Hauser, M., P. MacNeilage and M. Ware (1996). 'Numerical representation in primates'. *PNAS*, 93 (4): 1514–17.

Hauser, M. and J. Watumull (2017). 'The universal generative faculty: The source of our expressive power in language, mathematics, morality, and music'. *Journal of Neurolinguistics*, 43: 78–94.

Hauser, M., C. Yang, R. Berwick, I. Tattersall, M. Ryan, J. Watumull, N. Chomsky and R. Lewontin (2014). 'The mystery of language evolution'. *Frontiers in Psychology*, 7 May. doi:10.3389/fpsyg.2014.00401

Heß, D., J. Koch and B. Ronacher (2009). 'Desert ants do not rely on sky compass information for the perception of inclined path segments'. *Journal of Experimental Biology*, 212: 1528–34. doi:10.1242

Hills, T. and S. Butterfill (2015). 'From foraging to autonoetic consciousness: The primal self as a consequence of embodied prospective foraging'. *Current Zoology*, 61 (2): 368–81.

Hinzen, W. (2006). *Mind Design and Minimal Syntax*. Oxford: Oxford University Press.

Hinzen, W. (2007). *An Essay on Names and Truth*. Oxford: Oxford University Press.

Hinzen, W. (2012). 'The philosophical significance of Universal Grammar'. *Language Sciences*, 34: 635–49. doi:10.1016/j.langsci.2012.03.005

Hinzen, W. (2014a). 'On the rationality of case'. *Language Sciences*, 46: 133–51.

Hinzen, W. (2014b). 'What is un-Cartesian linguistics?' *Biolinguistics*, 8: 226–57.

Hinzen, W. (2016). 'On the grammar of referential dependence'. *Studies in Logic, Grammar and Rhetoric*, 46: 59. doi:10.1515/slgr-2016-0031

Hinzen, W., N. Mukherji and B. Boruah (2011). 'The character of mind'. *Biolinguistics*, 5: 3.

Hinzen, W. and M. Sheehan (2013). *The Philosophy of Universal Grammar*. Oxford: Oxford University Press.

Hiraiwa, K. (2017). 'The faculty of language integrates the two core systems of number'. *Frontiers in Psychology*, 8. doi:10.3389/fpsyg.2017.00351

Hoffman, D. (1998). *Visual Intelligence*. Norton. New York: W.W. Norton.

Hofstadter, D. (1980). *Godel, Escher, Bach: An Eternal Golden Braid*. New York: Vintage Books.

Hohwy, J. (2014). *The Predictive Mind*. Oxford: Oxford University Press.

Holden, C. (1998). 'No last word on human origins'. *Science*, 282: 1455.

Hornsby, J. (1998). *Simple Mindedness: In Defence of Naive Naturalism in the Philosophy of Mind*. Cambridge, MA: Harvard University Press.

Hornstein, N. (1989). 'Meaning and the mental: The problem of semantics after Chomsky'. In A. George (Ed.), *Reflections on Chomsky*, 23–40. Oxford: Basil Blackwell.

Hornstein, N. and P. Pietroski (2009). 'Basic operations: Minimal syntax-semantics'. *Catalan Journal of Linguistics*, 8: 113–39.

Huber, R. and M. Knaden (2018). 'Desert ants possess distinct memories for food and nest odors'. *PNAS*, 115 (41): 10470–4. doi:10.1073/pnas.1809433115

Hubel, D. and T. Weisel (1962). 'Receptive fields, binocular interaction and functional architecture in the cat's visual cortex'. *Journal of Physiology*, 160 (1): 106–54. doi:10.1113/jphysiol.1962.sp006837

Hublin, J., A. Ben-Ncer, S. Bailey, S. Freidline, S. Neubauer, M. Skinner, I. Bergmann, A. Le Cabec, S. Benazzi, K. Harvati and P. Gunz (2017). 'New fossils from Jebel Irhoud, Morocco and the pan-African origin of Homo sapiens'. *Nature*, 546 (8 June): 289–91. doi:10.1038/nature22336

Humboldt, W. (1836). *Uber die Verschiedenheit des Menschlichen Sprachbaues*. Berlin. Facsimile edition, Bonn: Verlag, 1960. English Tr. G. C. Buck and F. Raven, *Linguistic Variability and Intellectual Development*. Philadelphia: University of Pennsylvania Press, 1972.

Huybregts, R. (2017). 'Phonemic clicks and the mapping asymmetry: How language emerged and speech developed'. *Neuroscience and Biobehavioral Reviews*, 81 (Part B): 279–94.

Jackendoff, R. (1990). *Semantic Structures*. Cambridge, MA: MIT Press.

Jackendoff, R. (2002). *Foundations of Language: Brain, Meaning, Grammar, Evolution*. Oxford: Oxford University Press.

Jackendoff, R. and F. Lerdahl (2006). 'The capacity for music: What is it, and what's special about it?' *Cognition*, 100 (1): 33–72.

Jackson, F. (1998). 'Identity theory of mind'. *Routledge Encyclopaedia of Philosophy*. London: Taylor and Francis. Available online: https://www.rep.routledge.com/ articles/thematic/mind-identity-theory-of/v-1/sections/functionalism-and-the -identity-theory

Jenkins, L. (2000). *Biolinguistics: Exploring the Biology of Language*. Cambridge: Cambridge University Press.

Jenkins, L. (2004). 'Introduction'. In L. Jenkins (Ed.), *Variation and Universals in Biolinguistics*, xvii–xxii. Amsterdam: Elsevier.

Johansson, S. (2013). 'The talking Neanderthals: What do fossils, genetics and archaeology say?' *Biolinguistics*, 7: 35–74.

Johnson, D. and J. Bering (2006). 'Hand of god, mind of man: Punishment and cognition in the evolution of cooperation'. *Evolutionary Psychology*, 4: 219–33.

Jones, D. (2010). 'Human kinship, from conceptual structure to grammar'. *Behavioral and Brain Sciences*, 33: 367–416. doi:10.1017/S0140525X10000890

Jorgensen, L. (2012). 'Descartes on music: Between the ancients and the aestheticians'. *British Journal of Aesthetics*, 52 (4): 407–24.

Joordens, Josephine C. A., Francesco d'Errico, Frank P. Wesselingh, Stephen Munro, John de Vos, Jakob Wallinga, Christina Ankjærgaard, Tony Reimann, Jan R. Wijbrans, Klaudia F. Kuiper, Herman J. Mu¨cher, He´le`ne Coqueugniot, Vincent Prie´, Ineke Joosten, Bertil van Os, Anne S. Schulp, Michel Panuel, Victoria van der Haas, Wim Lustenhouwer, John J. G. Reijmer and Wil Roebroeks (2015). '*Homo erectus* at Trinil on Java used shells for tool production and engraving'. *Nature*, 518: 228–31.

Kaminsky, J., J. Call and J. Fischer (2004). 'Word-learning in a domestic dog: Evidence for "fast mapping"'. *Science*, 304 (5677): 1682–3.

Karmiloff-Smith, E. (1992). *Beyond Modularity: A Developmental Perspective on Cognitive Science*. Cambridge, MA: MIT Press.

Katz, J. and D. Pesetsky (2011). 'The identity thesis for language and music'. Available online: https://ling.auf.net/lingbuzz/000959

Kayne, R. (1994). *The Antisymmetry of Syntax*. Cambridge, MA: MIT Press.

Keil, F. (1979). *Semantic and Conceptual Development*. Cambridge, MA: Harvard University Press.

Kipper, S., R. Mundry, C. Sommer, H. Hultsch and D. Todt (2006). 'Song repertoire size is correlated with body measures and arrival date in common nightingales, *Luscinia megarhynchos*'. *Animal Behaviour*, 71: 211–17.

Klein, R. (2008). 'Out of Africa and the evolution of human behavior'. *Evolutionary Anthropology*, 17 (6): 267–81. https://doi.org/10.1002/evan.20181

Koster, J., H. van Riemsdijk and J. Vernaud (1978). *The GLOW Manifesto*. Reprinted in C. Otero (Ed.), *Noam Chomsky: Critical Assessments*. London: Routledge & Kegan Paul, 1994.

Kripke, S. (1980). *Naming and Necessity*. Cambridge, MA: Harvard University Press.

Krumhansl, C., P. Toivanen, T. Eerola, P. Toiviainen, T. Järvinen and J. Louhivuori (2000). 'Cross-cultural music cognition: Cognitive methodology applied to North Sami yoiks'. *Cognition*, 76: 13–58.

Krupenye, C., F. Kano, S. Hirata, J. Call and M. Tomasello (2016). 'Great apes anticipate that other individuals will act according to false beliefs'. *Science*, 354 (6308): 110–14.

Kunej, D. and I. Turk (2000). 'New perspectives on the beginnings of music: archeological and musicological analysis of a middle paleolithic bone "flute"'. In N. L. Wallin, B. Merker and S. Brown (Eds), *The Origins of Music*, 235–68. Cambridge, MA: MIT Press.

Landau, B. and L. Gleitman (1985). *Language and Experience: Evidence from the Blind Child*. Cambridge, MA: Harvard University Press.

Langendoen, D. (2003). 'Merge'. In A. Carnie, M. Willie and H. Harley (Eds), *Formal Approaches to Functional Phenomena: In Honor of Eloise Jelinek*, 307–18. Amsterdam: John Benjamins.

Legate, J. (2003). 'The configurational structure of a nonconfigurational language'. *Linguistic Variation Yearbook*, 1: 63–99.

Leiber, J. (1991). 'Cartesian linguistics?' In A. Kasher (Ed.), *The Chomskyan Turn*, 150–81. Oxford: Basil Blackwell.

Lerdahl, F. (2013). 'Musical syntax and its relation to linguistic syntax'. In M. Arbib (Ed.), *Language, Music, and the Brain: A Mysterious Relationship*. Strüngmann Forum Reports, 10. Cambridge, MA: MIT Press.

Lerdahl, F. (2015). 'Concepts and representations of musical hierarchies'. *Music Perception*, 33: 83–95.

Lerdahl, F. and R. Jackendoff (1983). *A Generative Theory of Tonal Music*. Cambridge, MA: MIT Press.

Li, X, T. Crow, W. Hopkins, Q. Gong, N. Roberts (2017). 'Human torque is not present in chimpanzee brain'. *NeuroImage*, 165: 1–9. doi:10.1016/j.neuroimage.2017.10.017

Lidz, J and A. Gagliardi (2015). 'How nature meets nurture: Universal grammar and statistical learning'. *Annual Review of Linguistics*, 1: 12.1–12.21. doi:10.1146/annurev-linguist-030514-125236

Lieberman, P. (2016). 'The evolution of language and thought'. *Journal of Anthropological Sciences*, 20 (94): 127–46. doi:10.4436/JASS.94029

Marantz, A. (1995). 'The minimalist program'. In G. Webelhuth (Ed.), *From GB to Minimalism*, 349–82. Oxford: Basil Blackwell.

Marchant, J. (2016). 'A journey to the oldest cave paintings in the world'. *Smithsonian Magazine*, January/February. https://www.smithsonianmag.com/history/journey -oldest-cave-paintings-world-180957685/

Marler, P. (2000). 'Origins of music and speech'. In N. Wallin, B. Merker and S. Brown (Eds), *The Origins of Music*, 31–48. Cambridge, MA: MIT Press.

Marr, D. (1982). *Vision*. New York: Freeman.

Marticorena, D., A. Ruiz, C. Mukerji, A. Goddu and L. Santos (2011). 'Monkeys represent others' knowledge but not their beliefs'. *Developmental Science*, 14 (6): 1406–16. doi:10.1111/j.1467-7687.2011.01085.x

Martins, P. and C. Boeckx (2016). 'What we talk about when we talk about biolinguistics'. *Linguistics Vanguard*. doi:10.1515/lingvan-2016-0007

Martins, P. and C. Boeckx (2019). 'Language evolution and complexity considerations: The no half-Merge fallacy'. *PLOS Biology*, 27 November. doi:10.1371/journal. pbio.3000389

Mcbrearty, S. and A. Brooks (2000). 'The revolution that wasn't: A new interpretation of the origin of modern human behavior'. *Journal of Human Evolution*, 39 (5, November): 453–563.

McDougall, I., F. Brown and J. Fleagle (2005). 'Stratigraphic placement and age of modern humans from Kibish, Ethiopia'. *Nature*, 433: 733–6. doi:10.1038/nature03258

McGonigle, B., M. Chalmers and A. Dickinson (2003). 'Concurrent disjoint and reciprocal classification by cebus apella in seriation tasks: Evidence for hierarchical organization'. *Animal Cognition*, 6: 185–97.

McLaughlin, J. (2005). 'Supervenience'. In *Stanford Encyclopaedia of Philosophy*. Online Edition plato.stanford.edu.

Merker, B. (2002). 'Music: The missing Humboldt system'. *Musicae Scientiae*, 6: 3–21.

Midgley, M. (1980). *Animals and Why They Matter*. London: Chapman and Hall.

Mikhail, J. (2007). 'Universal moral grammar: Theory, evidence and the future'. *Trends in Cognitive Sciences*, 11: 4.

Mikhail, J. (2009). 'Jurisprudence: A formal model of unconscious moral and legal knowledge'. *Psychology of Learning and Motivation*, 50: 29–100.

Miller, G. and N. Chomsky (1963). 'Finitary models of language users'. In R. Luce, R. Bush and E. Galanter (Eds), *Handbook of Mathematical Psychology*, Vol. II, 419–91. New York; London: John Wiley and Sons, Inc.

Miyagawa, S. (2021). 'Revisiting Fitch and Hauser's observation that Tamarin monkeys can learn combinations based on finite-state grammar'. *Frontiers in Psychology*, 12. doi:10.3389/fpsyg.2021.772291

Miyagawa, S., R. Berwick, K. Okanoya (2013). 'The emergence of hierarchical structure in human language'. *Frontiers in Psychology*, 4: 71. doi:10.3389/fpsyg.2013.00071

Miyagawa, S. and E. Clarke (2019). 'Systems underlying human and old world monkey communication: One, two, or infinite'. *Frontiers in Psychology*, 10.

Miyagawa, S., C. Lesure and V. Nóbrega (2018). 'Cross-modality information transfer: A hypothesis about the relationship among prehistoric cave paintings, symbolic thinking, and the emergence of language'. *Frontiers in Psychology*, 20 February. doi:10.3389/fpsyg.2018.00115

Miyagawa, S., S. Ojima, R. Berwick, K. Okanoya (2014). 'The Integration Hypothesis of human language evolution and the nature of contemporary languages'. *Frontiers in Psychology*, 5: 564. doi:10.3389/fpsyg.2014.00564

Moro, A. (2000). *Dynamic Antisymmetry*. Cambridge, MA: MIT Press.

Moro, A., M. Tettamanti, D. Perani, C. Donati, S. Cappa and F. Fazio (2001). 'Syntax and the brain: Disentangling grammar by selective anomalies'. *NeuroImage*, 13: 110–18.

Mukherji, N. (2000). *The Cartesian Mind: Reflections on Language and Music*. Shimla: Indian Institute of Advanced Study.

Mukherji, N. (2003). 'Is C_{HL} linguistically specific?' *Philosophical Psychology*, 16 (2): 289–308.

Mukherji, N. (2009a). 'Doctrinal dualism'. In P. Ghose (Ed.), *Materialism and Immaterialism in India and the West: Varying Vistas*, 509–22. New Delhi: Indian Council of Philosophical Research.

Mukherji, N. (2009b). 'Dawn of music theory in India'. In R. Singh (Ed.), *Trends in Linguistics, Annual Review of South Asian Languages and Linguistics*, 223–30. The Hague: Mouton de Gruyter.

Mukherji, N. (2010). *The Primacy of Grammar*. Cambridge, MA: MIT Press.

Mukherji, N. (2012). 'I sing my song, in Bengali (aami gaai gaan)'. *Anustup*, Festival Number (*Sharodiya Sankhya*).

Mukherji, N. (2017). *Reflections on Human Inquiry: Science, Philosophy, and Common Life*. Singapore: Springer Nature.

Mukherji, N. (2019). 'Sound of thoughts'. Talk at Heidelberg University, 13–14 February. Available online: https://www.academia.edu/44246153/Sound_of_Thoughts

Mukherji, N. (2021). 'On sound-meaning correlation'. In P. Kosta and K. Schlund (Eds), *Keynotes from the International Conference on Explanation and Prediction in Linguistics (CEP): Formalist and Functionalist Approaches*. Potsdam: University of Potsdam. Available online: lingbuzz/005472.

Mukherji, S. (2013). 'Generative musical grammar: A minimalist approach'. Ph. D thesis, Princeton University.

Muller, M. and R. Wehner (1988). 'Path integration in desert ants, Cataglyphis fortis'. *Proceedings of the National Academy of Sciences of the United States of America*, 85: 5287–90.

Murphy, E. (2016). 'The human oscillome and its explanatory potential'. *Biolinguistics*, 10: 6–20.

Murphy, E. (2018). 'Interfaces (traveling oscillations) + Recursion (delta-theta code) = Language'. In E. Luef and M. Manuela (Eds), *The Talking Species: Perspectives on the Evolutionary, Neuronal and Cultural Foundations of Language*, 251–69. Graz: Unipress Graz Verlag.

Musso, M., A. Moro, V. Glauche, M. Rijntjes, J. Reichenbach, C. Büchel and C. Weiller (2003). 'Broca's area and the language instinct'. *Nature Neuroscience*, 6: 774–81.

Nadel, L. and M. Piattelli-Palmarini (2003). 'What is cognitive science?' In L. Nadel (Ed.), *Encyclopedia of Cognitive Science*, Vol. 1, xiii–xli. London: Macmillan.

Nagel, T. (1997). *The Last Word*. New York: Oxford University Press.

Narendra, A. (2007). 'Homing strategies of the Australian desert ant *Melophorus bagoti* I. Proportional path-integration takes the ant half-way home'. *Journal of Experimental Biology*, 210: 1798–1803.

Narita, H. (2014). *Endocentric Structuring of Projection-free Syntax*. Amsterdam: John Benjamins.

Nelson, M., I. Karoui, K. Giber, X. Yang, L. Cohen, H. Koopman, S. Cash, L. Naccache, J. Hale, C. Pallier and S. Dehaene (2017). 'Neurophysiological dynamics of phrase-structure building during sentence processing'. *PNAS*, 114 (18, 2 May): E3669–678. doi:10.1073/pnas.1701590114

Nespor, M. (2001). 'About parameters, prominence, and bootstrapping'. In E. Dupoux (Ed.), *Language, Brain, and Cognitive Development: Essays in Honour of Jacques Mehler*, 127–42. Cambridge, MA: MIT Press.

Nevins, A., D. Pesetsky and C. Rodrigues (2009). 'Pirahã exceptionality: A reassessment'. *Language*, 85 (3): 671–81.

Newell, A. and H. Simon (1976). 'Computer science as empirical inquiry: Symbols and search'. *Communications of the ACM*, 19: 113–26.

Ormazabal, J. (2000). 'A conspiracy theory of case and agreement'. In R. Martin, D. Michaels and J. Uriagereka (Eds), *Step by Step: Essays on Minimalist Syntax in Honor of Howard Lasnik*, 235–60. Cambridge, MA: MIT Press.

Osherson, D. (Ed.) (1995). *An Invitation to Cognitive Science*. Vol. 1. Cambridge, MA: MIT Press.

Pallier, C., A. Devauchelle and S. Dehaene (2011). 'Cortical representation of the constituent structure of sentences'. *PNAS*, 108 (6, 8 February): 2522–7.

Patel, A. (2003). 'Language, music, syntax and the brain'. *Nature Neuroscience*, 6: 674–81. doi:10.1038/nn1082

Patel, A. (2008). *Music, Language, and the Brain*. New York: Oxford University Press.

Patel, A. (2019). 'Evolutionary music cognition: Cross-species studies'. In P. Rentfrow and D. Levitin (Eds), *Foundations in Music Psychology: Theory and Research*, 459–501. Cambridge, MA: MIT Press.

Pearce, E., C. Stringer and R. Dunbar (2013). 'New insights into differences in brain organization between Neanderthals and anatomically modern humans'. *Proceedings of the Royal Society, B* 280: 20130168.

Penn, D., K. Holyoak and D. Povinelli (2008). 'Darwin's mistake: Explaining the discontinuity between human and nonhuman minds'. *Behavioral and Brain Sciences*, 31 (2): 109–30. doi:10.1017/S0140525X08003543

Penn, D. and D. Povinelli (2007). 'On the lack of evidence that non-human animals possess anything remotely resembling a "theory of mind"'. *Philosophical Transactions of the Royal Society*, 362 (1480): 731–44.

Penrose, R. (1994). *Shadows of the Mind*. Oxford: Oxford University Press.

Peretz, I. (2001). 'The biological foundations of music'. In E. Dupoux (Ed.), *Language, Brain, and Cognitive Development: Essays in Honour of Jacques Mehler*, 435–45. Cambridge, MA: MIT Press.

Peretz, I., D. Vuvan, M. Lagrois and J. Armony (2015). 'Neural overlap in processing music and speech'. *Philosophical Transactions of the Royal Society London B Biological Sciences*, 370: 20140090. doi:10.1098/rstb.2014.0090

Pesetsky, D. (2007). 'Music syntax is language syntax'. Ms. web.mit.edu/linguistics/pe ople/ faculty/pesetsky/Pesetsky_Cambridge_music_handout.pdf (see also Katz and Pesetsky).

Petitto, L-A (2005). 'How the brain begets language'. In J. McGilvray (Ed.), *The Cambridge Companion to Chomsky*, 84–101. Cambridge: Cambridge University Press.

Phillips, J., W. Buckwalter, F. Cushman, O. Friedman, A. Martin, J. Turri, L. Santos and J. Knobe (2020). 'Knowledge before belief'. *Behavioral and Brain Sciences*, September. doi:10.1017/S0140525X20000618

Piattelli-Palmarini, M. and G. Vitiello (2015). 'Linguistics and some aspects of its underlying dynamics'. *Biolinguistics*, 9: 96–115. http://www.biolinguistics.eu

Pietroski, P. (2005). 'Meaning before truth'. In G. Preyer and G. Peters (Eds), *Contextualism in Philosophy*, 253–300. Oxford: Oxford University Press.

Pietroski, P. (2010). 'Concepts, meanings and truth: First nature, second nature and hard work'. *Mind and Language*, 25: 247–78.

Pietroski, P. (2020). 'Précis of *Conjoining Meanings: Semantics Without Truth Values*'. *Croatian Journal of Philosophy*, XX: 60.

Pinker, S. (1997). *How the Mind Works*. New York: Norton.

Pinker, S. (1998). 'Language and consciousness, part 1'. Available online: https://www .youtube.com/watch?v=UZDeYe93rFg

Pinker, S. and R. Jackendoff (2005). 'The faculty of language: What's special about it?' *Cognition*, 95 (2): 201–36.

Poeppel, D. (2012). 'The maps problem and the mapping problem: Two challenges for a cognitive neuroscience of speech and language'. *Cognitive Neuropsychology*, 29 (1–2): 34–55.

Poeppel, D. and D. Embick (2005). 'Defining the relation between linguistics and neuroscience'. In A. Cutler (Ed.), *Twenty-First Century Psycholinguistics: Four Cornerstones*. Mahwah: Lawrence Erlbaum.

Post, E. (1921). 'Absolutely unsolvable problems and relatively undecidable propositions – account of an anticipation'. In M. Davis (Ed.), *The Undecidable: Basic Papers on Undecidable Propositions, Unsolvable Problems and Computable Functions*, 340–433. New York: Raven Press, 1965.

Povinelli, D. (2000). *Folk Physics for Apes: The Chimpanzee's Theory of How the World Works*. Oxford: Oxford University Press.

Premack, D. (1986). *Gavagai or the Future History of the Animal Language Controversy*. Cambridge, MA: MIT Press.

Premack, D. and A. Premack (2003). *Original Intelligence: Unlocking the Mystery of Who We Are*. New Delhi: McGraw-Hill.

Premack, D. and G. Woodruff (1978). 'Does the chimpanzee have a theory of mind?' *Behavioral and Brain Sciences*, 1 (4): 515–26.

Prinz, J. (2006). 'Is the mind really modular?' In R. Stainton (Ed.), *Contemporary Debates in Cognitive Science*, 22–36. London: Blackwell.

Putnam, H. (1999). *The Threefold Cord: Mind, Body and World*. New York: Columbia University Press.

Pylyshyn, Z. (1984). *Computation and Cognition*. Cambridge, MA: MIT Press.

Quine, W. (1960). *Word and Object*. Cambridge, MA: MIT Press.

Quine, W. (1969). 'Reply to Chomsky'. In D. Davidson and J. Hintikka (Eds), *Words and Objections*, 302–11. Dordrecht: D. Reidel.

Quintana O. (2019). 'Does the Y-model for language work for music?' P. Eismont, O. Mitrenina, A. Pereltsvaig (Eds), *Language, Music and Computing. LMAC 2017. Communications in Computer and Information Science*, vol 943. Cham: Springer. doi:10.1007/978-3-030-05594-3_1

Raffman, D. (1993). *Language, Music and Mind*. Cambridge, MA: The MIT Press.

Ramus, F., M. Hauser, C. Miller, D. Morris and J. Mehler (2000). 'Language discrimination by human new-borns and by cotton-top tamarin monkeys'. *Science*, 288: 349–51.

Raichlen, D. and J. Polk (2013). 'Linking brains and brawn: Exercise and the evolution of human neurobiology'. *Proceedings of the Royal Society B: Biological Sciences*, 280 (1750): 20122250. doi:10.1098/rspb.2012.2250

Reimsdijk, H. (2007). 'Interview with Kleanthes Grohmann'. *Biolinguistics*, 1: 137–49.

Reinhart, T. (2006). *Interface Strategies: Optimal and Costly Computations*. Cambridge, MA: MIT Press.

Rizzi, L. (2016). 'Labeling, maximality and the head-phrase distinction'. *The Linguistic Review*, 33 (1): 103–27. doi:10.1515/tlr-2015-0016

Roffman I., S. Savage-Rumbaugh, E. Rubert-Pugh, A. Ronen and E. Nevo (2012). 'Stone tool production and utilization by bonobo-chimpanzees (Pan paniscus)'. *PNAS*, 109 (36, 4 September): 14500–3.

Rohrmeier, M. (2011). 'Towards a generative syntax of tonal harmony'. *Journal of Mathematics and Music*, 5: 35–53. doi:10.1080/17459737.2011.573676

Rumelhart, D. and J. McClelland (1986). *Parallel Distributed Processing, Volume 1: Explorations in the Microstructure of Cognition: Foundations*. Cambridge, MA: MIT Press.

Russell, B. (1919). 'The philosophy of logical atomism'. *Monist*. Reprinted in R. Marsh (Ed.), *Logic and Knowledge*. London: George Allen and Unwin, 1956, 177–281.

Ryle, G. (1949). *The Concept of Mind*. London: Penguin Books.

Sahle, Y. and A. Brooks (2019). 'Assessment of complex projectiles in the early Late Pleistocene at Aduma, Ethiopia'. *Plos One*. https://journals.plos.org/plosone/article ?id=10.1371/journal.pone.0216716

Sauerland, U. and A. Alexiadou (2020). 'Generative grammar: A meaning first approach'. *Frontiers in Psychology*, 11: 3104. doi:10.3389/fpsyg.2020.571295

Schino, G., B. Tiddi and P. di Sorrento (2006). 'Simultaneous classification by rank and kinship in Japanese Macaques'. *Animal Behaviour*, 71: 1069–74.

Searle, J. (1980). 'Minds, brains and programmes'. In *Behavioural and the Brain Sciences* 3. Reprinted in J. Haugeland (Ed.), *Mind Design II: Philosophy, Psychology, Artificial Intelligence*. Cambridge, MA: MIT Press, 1997, 183–204.

Searle, J. (1992). *The Rediscovery of the Mind*. Cambridge, MA: MIT Press.

Searle, J. (1998). 'Animal minds'. *Etica & Animali*, 9: 37–50.

Seidl, T. and R. Wehner (2006).'Visual and tactile learning of ground structures in desert ants'. *Journal of Experimental Biology*, 209 (17): 3336–44. doi:10.1242/jeb.02364

Seidl, T. and R. Wehner (2008). 'Walking on inclines: How do desert ants monitor slope and step length?' *Frontiers in Zoology*, 5: 8.

Sells, P. (1985). *Lectures on Contemporary Syntactic Theories*. CSLI, Stanford: Stanford University.

Seyfarth, R., D. Cheney and T. Bergman (2005). 'Primate social cognition and the origins of language'. *Trends in Cognitive Sciences*, 9: 265–6.

Sheiber, S. (Ed.) (2004). *The Turing Test: Verbal Behaviour as the Hallmark of Intelligent*. Cambridge, MA: The MIT Press.

Singer, P. (1976). *Animal Liberation*. London: Jonathan Cape.

Spelke, E. (2000). 'Core knowledge'. *American Psychologist*, 55 (11): 1233–43. doi:10.1037/0003-066X.55.11.1233

Spelke, E. (2003). 'What makes us smart? Core knowledge and natural language'. In D. Gentner and S. Goldwin-Meadow (Eds), *Language in Mind: Advances in the study of language and thought*. Cambridge, MA: The MIT Press.

Spelke, E. (2011). 'Natural number and natural geometry'. In S. Dehaene and E. Brannon (Eds). *Space, Time and Number in the Brain*, Chapter 18, 287–317. Cambridge, MA: Academic Press.

Sperber, D. (1994). 'The modularity of thought and the epidemiology of representations'. In L. Hirschfeld and S. Gelman (Eds), *Mapping the Mind: Domain Specificity in Cognition and Culture*, 39–67. Cambridge: Cambridge University Press.

Soames, S. and D. Perlmutter (1979). *Syntactic Argumentation and the Structure of English*. Berkeley: University of California Press.

Steck, K., B. Hansson, M. Knaden (2011). 'Desert ants benefit from combining visual and olfactory landmarks'. *Journal of Experimental Biology*, 214: 1307–12. doi:10.1242/jeb.053579

Stewart, I. (1995). *Nature's Numbers: Discovering Order and Pattern in the Universe.* London: Weidenfeld and Nicolson.

Stewart, I. (2001). *What Shape is a Snowflake?* London: Weidenfeld and Nicolson.

Stout, D. (2011). 'Stone toolmaking and the evolution of human culture and cognition'. *Philosophical Transactions of Royal Society of London B Biol Sci.*, 366 (1567, 12 April): 1050–9.

Strawson, P. (1959). *Individuals.* London: Methuen.

Streidter, G. (2004). *Principles of Brain Evolution.* Oxford: Oxford University Press.

Stringer, C. (2011). *The Origin of Our Species.* London: Allan Lane.

Studdert-Kennedy, M. and H. Terrace (2017). 'In the beginning: A review of Robert C. Berwick and Noam Chomsky's *Why Only Us*'. *Journal of Language Evolution*, 2 (2): 114–25. doi:10.1093/jole/lzx005

Tattersall, I. (1995). *The Fossil Trail: How We Know What We Think We Know about Human Evolution.* New York: Oxford University Press.

Tattersall, I. (2012). *Masters of the Planet: The Search for Our Human Origins.* New York: Palgrave Macmillan.

Tattersall, I. (2016). 'A tentative framework for the acquisition of language and modern human cognition'. *Journal of Anthropological Sciences*, 94: 157–66. doi:10.4436/JASS.94030

Tattersall, I. (2017). 'How can we detect when language emerged?' *Psychonomic Bulletin & Review*, 24 (1): 64–7. doi:10.3758/s13423-016-1075-9

Tattersall, I. (2018). 'Brain size and the emergence of modern human cognition'. In J. Schwartz (Ed.), *Rethinking Human Evolution*, 319–34. Cambridge, MA: MIT Press.

Tattersall, I. (2019). 'The minimalist program and the origin of language: A view from paleoanthropology'. *Frontiers in Psychology*, 02 April. doi:10.3389/fpsyg.2019.00677

Terrace H. S., L. A. Petitto, R. J. Sanders and T. G. Bever (1979). 'Can an Ape create a sentence?' *Science*, 23 (206, Issue 4421): 891–902. doi:10.1126/science.504995

Thornton, C. (2016). 'Three ways to link Merge with hierarchical concept-combination'. *Biolinguistics*, 10: 78–106.

Turing, A. (1937). 'On computable numbers, with an application to the *entscheidungsproblem*'. *Proceedings of the London Mathematical Society*, Series 2, 42: 230–65.

Turing, A. (1950). 'Computing machinery and intelligence'. *Mind*, 59: 433–60.

Turing, A. (1952). 'The chemical basis of morphogenesis'. *Philosophical Transactions of the Royal Society of London, Series B*, 237: 37–72. In P. Saunders (Ed.), *The Collected Works of A. M. Turing: Morphogenesis.* Amsterdam: North-Holland, 1992.

Uomini, N. and G. Meyer (2013). 'Shared brain lateralization patterns in language and Acheulean stone tool production: A functional transcranial Doppler ultrasound study'. *PLoS One*, 8: e72693. doi:10.1371/journal.pone. 0072693

Uriagereka, J. (2008). *Syntactic Anchors on Semantic Structuring.* Cambridge: Cambridge University Press.

Varley, R., N. Klessinger, C. Romanowski and M. Siegal (2005). 'Agrammatic but numerate'. *PNAS*. Available online: www.pnas.org_cgi_doi_10.1073_pnas .0407470102

Van Gelder, T. (1997). 'Dynamics and cognition'. In J. Haugeland (Ed.), *Mind Design II*, 421–50. Cambridge, MA: MIT Press.

Vijaykrishnan, K. (2007). *The Grammar of Carnatic Music*. Berlin: Mouton de Gruyter.

Wang, H. (1987). *Reflections on Kurt Godel*. Cambridge, MA: MIT Press.

Wasow, T. (1985). '"Postscript" to sells (1985)'. Reprinted in C. Otero (Ed.), *Noam Chomsky: Critical Assessments*, Vol. 1. London: Routledge and Kegan Paul, 1994.

Watumull, J., M. Hauser, I. Roberts and N. Hornstein (2014). 'On recursion'. *Frontiers in Psychology*, 08 January. doi:10.3389/fpsyg.2013.01017

Wehner, R. and M. Srinivasan (1981). 'Searching behavior of desert ants, genus *Cataglyphis* (Formicidae, Hymenoptera)'. *Journal of Comparative Physiology*, 142: 315–38.

Williams, B. (1985). *Ethics and the Limits of Philosophy*. Cambridge, MA: Harvard University Press.

Wilson, M. (1978). *Descartes*. London: Routledge and Kegan Paul.

Wilson, R. and F. Keil (Eds) (1999). *The MIT Encyclopedia of the Cognitive Sciences*. Cambridge, MA: MIT Press.

Wintergerst, S. and B. Ronacher (2012). 'Discrimination of inclined path segments by the desert ant *Cataglyphis fortis*'. *Journal of Comparative Physiology*, 198: 363–73.

Wittgenstein, L. (1931/1958). *The Blue and Brown Books*. Oxford: Blackwell.

Wittgenstein, L. (1953). *Philosophical Investigations*. G. Anscombe (Trans.). Oxford: Blackwell Publishers.

Wittlinger, M., R. Wehner and H. Wolf (2006). 'The ant odometer: Stepping on stilts and stumps'. *Science*, 312 (5782, 30 June): 1965–67. doi:10.1126/science.1126912

Wolf, H. and R. Wehner (2000). 'Pinpointing food sources: Olfactory and anemotactic orientation in desert ants, *Cataglyphis fortis*'. *Journal of Experimental Biology*, 203: 857–68.

Yablo, S. (1990). 'The real distinction between mind and body'. *Canadian Journal of Philosophy*, 16: 149–201.

Index

Lightning Source UK Ltd.
Milton Keynes UK
UKHW021545091122
411892UK00003B/53